Applied Strategic Planning:

A Comprehensive Guide

Applied Strategic Planning

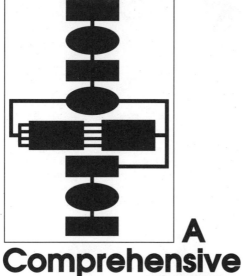

A Comprehensive Guide

Leonard D. Goodstein, Ph.D.
Timothy M. Nolan, Ph.D.
J. William Pfeiffer, Ph.D., J.D.

McGraw-Hill, Inc.

New York   San Francisco   Washington, D.C.   Auckland   Bogotá
Caracas   Lisbon   London   Madrid   Mexico City   Milan
Montreal   New Delhi   San Juan   Singapore
Sydney   Tokyo   Toronto

Library of Congress Cataloging-in-Publication Data

Goodstein, Leonard David.
    Applied strategic planning : how to develop a plan that really
works / Leonard D. Goodstein, Timothy M. Nolan, J. William Pfeiffer.
      p.   cm.
    Includes index.
    ISBN 0-07-024020-5 (alk. paper)
    1. Strategic planning.   I. Nolan, Timothy M.   II. Pfeiffer, J.
William.   III. Title.
HD30.28.G66   1993
658.4'012—dc20   93-1205
                                                          CIP

    6 7 8 9 0 DOC/DOC 9 9 8 7 6

ISBN 0-07-024020-5

*The sponsoring editor for this book was Philip Ruppel, the editing
supervisor was Kimberly A. Goff, and the production supervisor was
Donald F. Schmidt. This book was set in Caledonia.*

Printed and bound by R. R. Donnelley & Sons Company.

This book was previously published in 1992 under the title *Applied Strategic
Planning: A Comprehensive Guide* by Pfeiffer & Company.

 This book is printed on recycled, acid-free paper containing a
minimum of 50% recycled de-inked fiber.

Contents

The Plan

In the beginning was the plan.
And then came the assumptions.
And the assumptions were without form.
And the plan was completely without substance,
And darkness was upon the face of the workers.
And they spake unto their marketing manager, saying,
> "It is a pot of crap, and it stinketh."

And the marketing manager went unto the strategists and sayeth,
> "It is a pile of dung, and none may abide the odor thereof."

And the strategists went unto the business managers and sayeth unto them,
> "It is a container of excrement, and it is very strong,
> such that none may abide by it."

And the business managers went unto the director and sayeth unto him,
> "It is a vessel of fertilizer, and none may abide its strength."

And the director went unto the vice president and sayeth,
> "It contains that which aids plant growth, and it is very
> strong."

And the vice president went unto the senior vice president and sayeth,
> "It promoteth growth, and it is powerful."

And the senior vice president went unto the president and sayeth unto him,
> "This powerful new plan will actively promote the growth
> and efficiency of the company and the business in general."

And the president looked upon the plan and saw that it was good,
> AND THE PLAN BECAME POLICY.

Author Unknown*

---

*If anyone claims to be the author of this piece or knows who the author is, please send us the information and we will be happy to give credit where it is due in the next printing of this book.

Preface

The Applied Strategic Planning process was created out of our experience with organizations involved in planned change efforts. As consultants concerned with organizational effectiveness, we recognized what was necessary to achieve effective change. We developed our Applied Strategic Planning model with a careful eye toward weaving these insights into the process.

This book is intended to be a straightforward, comprehensive guide to conducting Applied Strategic Planning. It outlines, in a step-by-step fashion, how the strategic planning process should be conducted. The book is intended for managers, especially senior managers concerned with the overall direction of their organization. It is also directed at professional consultants, both internal and external, who are confronted with the task of managing or facilitating a strategic planning process for an organization.

This book is a complete revision and extension of our earlier book, *Applied Strategic Planning: A How To Do It Guide.* The modifications and additions represent our accumulated wisdom obtained from an additional six years of using the Applied Strategic Planning model with over sixty different clients. Our work has also been extensively influenced by the contributions of our colleagues in planning, Wayne Widdis, Jack Knight, and Bruce Dunn, to whom we acknowledge our indebtedness. The earlier version of this book included a number of activities that were intended to be used as part of the Applied Strategic Planning process. The development of both the model and the variety of activities that could be used to apply the model has been so extensive that it made that merger impossible in the present case. Therefore we have split off the activities into a separate volume, *Applied Strategic Planning: The Consultant's Kit.*

This volume provides the reader with both an overall understanding of the process of Applied Strategic Planning and the required steps and technology for using the model in a strategic planning process. A careful reading of this book will help line managers understand why strategic planning is necessary, why the Applied Strategic Planning model offers distinct advantages over any alternative model, and how the model should be applied. A careful reading of this book, faithful adherence to the Applied Strategic Planning model, and effective use of the activities included in the *Consultant's Kit* should enable a competent consultant who is relatively inexperienced in strategic planning to successfully manage an organization's planning process.

The Applied Strategic Planning model, which first appears in this book on page 8, represents the synthesis of our combined experience as consultants and trainers in this arena for the past eighteen years. Although our model is based on existing models, it differs from the others in several important ways. The four major differences are the values scan, organizational culture, strategic business modeling, and integrating business and functional plans. Implementation (hence "Applied" Strategic Planning) is the acid test of the model's success. Not only is implementation the final phase of the model, but "application considerations" are important throughout all the other phases. Another important ingredient of this model is "environmental monitoring," which is an ongoing process that continues from the beginning to the end of the . planning period—and beyond.

A unique aspect of the model is the systematic way in which values clarification is explicitly confronted very early in the process. Although other models of strategic planning may give some attention to the underlying values that drive the planning process, our model gives values a seminal focus and provides specific technology for integrating values into the fabric of strategic planning that is lacking in other models. Our approach requires a greater focus on the psychological components of the planning process, especially during the values scan, mission formulation, and the proactive futuring of strategic business modeling. We have taken this approach since it contributes significantly to the successful implementation of the final strategic plan.

Applied Strategic Planning involves a shift in focus from fire fighting and crisis management to a proactive consideration of the future and "down-board" thinking (as explained in Chapter 1). Our definition of strategic planning—"the process by which the guiding members of an organization envision its future and develop the necessary procedures and operations to achieve that future"—requires a greater emphasis on process consultation than other models typically require. Applied Strategic Planning is very different from mere long-range planning, for it is not just an extrapolation of the present. This envisioning process has special importance for strategic planning in today's turbulent environment. It allows the organization to take charge of its own destiny and create its own future rather than passively wait for the future to arrive.

Our approach is also more process oriented than most of the others now available; it gives more attention to having the plan successfully implemented and less attention to the plan itself. It is also clearly sequenced, with each phase of the process building on the preceding phase.

The involvement of the planning team (which is composed of key organizational members), the regular participation of other key organizational stakeholders, the in-depth examination of the social and psychological underpinnings of the organization, the continuous environmental surveillance, and the constant focus on implementation considerations produce a broader and yet more detailed and more immediately applicable plan than those that result from the use of other models.

Managers and consultants may be interested in a number of other products that have been developed to support the Applied Strategic Planning process. These include *Applied Strategic Planning: The Consultant's Kit,* discussed above, *Applied Strategic Planning: An Introduction,* and *Applied Strategic Planning: An Overview.*

No book ever appears without the assistance of many people. As mentioned, our colleagues Wayne Widdis, Jack Knight, and Bruce Dunn were especially helpful in sharing their experiences and ideas. David Hills brought his light-hearted and good-natured humor to illustrate our model with his sketches; and our editor, Mary Kitzmiller, brought a special level of both competence and commitment to this volume. We express our deep-felt gratitude to all of them.

Leonard D. Goodstein
Washington, DC

Timothy M. Nolan
Milwaukee, Wisconsin

J. William Pfeiffer
San Diego, California

November, 1991

Applied Strategic Planning:

A Comprehensive Guide

Chapter One

Introduction to
Applied Strategic Planning

Alice: Which way should I go?
Cat: That depends on where you are going.
Alice: I don't know where I'm going!
Cat: Then it doesn't matter which way you go!!

Lewis Carroll
1872
Through the Looking-Glass

Most organizations do some kind of long-range or strategic planning, and the formal strategic planning process has been used for over thirty years. However, our experience as consultants to a wide variety of organizations has convinced us that most strategic planning processes are poorly conceptualized and poorly executed; the process is often not very creative and it is tactical rather than strategic in nature; and the so-called strategic plan rarely impacts the day-to-day decisions made in the organization. To be successful, a strategic planning process should provide the criteria for making day-to-day organizational decisions and should provide a template against which all such decisions can be evaluated. This standard for evaluating the adequacy of an organization's strategic planning process is strict, and only a few organizations would successfully meet it. This book provides a detailed and comprehensive guide to assist organizations to develop a strategic planning process that can meet that criteria—if it is carefully followed.

When managers are asked about their organization's strategic plan, they frequently look pained or embarrassed and begin to search through their desk drawers or filing cabinets to find the plan, which is obviously nonfunctional. All too often, strategic planning is seen as a top-management exercise that has little or nothing to do with the actual running of the organization. Kastens (1979) makes similar points in a direct, confrontational fashion.

Strategic Plans Should Impact Day-to-Day Decisions

According to our colleague Wayne Widdis, there are two kinds of important decisions that organizations make: strategic decisions and strategically driven decisions. The organization's senior management needs to be intimately involved with the first of these, because that is clearly an executive function, perhaps the most important executive function. The senior management needs to make certain that the second (strategically driven decisions) are properly made and implemented. This is strategic management: the execution of the strategic plan. Applied Strategic Planning is intended to build or increase the strategic-management capacity of the organization by involving senior management directly in the planning process. Nevertheless, involvement is not enough. Top management must be united and committed to the strategy that this process develops. That unity of commitment is the single most important factor in implementing the strategy.

SOME DEFINITIONS

Planning is the process of establishing objectives and choosing the most suitable means for achieving these objectives prior to taking action. As Russell Ackoff, professor at the Wharton Business School and a noted strategic planning consultant, notes, "Planning...is **anticipatory decision-making**. It is a process of deciding...before action is required" (Ackoff, 1981).

In contrast, we define strategic planning as "**the process by which the guiding members of an organization envision its future and develop the necessary procedures and operations to achieve that future.**" This vision of the future state of the organization provides both a direction in which the organization should move and the energy to begin that move. This envisioning process is very different from long-range planning. Usually, long-range planning is simply the extrapolation of current business trends. Envisioning is more than an attempt to anticipate the future and prepare accordingly. It involves a belief that aspects of the future can be influenced and changed by what we do now. The model of strategic planning presented in this book helps an organization to understand that the strategic planning process does more than plan for the future; it helps an organization to *create* its future. Chapter 2 presents a further discussion of the envisioning process.

Six critical factors need to be involved in any comprehensive understanding of the concept of strategic planning. First, strategy is a coherent, unifying, and integrative pattern of decisions. This means that strategy development is conscious, explicit, and proactive. Second, strategy is a means of establishing an organization's purpose in terms of its long-term objectives, action plans, and allocation of resources. The allocation of resources is perhaps the true *acid test* of the organization's strategic plan. Third, strategy is a definition of an organization's competitive domain: what business the organization really is in. However, this is not as simple a question as it appears on the surface. Fourth, strategy is a response to internal strengths and weaknesses and to external opportunities and threats in order to develop a competitive advantage. Fifth, strategy becomes a logical system for differentiating executive and managerial tasks and roles at corporate, business, and functional levels, so that structure follows function. Sixth, strategy is a way of defining the economic and noneconomic contribution the organization will make to its stakeholders, its raison d'etre. The process of strategic planning outlined in this book deals with each of these six factors, although not in the order listed above.

For our purposes, *tactical planning* and *operational planning* are synonymous. Both relate to *how* to get the job done, whereas strategic planning is concerned with *what* shall be done. That is, both tactical and operational plans are concerned with the setting of specific, measurable objectives and milestones to be achieved by divisions, departments, work groups, and individuals within the organization, typically in a shorter and more specific time frame. While the Applied Strategic Planning process involves such tactical and operational planning, this type of planning occurs in the context of organization-wide action plans that advance the achievement of the overall strategic plan. Chapter 12 ("Integrating Action Plans—Horizontally and Vertically") returns to tactical and operational planning and considers how the various plans that have been developed can be integrated.

Strategic planning needs to answer three basic questions for an organization (Gup, 1979). The first of these, "Where are you going?" was raised by the quotation from Lewis Carroll on the first page of this chapter. Without a clear sense of direction—without a mission statement, clarity about the scope of operations, and a set of specific goals and objectives—an organization, like Alice, is adrift. The second question is "What is the environment?" In answering this question the organization is forced to take a hard, objective look at itself, its external environment, its competitors, and the threats and opportunities that these pose. Furthermore, the organization must measure the gap between its goals or objectives and its capacity to attain those goals or objectives. The final question that strategic planning must answer is "How do you get there?" That is, what are the specific business models that can enable the organization to reach its goals and how do the organization's resources need to be allocated to make these models work? How these questions can be truthfully answered in a way that positively impacts the fate of an organization is the substance of this book.

MARKETING MYOPIA

The need for envisioning, which is central to our definition of strategic planning, is highlighted in the classic article "Marketing Myopia" (Levitt, 1960). By *marketing myopia,* Levitt means a nearsighted view of marketing in terms of the goods or services provided rather than a broader view in terms of needs to be served. In his seminal article he points out that the failure of the railroads to see themselves as being in the transportation business was the critical reason for their decline in importance. The railroads did not decline because the need for moving people and freight disappeared. Rather these needs are now served in

Some Organizations Have Buggy-Whip Myopia

other ways—by airplanes, automobiles, trucks, and buses. Had the railroads defined their mission as transportation rather than railroading, they might very well now have truck, airline, and bus divisions and still be a major economic, political, and social American institution. The only North American railroad that seemed to have successfully understood and solved this problem was the Canadian Pacific Railroad, which has evolved such a configuration and is a large, successful organization.

Strategic planning is much more than just an envisioning process. It requires setting clear goals and objectives and attaining those goals and objectives during specified periods in order to reach the planned future state. Thus, these targets must be developed within the context of the desired future state and must be realistic, objective, and attainable. The goals and objectives developed in the strategic planning process should provide an organization with its core priorities and a set of guidelines for virtually all day-to-day managerial decisions.

Our definition of strategic planning focuses on the *process* of planning, not the plan that is produced. Although an organization's documents may delineate mission statements, strategic goals, critical success indicators, functional objectives, and so on, successful strategic planning is characterized by the process of self-examination, the confrontation of difficult choices, the setting of priorities, and the like. Documents too often are merely filed away until a revision is mandated by some external force.

Strategic planning is a reiterative process. Strategic planning and *strategic management*—which we define as the day-to-day implementation of the strategic plan—are the most important, never-ending jobs of management, especially top management. Once a strategic planning cycle is completed, the task of management is to ensure its implementation and then to decide on when to begin the next planning cycle. The future, by definition, always faces us; thus, organizations must always be in the simultaneous processes of planning and implementing their plans. Planning is what we need to do before taking actions.

WHY DO STRATEGIC PLANNING?

The single most important answer to the question of "Why do strategic planning?" is that it provides a framework for action that is embedded in the mind-sets of the organization and its employees. Strategic planning provides a framework for managers and others in the organization to assess strategic situations similarly, discuss the alternatives in a common language, and decide on actions (based on a shared set of values and understandings) that need to be taken in a reasonable period of time. A short version of this answer is that the only valid reason for strategic planning is to build the strategic-management capacity of the organization.

Strategic planning also enables the organization's leaders to unleash the energy of the organization behind a shared vision and a shared belief that the vision can be fulfilled. Strategic planning increases the capacity of the organization to implement the strategic plan completely on a timely basis. Strategic planning also helps the organization develop, organize, and utilize a better understanding of the environment in which it operates, or the industry or arena in which it operates, of its customers—current and potential—and of its own capabilities and limitations.

Strategic planning provides an opportunity on at least an annual basis to constantly adjust to current events and actions by competitors. Furthermore, strategic planning should provide the proper incentives to attract and properly motivate key managers in the organization. Strategic success must occur on both the individual and organizational level.

A necessary component of effective strategic planning is called *down-board thinking*. This concept is analogous to the way world-class chess players think. They must not only decide on their immediate moves, but they must look "down board" and consider their opponents' possible responses to their moves and plan a number of moves ahead. So it is with strategic planning: The planning team must look down board, consider the implications of its plans, and then base additional plans on those implications.

WHAT STRATEGIC PLANNING IS NOT

Having defined strategic planning and why it should be done, we feel compelled to suggest what strategic planning is *not*. First, and most importantly, strategic planning is not forecasting. Forecasting involves the extrapolation of present business trends into the future. Strategic planning is necessary precisely because such extrapolations from the present to the future are rarely correct, even for the short term. Organizational environments are constantly changing, and most experts on these environments agree that the pace of these changes is exponentially increasing. Whatever utility simple forecasting might have had in the past, it will be sharply reduced in the future.

Strategic planning is not the simple application of quantitative techniques to business planning. Rather strategic planning requires creativity, analysis, honesty, and a level of soul searching that could not be farther from quantitative analysis. Although some quantitative analyses are necessary for a complete strategic planning process, these are never the core of the process.

Strategic planning does not deal only with future decisions. Instead, strategic planning is concerned with making decisions today that will affect the organization and its future.

Furthermore, strategic planning does not eliminate risk. Rather, strategic planning helps managers assess the risks that they must take by gaining a better understanding of the parameters involved in their decisions.

A NEW STRATEGIC PLANNING MODEL

The model of strategic planning presented in this book is based on existing models; but it differs in content, emphasis, and process. This model (Figure 1-1) is especially useful for medium-sized and small organizations, and it is as useful for governmental agencies and not-for-profit organizations as it is for business and industrial organizations. Using this model for strategic planning will provide both new direction and new energy to the organization. The model differs from others in its continual concern with application and implementation—not only

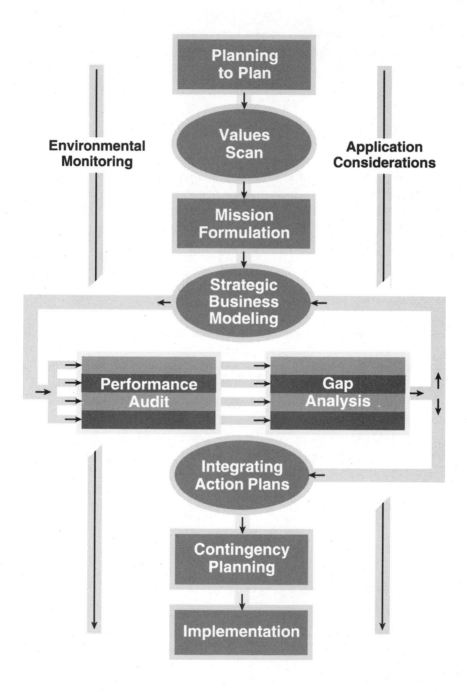

Figure 1-1. The Applied Strategic Planning Model

after its completion, but at every step along the way; hence the title "Applied Strategic Planning." This model also differs from others in its emphasis on values-driven decision making and its heavy focus on creatively envisioning the ideal organizational future.

The model involves nine sequential phases, with two of these phases (performance audit and gap analysis) essentially two differentiated aspects of a single phase; the model also includes two continuous functions (environmental monitoring and application considerations), both of which are involved at each of the sequential phases. The Applied Strategic Planning model places three of the sequential phases (values scan, strategic business modeling, and integrating action plans) in ovals rather than rectangles to differentiate those elements that are different from the usual approaches to strategic planning. We emphasize them in this manner because we believe they represent our model's distinctive competency, a topic we will return to later.

In the sequential steps, after gap analysis, there is a choice (represented in the model by arrows). If the gaps between the strategic business model and the performance audit identified in the gap analysis can be readily resolved, the process can move on to the next phase—integrating action plans. If this is not the case, the strategic business modeling phase must be revisited.

This chapter provides an overview of the model and its utility. The succeeding chapters examine each phase of the model in greater detail.

Planning to Plan

The prework of the Applied Strategic Planning process involves answering a host of questions and making a number of decisions, all of which are critically important to the eventual success or failure of the entire planning process. The following questions are typical of those that should be asked:

- How much commitment to the planning process is present?
- Who should be involved?
- How will we involve the absent stakeholders?
- How does the organization's fiscal year fit the planning process?
- How long will it take?
- What information is needed in order to plan successfully?
- Who needs to develop the data?

Planning to plan includes developing answers to these questions and making the necessary decisions to implement those answers prior

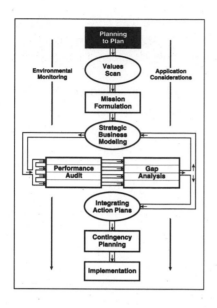

to the initiation of any actual planning process. It is critically important not to rush into the actual planning process without clarifying the various expectations held by people in the organization about planning, without considering who is and is not involved, and so on. These issues must be resolved before even the decision to plan can be made.

The first step in planning to plan is to make certain that there is organizational commitment to the process—that the organization's key players, especially the chief executive officer (CEO) or executive director, view the planning process as important and are willing to invest time and effort in that process in a way that is visible to the rest of the organization. Without that kind of obvious commitment to the planning process by the power structure of the organization, there can be no successful strategic planning.

Once commitment from the chief executive officer is secured, the next concern is to identify the planning team. The CEO should be involved, especially in the early stages, as should other key people in the organization. The model presented here requires top-management involvement on a continuous basis. At the same time, both input to the process and reactions to decisions that are being reached must be solicited from a broadly representative group of people in the organization.

To be effective, a planning team should be able to observe and process its own group dynamics. This means that the planning team probably should not exceed ten to twelve permanent members. Who should be involved, what the selection process should be, how to deal with organizational members who feel that they should have been included, and how to solicit input and feedback regularly from various segments of the organization are matters that need to be addressed with both candor and sensitivity by those initiating the strategic planning process. Among the factors to be considered in making these decisions are the size of the organization, its structure, the various stakeholder groups, and the organization's history in dealing with issues of general organizational importance. Again, these issues should be resolved prior to the initiation of any actual planning.

Although some recommend that the planning process be assigned to a staff group, we believe that deciding the future course of an organization *is* the task of top management—a task that cannot and should not be delegated. The proper role of staff in this process is to serve as a resource to the management planning group, conduct research, generate data, and develop alternative ways of integrating and implementing the action steps that emerge from the planning process. Chapter 5 ("Planning to Plan") deals with this phase.

Environmental Monitoring and Application Considerations

The Applied Strategic Planning model involves both discrete and continuous phases. The continuous processes are environmental monitoring and application considerations, that is, managing those issues that need to be addressed immediately as they emerge from the considerations of the planning group. These are briefly considered before our discussion returns to the discrete phases.

Environmental Monitoring

Throughout their existence, organizations need to be aware of what is happening in their environments that might affect them, and this is especially true throughout the planning process. Four separate but overlapping environments, in particular, need to be monitored:

1. The macro environment;
2. The industry environment;
3. The competitive environment; and
4. The organization's internal environment.

During the planning process, information about each of these environments must be available to conduct the values scan, to draft the mission statement, to formulate the strategic business model, to identify the competition, and so on.

The environmental monitoring process will also identify a variety of factors, both internal and external to the organization, to be considered as part of the strategic planning process. In fact, one of the extra benefits of strategic planning is that the organization gains a better understanding of how environmental monitoring should be done.

Factors to be considered as part of the macro-environmental-monitoring process include social factors such as demographics, technological factors such as the large-scale use of microcomputers, economic factors such as interest rates, and political factors such as changes in governmental regulation. Among the factors to be considered as part of the industry environment are the structure of the industry, how the industry is financed, the degree of governmental presence, the typical products used in the industry, and the typical marketing strategies of the industry. Monitoring the competitive environment includes factors such as consideration of competitor profiles, market-segmentation patterns, and research and development. Among the factors to be considered as part of the internal organizational environment are the structure of the company, its history, and its distinctive strengths and weaknesses. Predicting how each of these areas might affect the organization over time is an essential part of Applied Strategic Planning and needs to be considered in each phase. Perhaps the most important single decision to be made as part of environmental monitoring is deciding *what* important aspects of the environment should be regularly monitored.

The environmental monitoring process should be continual, so that appropriate information about what is happening or about to happen in the various environments is always available. Strategic planning provides an opportune time for a major use of this data. Learning not only to collect relevant information, but to organize, interpret, and use this information is critical to strategic success.

Application Considerations

While implementation is the final step of the model, and the overall strategic plan cannot be implemented until integration and checking occurs, there is a continual need for application and implementation throughout the planning process. Every phase of the planning process contains application aspects, and these should be addressed during that phase, not postponed until the final implementation phase. For example, in the planning to plan phase, absent stakeholders need to be informed about the initiation of the planning process and their assent to the process must be secured; if the values scan identifies incongruous values in segments of the organization, these need to be addressed as soon as they are identified; and the mission statement should be distributed for comments and suggestions before it is accepted, and no further planning should be done until there is consensus on the mission statement.

Chapter 6 ("Environmental Monitoring and Application Considerations") discusses these topics in more detail, and each chapter will raise the issues of environmental monitoring and application considerations that are appropriate for that particular phase of the process.

Values Scan

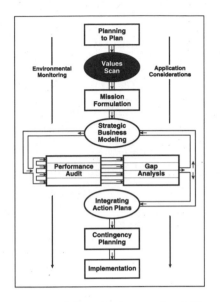

A values scan is an examination of the values of the members of the planning team, the current values of the organization, the organization's philosophy of operations, the assumptions that the organization ordinarily uses in its operations, the organization's preferred culture, and, finally, the values of the stakeholders in the organization's future. In this values scan, the planning team moves from an individual focus to a broader examination of the organization and how it works as a social system. The values scan is the first formal step of the Applied Strategic Planning model and is entirely different from that found in most strategic planning models.

Personal Values

An important part of this phase involves an examination of the personal values of the individual members of the team. Rokeach (1973, p. 5) defines a value as "an enduring belief that a specific mode of conduct or end-state of existence is personally or socially preferable to an opposite or converse mode of conduct or end-state of existence." An individual for whom risk taking is an important personal value will envision a very different organizational future than will a person who holds security as a high personal value. Likewise, the goals and dreams of an individual who holds professional reputation as a value and is less interested in power will be different from those of a person with opposite priorities.

These differences have clear implications for the organization's future direction, structure, and decision-making processes and for all other work of the management team. If the differences in values are not identified, clarified, and understood, there can be little agreement about how the organization's future meets the personal expectations of the individual members of the management group. Once there is clarity on the personal values of the members of the planning team and an agreement on how their differences in values can be managed, the strategic planning process can move ahead. This phase of Applied Strategic Planning is very much a values-clarification process, and the actual strategic plan represents the operational implementation of the shared values-based vision of the management team.

Organizational Values

Once the individual values of the management planning team have been worked through, the desired values of the organization as a whole must be considered. These organizational values will be played out in the future behavior of the organization. To avoid an overly abstract discussion of these preferred future behaviors, the group may want to identify some recent organizational decisions that caused them pride and some that caused them concern or shame. The sharing of these feelings and an exploration of the underlying reasons for them will demonstrate to the planning group that all management decisions *are*, in fact, values based.

Philosophies of Operations

An organization's values sometimes are organized and codified into the organization's *philosophy of operations,* that is, the way the organization approaches its work. Some organizations have explicit, formal statements of philosophy, such as the "Five Principles of Mars" (Figure 1-2). This statement by the multinational food and candy corporation contains only five short sentences on quality, responsibility, mutuality, efficiency, and freedom; and it stresses the importance of the consumer.

This type of formal statement integrates the organization's values into the way it does business. Values-driven organizations such as Mars spend a great deal of time and energy in disseminating and tracking the impact of their philosophies on all organizational behavior. All employees of the organization are expected to know the philosophy and use it in their daily work, and typically there are serious sanctions against any violation of the philosophy by an organizational member.

All organizations have philosophies of operation, whether or not those philosophies are stated explicitly. If an organization has an implicit philosophy of operations, then part of the strategic planning process is to make that philosophy explicit. The strategic plan must fit the philosophy, or the philosophy needs to be modified.

An organization's philosophy of operations includes a series of assumptions about the way things work and the way in which decisions are made. A typical assumption in the profit-making sector is "No profit can be made doing business with the government," or "Allowing a labor union to organize our hourly production people would destroy this

---

1. Quality
The consumer is our boss, quality is our work, and value for money is our goal.

2. Responsibility
As individuals, we demand total responsibility from ourselves; as associates, we support the responsibilities of others.

3. Mutuality
A mutual benefit is a shared benefit; a shared benefit will endure.

4. Efficiency
We use resources to the fullest, waste nothing, and do only what we can do best.

5. Freedom
We need freedom to shape our future; we need profit to remain free.

Figure 1-2. The Five Principles of Mars

company." In the not-for-profit sector, typical assumptions include "If we do not spend all of this year's budget, it will be cut next time," and "You have to go along to get along." Other general assumptions are that the organization's growth is assured by an expanding and more affluent population or that there never will be a satisfactory substitute for the organization's major product or service.

Unless such assumptions are examined in terms of their current validity and relevance—whether or not they ever were true or relevant—the organization will continue to assume that they are true and operate accordingly. Thus, an important part of the strategic planning process is to identify the assumptions that the organization makes about its environment, its markets, its operations, and how things do or should work and to examine their validity.

Culture

Organizations develop cultures in a fashion similar to the way societies in general develop cultures. Schein (1990) defines culture as (a) a pattern of basic assumptions, (b) invented, discovered, or developed by a given group, (c) as it learns to cope with its problems of external adaptation and internal integration, (d) that has worked well enough to be considered valid and, therefore (e) is taught to new members as the (f) correct way to perceive, think, and feel in relation to those problems. Schein goes on to point out that, in analyzing an organization's culture there are three levels in which the culture manifests itself: (1) observable artifacts, including behavior; (2) values; and (3) the basic underlying assumptions. Of these factors—which lie at the heart of most of our actions in social systems—only the artifacts are directly observable. All the rest—much of which is unconscious—must be inferred from those observables, including values that can be assessed only indirectly.

Behavioral evidence about the organization's culture abounds—in the organization's physical structures and sites, in how it greets or guards itself from outsiders, in its war stories told about the good (or bad) old days, in those regarded as the organization's heroes and villains, in the rites and rituals of the organization, and so on. But all this must be decoded; and this decoding is difficult, because it involves drawing inferences about the underlying meaning and significance of behavior, a frequently controversial task. Thus, it often becomes one of the tasks that need to be initiated and managed by the strategic planning consultant.

An organization's culture provides the social context in and through which the organization performs its work. It guides the organization's members in decision making, how time and energy are invested, which facts are examined with care and which are summarily rejected, which options are looked favorably upon from the start, which types of people are selected to work for and in the organization, and how practically everything else is done in the organization.

The culture of an organization will either facilitate or hinder both the strategic planning process and the implementation of the plan that process produces. A formal assessment of the organization's culture and its potential impact on the implementation of the strategic plan is ordinarily performed as part of the performance audit and gap analysis phases of Applied Strategic Planning. Nevertheless, a discussion of the organization's culture—especially the roots of that culture in the assumptions, values, and beliefs of the management team—often begins during the values scan. It is a useful and important part of that phase and provides a link to issues discussed in Chapter 3 ("Culture and Applied Strategic Planning"), Chapter 7 ("Values Scan"), Chapter 8 ("Mission Formulation"), Chapter 9 ("Strategic Business Modeling"), Chapter 10 ("Performance Audit"), and Chapter 11 ("Gap Analysis").

Stakeholder Analysis

Scanning an organization's values requires a stakeholder analysis. Stakeholders are those individuals, groups, and organizations who will be impacted by or interested in the organization's strategic plan. They must be identified, and their concerns must be determined (that is, how their resources, status, freedom of action, relationships, and activities may appear to them to be impacted by shifts or changes in the organization's direction). Stakeholders typically include employees (including managers), clients or customers, suppliers, governments, unions, creditors, owners, shareholders, and members of the community who believe that they have a stake in the organization, regardless of whether or not such a belief is accurate or reasonable.

Once the stakeholders are identified, the impact of various future states on different stakeholders can be considered as they are developed as part of the strategic planning process. It is important to identify who the planning team regards as significant stakeholders early in the values scan. If this is not done until later in the process, a more selective list may emerge. The stakeholders are the various constituencies that need to be considered by the strategic planning team.

The values scan is the most important and one of the most difficult phases of the Applied Strategic Planning process. It requires in-depth analysis of the most fundamental beliefs that underlie organizational life, especially organizational decision making. Such analysis is rare in the experience of many managers and thus can be a long and painful experience. But without such confrontation, unresolved differences in assumptions, values, beliefs, and philosophy will surface continually in the planning process, blocking forward movement and interfering with the development of a functional strategic plan. Once the differences in the management group are surfaced and clarified, and some level of agreement reached about how differences are to be managed in the future so that they do not interfere with the planning process, it is time to move on to the next phase of the process. Chapter 7 provides a more in-depth examination of the values-scanning process.

Mission Formulation

Mission formulation involves developing a clear statement of what business the organization is in (or plans to be in)—a concise definition of the purpose that the organization is attempting to fulfill in society and/or the economy. In formulating its mission, an organization must answer four primary questions:

1. *What* function(s) does the organization perform?
2. For *whom* does the organization perform this function?

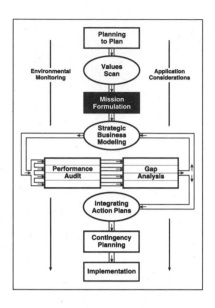

3. *How* does the organization go about filling this function?

4. *Why* does this organization exist?

Most organizations tend to answer the "what" question in terms of the goods or services produced for customers. Manufacturers of detergents see themselves in the "soap business," and gasoline producers see themselves as in the "oil business." As Levitt (1960) pointed out decades ago, such myopia blocks organizations both from seeing new opportunity for growth and expansion and from responding to threats and challenges.

The recommended alternative is to answer the question in terms of the customer or client needs that the organization attempts to meet. If an organization identifies itself as meeting certain customer needs, it will be more sensitive to identifying and treating those needs, more likely to develop new products and services to meet those needs, and less likely to experience obsolescence and decline. If a detergent manufacturer sees itself as being in the business of providing a mechanism for helping people to clean their garments, or if gasoline producers see themselves as being in the business of providing sources of energy to consumers, many new options are open to them—ultrasonic cleaners, solar and wind-power generators, and so on.

In the not-for-profit sector, answering the question of *what* function the organization serves is critical. For example, once a certain metropolitan library became clear that its function was the dissemination of information, and not merely distributing books, options for new services became apparent, as did new community support.

Successful organizations try to identify value-satisfying goods and services that meet the needs of the public and include these considerations in their mission formulations. A major issue in mission formulation typically is achieving consensus on how broadly or narrowly to answer the "what" question.

Identifying the "who" is the second concern of mission formulation. No organization, no matter how large, can meet all the needs of all possible clients or customers. The mission formulation requires a clear identification of what portion of the total potential customer base an organization identifies as its primary target. The process of sorting out the potential customer or client base and identifying which portion should be sought out by the organization typically is called *market segmentation.*

Markets can be segmented in many ways: geographically, financially, ethnically, and so on. The needs of Sun Belt consumers are different from those of Frost Belt consumers. Federal Express serves customers who are willing to spend more than the price of ordinary postage to ensure next-day delivery of packages. Kosher foods have devout consumers, as do soul foods. Historically, General Motors has had five traditional automobile lines, each designed for consumers in different economic strata.

Understanding the marketplace is also important for the not-for-profit sector, especially those that are publicly funded. Clarity about the two kinds of critical clients—those who control the funding sources and those who are the recipients of the organization's service—and about meeting the needs and expectations of both sets of clients is an important ingredient of success in this arena.

Once the planning team has identified what the organization does and for whom, the next step is deciding how the organization will proceed to achieve these targets. The "how" can involve a marketing strategy, such as being the low-cost producer or the technological leader or the high-quality manufacturer; it may involve a distribution system, such as regional warehouses or evening classes in factories or no-appointment medical-treatment facilities. It may involve customer service or personalized selling or any of a variety of processes through which an organization can deliver products or services to a defined consumer group.

The question of *why* an organization performs the functions that it does—the existential question—frequently is an important one for both profit-oriented and not-for-profit organizations. Many organizations feel that they need to include some simple statement of their raison d'etre as part of their mission statements. It can appear as the "heart" in the diagram of the triangular relationship of the "what," "who," and "how" questions (see Figure 8-1 in the chapter on Mission Formulation). For example, the mission statement of the Johnsonville Sausage Company of Sheboygan Falls, Wisconsin, includes the following: "We, here at Johnsonville, have a moral responsibility to become the best sausage company ever established..." while the Center for Creative Leadership in Greensboro, North Carolina, states, "Our mission is to encourage and develop creative leadership and effective management for the good of society overall." Although not all organizations choose to include such a statement—nor should they be required to do so, although we recommend it—such statements are often a natural outgrowth of the organizational-level values scan, and the Applied Strategic Planning model promotes the inclusion of such a statement.

Developing a mission statement can be an extremely difficult and time-consuming task, but it is one that the planning group must complete before moving to the next step. Developing, editing, and reaching consensus on such a statement requires skill, patience, and understanding. However, the mission statement provides an enormous bonus to an organization: It clearly charts its future direction and establishes a basis for organizational decision making. The next step is for each major unit of the organization to develop its own mission statement. Unit mission statements should be more focused and more limited than that of the total organization, but they must be clearly derived from the organizational mission statement. The process of mission formulation is covered in greater detail in Chapter 8.

Strategic Business Modeling

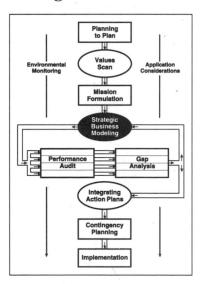

Strategic business modeling involves the organization's initial attempt to spell out in some detail the paths by which the organization's mission is to be accomplished. Strategic business modeling is not an extrapolation of what the organization is now doing. It is not a long-range plan to do more of the same, only better. In this phase of the process, the planning team is asked to conceptualize a series of specific future scenarios. It is also asked to identify the steps necessary for achieving those scenarios, who will be responsible for those steps, and when those steps can be accomplished. The strategic business models that are developed should reflect the values and the overall mission created in the earlier phases of the planning process.

Strategic business modeling thus involves establishing the quantified business objectives of the organization. The process of strategic business modeling consists of four major elements:

1. Identifying the major lines of business (LOBs) or strategic profile that the organization will develop to fulfill its mission.
2. Establishing the critical success indicators (CSIs) that will enable the organization to track its progress in each LOB that it intends to pursue.
3. Identifying the strategic thrusts by which the organization will achieve its vision of the ideal future state. Strategic thrusts are organizational goals that are neither LOBs nor the CSIs to assess those goals, although strategic thrusts typically can impact LOBs and usually are trackable by CSIs. Examples of strategic thrusts include the development of a total quality management process, the creation of a fully functioning human resources department, and the installation of a point-of-sale inventory system.
4. Determining the culture necessary to support those LOBs, CSIs, and strategic thrusts.

Each of these four elements must be determined and independently worked through during the next two formal phases (i.e., performance audit and gap analysis) of Applied Strategic Planning and, where necessary, looped back and revised before moving on to the next element.

Lines of Business

The LOB analysis involves deciding the mix of products and/or services the organization will offer in the future. After each such LOB is identified, the relative size of that LOB must be agreed on—in terms of gross revenue, marketing required, profit potential, investment required, and so on. The LOB analyses allow an organization to change its product/service mix—to drop those that no longer meet market needs, that have become unprofitable, that require too much investment to maintain, etc. For example, as a result of its strategic business modeling, a law firm decided to abandon its maritime-law and patent-law practices, as the volume of such work no longer justified maintaining these as LOBs. A government agency decided on the basis of its planning process to reduce its heavy focus on MIS consulting and to begin instead to focus on general-management consultation.

Critical Success Indicators

As the organization conceptualizes its future, it must identify the specific means of measuring its progress toward that future, setting critical success indicators (CSIs) for each LOB and then for the organization as a whole. The CSIs are typically a mix of hard financial figures—such as sales, margins, and return on investment (ROI)—and soft indices of success—such as employee morale and opinions of customers about service. Other measures, such as the number of new product launches or new markets established, can be included as long as they are clear, quantifiable, and trackable.

Strategic Thrusts

Strategic thrusts typically are tasks, processes, or goals that are seen as necessary steps in the achievement of the organization's total strategic plan. These strategic thrusts may be short-term, focused activities or long-term, far-reaching ones, ranging from the improvement of the organization's inventory control system to the development of rather complex organizational structures. However, regardless of their scope or nature, they must be in full alignment with the organizational culture that is determined to be necessary for success.

For example, one of our clients saw the need to create a fully functioning human resources development capacity within the organization. This involved a human resources need analysis and a complete redesign of the recruitment, orientation, compensation, development, and promotion processes. It even included the development of an in-company training school. The resulting shift in decision making regarding human resources and the enhanced alignment between resource needs and capabilities had a profoundly positive effect on the organization's chances of success in achieving its overall strategic goals.

Culture

Relative to determining the necessary culture two questions are important:
1. What common understanding do members of the organization need to share to support these LOBs, CSIs, and strategic thrusts?
2. What are the cultural specifications necessary to achieve success?

For example, a major international airline set as one of its CSIs a 20-percent increase in customer satisfaction—as measured by reductions in passenger complaints, reports from focus groups and questionnaires, employee reports, and a variety of other sources. To achieve such a dramatic increase in customer satisfaction, a market-oriented culture was required. This culture had to be sensitive to the critical importance of meeting passenger needs and of being willing and able to provide "seamless" service.

After the culture requirement has been set, the degree to which such a culture is present or absent in the organization is ascertained in the performance audit phase of Applied Strategic Planning.

Priorities need to be set for these CSIs to make certain that the most important indices of being on track have been established and will be closely monitored over time. A tentative timetable for reaching particular levels for each of these indices also must be established. The performance audit and the gap analysis phases examine the current resources of the organization to meet these new requirements, and the planning team must determine to what degree the CSIs are likely to be achieved.

That Applied Strategic Planning is distinctively different from long-range planning becomes most clear in the strategic business modeling process. Long-range planning tends to be merely an extension of what an organization is doing already, almost like a spreadsheet extension of the previous year's results. An international airline may plan to sell more tickets through its existing distribution network, or a hospital may

WE CAN'T EXPECT HER TO BE REAL JOLLY. THIS IS THE DAY THEY CONFRONT THE ORGANIZATIONAL CULTURE.

The Necessary Culture Must Be Determined

plan to open a suburban branch; but both of these plans involve only slight variations in or expansion of the product or service offered in existing markets. Such typical long-range planning often is myopic and unduly constraining. When an organization focuses heavily on that area of the market that it currently occupies, it overlooks other possible markets. Thus, for example, the airline might decide to enter the small-package delivery business, while the hospital might consider preventative health programs. Applied Strategic Planning, with its emphasis on stepping back and envisioning the ideal future of the organization, enables the organization to confirm current directions that are part of a viable future and to explore new directions that would not emerge naturally from the present day's work.

Several considerations are critical to the success of this stage. First, the modeling must be congruent with and build on the identified values and mission of the organization. Second, the modeling must be done in a context of proactive futuring: the belief that, although no one can fully predict the future, it is possible to anticipate significant aspects of the future, to conceptualize a desired end state for the organization (by taking into account those anticipated aspects), and to work proactively to make that desired future state occur. Within this context, the organization takes responsibility for its own future rather than assigning that responsibility to unseen external forces. Third, strategic business modeling involves a heavy emphasis on focused creativity, a free-flowing generation of ideas that involves many alternative options for the organization to consider. Success in this phase of the process is most likely to be attained when there is a maximum creative output within mission-focused, *realistic* boundaries. The next steps of the planning process—performance audit and gap analysis—are intended to identify whether or not the organization has the necessary resources, as *commitment* alone is not sufficient to achieve success. Chapter 9 returns to the development of strategic business plans.

Performance Audit

Once the planning team has envisioned the organization's future, it must develop a clear understanding of the organization's current performance in a process called the *performance audit*. It is important that the envisioning of the future precede any in-depth analysis of the organization's current performance and capacity. Otherwise, such an analysis is likely to limit the options that the planning team considers. Visions not based on reality are hallucinations. The performance audit is intended to prevent hallucinations.

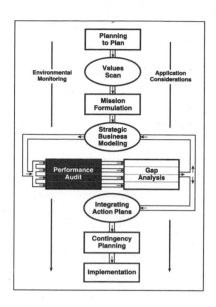

The performance audit is a focused effort that involves the simultaneous study of the organization's internal strengths and weaknesses and of the external opportunities and threats that may positively or negatively effect the organization in its efforts to achieve a desired future. The acronym SWOT represents these four factors (strengths, weaknesses, opportunities, threats) that must be considered in an effective performance audit. The SWOT analysis is the major way of validating the strategic business model.

The internal performance audit examines the *recent* performance of the organization in terms of the basic performance indices—cash flow, growth, staffing patterns, quality, technology, operations, service, profit, ROI, cash flow, and so on—that have been identified as critical in the strategic profile. The purpose of the performance audit is to provide the data for the *gap analysis*—determining the degree to which the strategic business model is realistic and workable.

What is necessary here is detached objectivity and a willingness to evaluate realistically the internal strengths and weakness of the organization, as painful as such an analysis may be. An important part of this internal analysis is the evaluation of the organization's present structure: Is the present organizational structure likely to support the new mission and LOBs?

Any data that can help the organization to better understand its present capabilities for doing its work should be included in the performance analysis. Such data might include life cycles of existing products, employee productivity, scrap rate, inventory turnover, facilities (including capacity and condition), and management capability. The important question that the performance audit must answer is whether or not the organization has the capability to implement its strategic business plan successfully and thus achieve its mission. Therefore, in planning the performance audit, the team must pay special attention to securing the hard data that will indicate the organization's capacity to move in the identified strategic direction.

The performance audit must also include information about the forces outside the organization that may impact success in reaching its goals—the opportunities and threats of the SWOT analysis. During this external analysis, the planning team must study competitors, suppliers, markets and customers, economic trends, labor market conditions, and governmental regulations on all levels that can affect the organization positively or negatively. This information should include a consideration of both current and future trends—a longitudinal perspective. In chess, this consideration is called "down-board thinking"; that is, the player thinks, "If I do this, my opponent will do that, then I will need to..." In strategic planning, the team needs to say, "If we do this, our competitor (or customers or supplier or governmental agency) will do that, then we will need to..."

Competitor Analysis

One of the most important sets of data is the competitor analysis, which profiles organizations that are in the same business or aiming for the same market segment of clients or customers. The competitor analysis should include "creative crossovers"—items that are sold or services that are delivered for similar reasons. For example, one of the chief competitors of Cross pens during the holiday seasons is not another pen manufacturer but the billfold industry, because both pen-and-pencil sets and billfolds are frequently purchased as holiday gifts for men. Because the competitor analysis requires some research, each member of the planning team should have responsibility for an analysis of one to three competitors. This responsibility will also increase the members' awareness of the marketplace.

Much, but not all, of the data required for the internal performance audit will be available in organizations that have good management information systems, including financial reporting systems. Furthermore, although data bases may be available (inside or outside the organization), the organization may need to hire or reassign financial staff to research, validate, and analyze the data. This is a crunch point in many organizations: the ability—in terms of time, personnel, expertise, and so on—to handle and report on the data. However, it is a critical step that must be completed adequately.

One major emphasis of the performance audit should be a strategic business unit (SBU) analysis. An SBU is a division, department, or product line that is a business unto itself within the organization; for example, the loan department in a bank, the home-furnishings division of a large department store, or the pharmacy in a large drug store. The

SBU analysis should identify which aspects of the business are losing money, how strengths can be reinforced and weaknesses eliminated, and so on. Line-of-business analyses need to be performed in each of these SBUs as well as in the overall organization.

It should be obvious by now that the performance audit and subsequent analysis are some of the most detailed and time-consuming aspects of Applied Strategic Planning. However, without this important, detailed information, the basis for planning is incomplete and shaky. In addition, the need for candor, openness, and non-defensiveness during the performance audit cannot be overestimated. An organization that fools itself during the performance audit is almost certain to find itself with an unworkable plan. Obviously, under such circumstances, the time and effort put into the strategic planning process will result in a travesty. The performance audit is discussed in detail in Chapter 10.

Gap Analysis

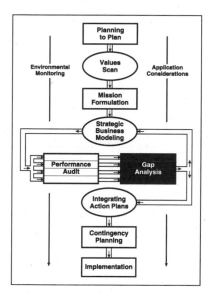

After the performance audit is complete, it is necessary to identify gaps between the current performance of the organization and the desired performance required for the successful realization of its strategic business model. This gap analysis is a comparison of the data generated during the performance audit with that requisite for executing its strategic plan; that is, a *reality test*. Furthermore, the gap analysis requires the development of specific strategies to close each gap identified.

For each gap that cannot be closed by a readily apparent strategy, the planning team must *return* to the strategic business modeling phase and rework the model until the gap can be closed. For this reason, the Applied Strategic Planning Model shows arrows in two directions following the gap analysis: those proceeding to the integrating action plans phase and those returning to strategic business modeling. When gaps remain, several repetitions of this process may be necessary before the gaps can be closed. Sometimes the mission statement has to be modified.

If the gap analysis reveals a substantial disparity between the performance audit and the strategic profile or the strategies identified for achieving it, the design or functioning of the organization may need to be re-examined. Obviously, either the strategic business model or the organization (or both) needs to be modified in order to close the gaps between the plan and the organization's capacity.

In general, there are four basic approaches to closing gaps between the organization's current and desired state:

1. Lengthen the time frame for accomplishing the objective. This approach is used when the current allocation of resources is appropriate but more time is needed to achieve the goal than initially planned.
2. Reduce the size or scope of the objective. This approach is viable if the vision is appropriate but lesser or somewhat modified objectives are more achievable and less risky.
3. Reallocate resources to achieve goals. This approach is appropriate if these goals can be achieved only by focusing existing resources that have been spread too thin.
4. Obtain new resources. This approach is appropriate when new talent, products, markets, or capital are necessary to achieve desired goals.

Each of these approaches should be considered carefully each time a gap is encountered and needs to be closed.

Events never quite work out quite as anticipated, but strategic plans need to be developed nevertheless. The typical planning process focuses, appropriately, on the highest-probability events, but this focus can result in an incomplete set of plans. Contingency planning (a later phase of Applied Strategic Planning) involves the development of specific action(s) when lower-probability events occur, but only those lower-probability events that would have important consequences for the organization.

A significant issue in the gap analysis is whether or not there is alignment between the strategic business model and the values scan. Such a comparison is necessary to ascertain that the actions the organization is proposing to take are consistent with its culture. As noted earlier, plans that do not take into account and build on the organization's culture are not likely to succeed. This portion of the gap analysis requires the same degree of openness, candor, and confrontation that should have typified the original values scan. The gap analysis is important because it clearly contrasts the organization's *wants* against reality. In effect, it is the anchor that keeps the plan from floating off in an unguided, or misguided, direction. Chapter 11 provides detailed coverage of gap analysis.

Integrating Action Plans

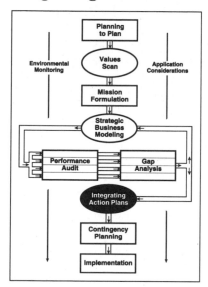

Once the gaps revealed in the gap analysis phase have been closed to a manageable level, two important issues need to be addressed:

1. The grand strategies or master business plans must be developed for each of the LOBs.
2. The various units of the organization—functional and business—need to develop detailed operational plans based on the overall organizational plan. These unit plans must reflect the grand strategy and must include budgets and timetables.

A grand strategy is a comprehensive general approach that guides the actions of an LOB. Grand strategies indicate how the strategic plans of each of the LOBs are to be accomplished. Pierce and Robinson (1991) identify the following twelve grand strategies:

1. Concentrated growth, that is, focusing on a single product that has been a profitable mainstay of the organization.
2. Market development, that is, adding new customers in related markets.
3. Product development, that is, creating new, but related products that can be sold to existing markets.
4. Innovation, that is, creating products that are so new and superior that existing products become obsolete.
5. Horizontal integration, that is, acquiring or merging with a similar organization in order to reduce competition.
6. Vertical integration, that is, either developing an internal supply network (backward vertical integration) or developing an inter-

nal distribution system that puts the organization closer to its end users (forward vertical integration).

7. Joint venture, that is, teaming up with another organization to develop a new product or market.
8. Concentric diversification, that is, acquiring or merging with organizations that are compatible with the organization's technology, markets, or products.
9. Diversification, that is, acquiring or merging with an organization that counterbalances its own strengths and weaknesses.
10. Retrenchment, that is, reversing the negative trends in profits through a variety of cost-cutting methods.
11. Divestiture, that is, selling off or closing down a segment of the organization.
12. Liquidation, that is, selling off the organization for its tangible assets and closing it down.

Deciding which of these grand strategies best fits both the organization as a whole and each of the LOBs in meeting their goals is an important part of Applied Strategic Planning.

For organizations that are arrayed in business units, in each of the separate business units detailed business plans (based on the newly established strategic directions) need to be developed. On the functional level, financial plans, sales and marketing plans, human and capital resources plans, and so on, are needed. For example, in a human resources plan, current and future needs for staffing on the managerial, supervisory, technical, production, and administrative levels would be developed for the time period of the plan. Such a plan would take into account employee turnover, staffing needs, recruitment and training programs, and costs and would include contingency plans.

Each action plan developed by a functional group or business unit in the organization also must be understood and agreed to by each of the other functional groups in the organization. This process often is difficult, because once the model is developed and plans are made, each part of the organization begins to compete for limited resources in order to attain its objectives, achieve the planned growth, and so on. Several departments simultaneously may require the services of the graphics department, need a new computer program, or produce something that requires the support of the sales staff or the mailing department. All these actions have timing and budget implications as well. It is imperative that all functional units in the organization understand the impact of such competition and agree to the planned allocation of resources both to their own units and to the other functional units.

The planning team then will identify the gaps in and between the combined action plans, how these can be closed, and what the impact of the gaps might be on the successful execution of the strategic business model. The integration of the action plans involves putting together all the pieces in order to ascertain how the overall plan will work and where the potential trouble spots are. Most of these integration issues must be resolved during the budgetary process.

Each constituent plan must be checked against the organizational values scan and mission statement to determine whether the proposed actions and directions are consistent with what the organization has said it wants to be. This check may reveal a need for further clarification of the values, mission, and strategic business model of the organization so that all plans are developed with the same overall objectives and assumptions. Chapter 12 returns to the integration process.

Contingency Planning

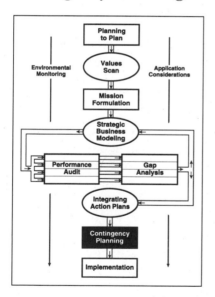

Aside from universal external threats such as war or economic collapse, each type of business or organization is subject to a specific set of contingencies that must be planned for. For example, producers of building materials are heavily influenced by new housing starts, which in turn are a function of interest rates and general economic conditions. In developing its strategic business model, a producer of building materials may identify several alternative futures, each based on different volumes of housing starts. Scenarios may be developed for each major possibility. Housing starts, in turn, are influenced by a variety of governmental actions. For example, the elimination of mortgage deductions on personal income taxes would be a threat to housing starts in both the United States and the United Kingdom, while a large governmental program to subsidize single-family homes would be an opportunity. The strategic business model of the building-materials producer would assume that neither of these two events would be likely to occur, but contingency plans would be developed on the basis of both possibilities.

Contingency planning involves the following:

1. Identifying the most important internal and external threats to and opportunities for the organization, especially those involving other than the most-likely scenarios.
2. Developing trigger points to initiate action steps for each contingency.
3. Agreeing on which action steps will be taken for each of these trigger points.

Among the kinds of internal threats that are often identified by planning teams are the death or severe disability of an "irreplaceable" key staff member—the director of research and development or the orchestra's principal soloist—and the destruction of a key facility—such as a manufacturing plant or the computer room.

Internal opportunities would include the unanticipated opportunity to commercialize a chance invention or a cash infusion by the settlement of long-standing litigation, whereas external opportunities would include the sudden opening of new markets—such as those in Eastern Europe—or the availability of new technology or equipment. Certainly not all such contingencies can be anticipated, but careful attention to the early warning signs of such critically important changes can assist an organization in both conducting and executing effective contingency plans.

Contingency planning is based on the assumption that the ability to forecast accurately the significant factors that will affect the organization is somewhat limited, especially in terms of variations in those factors. However, the planning team should be able to identify the factors themselves, such as interest rates, employment, housing starts, and foreign-currency exchange rates, and develop alternative plans based on possible variations in these factors. Thus, contingency planning provides the organization with a variety of business modeling strategies that can be used with a variety of scenarios, each of which can be evaluated and planned for. The SWOT analysis performed earlier as part of the performance audit should provide a useful road map to help identify key areas in contingency planning.

Contingency planning should also identify a number of key indicators that will trigger an awareness of the need to re-examine the adequacy of the strategy currently being followed. A *trigger point* could be an actual or anticipated increase in the price of fuel or a critical raw material or in the interest rate, or it could be a sharp, unexpected positive turnaround in the economy that offers an opportunity for expansion and growth. When a trigger point is identified as having been reached, two levels of response should be generated:

1. Higher-level monitoring. No precipitant action should be taken; in fact, no action may be required. However, the possibility of a need for a change in main-line assumptions should be noted, and indicators should be watched.
2. Action. At this level, the decision is made that conditions are different, and some contingency plan is implemented or some aspect of a strategy is modified.

The end of 1990 and the early months of 1991 saw a rapid increase in the price of oil and the threat and then the reality of war in the Gulf while the world economy was experiencing a recession—all of which had profound consequences for airlines, both domestic and international. Had the airlines had adequate contingency plans with any or all of these variables as trigger points, they could have taken earlier and more functional actions, saving several of them from having to seek the protection of bankruptcy. Chapter 13 provides a detailed examination of how to plan for contingencies.

Implementation

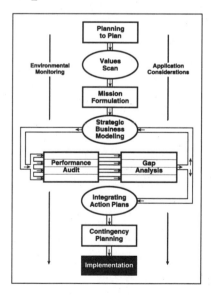

The implementation of the strategic plan involves the *concurrent* initiation of several tactical/operational plans designed at the unit and functional level *plus* the monitoring and integration of these plans at the organizational level. In the implementation phase, all stakeholders need to be informed that the strategic plan is now being implemented, and they need to agree to support that implementation. The necessary changes in the management-control system, the information system, and the organizational culture needed to execute the strategic plan must also be initiated.

The final implementation involves the initiation of the several action plans designed at the functional level and their integration at the top of the organization. This may, for example, involve new construction, initiation of management development or technical training, increased research and development, or marketing new products or services. All parts of the organization should feel that there is activity on all levels of the organization that will bring about the successful completion of the organization's mission.

Applied Strategic Planning Means "Creating the Future"

The most important test of implementation, however, is the degree to which organizational members, especially managers, integrate the strategic plan into their everyday management decisions. A strategic plan is being implemented when the initial response of a manager confronted by a decision is to consider whether an answer is found in the organization's strategic plan. Although guidelines for every decision will not be provided by the planning process, consideration of the plan as the first step in decision making is the best evidence of the plan's implementation. The process of implementation is the subject of Chapter 14, and implementation considerations are also discussed where appropriate throughout the book.

SUMMARY

Applied Strategic Planning is the process by which the guiding members of an organization envision its future and develop the necessary procedures and operations to achieve that future. This vision of the organization's future state provides a direction in which the organization should move and the energy to begin that move. Although most organizations do some kind of long-range or strategic planning, usually these planning processes are poorly conceptualized and poorly implemented. Furthermore, their strategic plans rarely impact day-to-day decisions. A necessary component of effective strategic planning is "down-board thinking." Not only should a planning team decide on its immediate moves, but it should also look down board and consider the consequences of these moves in light of how the competition and other environmental factors will respond. The Applied Strategic Planning model used in this book differs from existing models in content, emphasis, and process. It contains the following phases: planning to plan, values scan, mission formulation, strategic business modeling, performance audit, gap analysis, both the vertical and horizontal integration of plans, contingency planning, and implementation. It also provides for applying the plan throughout the planning process and for continually monitoring the environment.

REFERENCES

Ackoff, R. (1981). *Creating the corporate future.* New York: John Wiley.

Gup, B.E. (1979). Begin strategic planning by asking three questions. *Managerial Planning, 35,* 28-31. Reprinted in J.W. Pfeiffer (Ed.). (1991). *Strategic planning: Selected readings* (rev. ed.). San Diego, CA: Pfeiffer & Company.

Kastens, M.L. (1979, July-August). The whys and how of planning. *Managerial Planning,* pp. 33-35. Reprinted in J.W. Pfeiffer (Ed.). (1991). *Strategic planning: Selected readings* (rev. ed.). San Diego, CA: Pfeiffer & Company.

Levitt, T. (1960, July-August). Marketing myopia. *Harvard Business Review,* pp. 45-56. Reprinted in *Harvard Business Review,* (1975, September-October), pp. 26-28, 33-34, 38-39, 44, 173-174. Also reprinted in J.W. Pfeiffer (Ed.). (1991). *Strategic planning: Selected readings* (rev. ed.). San Diego, CA: Pfeiffer & Company.

Pierce, J., & Robinson, E. (1991). *Strategic management.* Homewood, IL: Irwin.

Rokeach, M. (1973). *The nature of human values.* New York: Free Press.

Schein, E.G. (1990). Organizational culture. *American Psychologist, 45,* 109-119.

Chapter Two

The Process of Envisioning

...I still have a dream. It is a dream deeply rooted in the American dream.

I have a dream that one day this nation will rise up and live out the true meaning of its creed: "We hold these truths to be self-evident; that all men are created equal."

I have a dream that one day on the red hills of Georgia the sons of the former slaves and the sons of former slaveowners will be able to sit down together at the table of brotherhood.

I have a dream that one day even the state of Mississippi, a desert state sweltering with the heat of injustice and oppression, will be transformed into an oasis of freedom and justice.

I have a dream that my four little children will one day live in a nation where they will not be judged by the color of their skin but by the content of their character.

I have a dream today.

Martin Luther King, Jr.
August 28, 1963
Washington, D.C.
(See Bishop, 1971)

We have defined Applied Strategic Planning as the process by which the guiding members of an organization envision its future and develop the necessary procedures and operations to achieve that future. This chapter will further explore the concept of envisioning and its central role in strategic planning.

ENVISIONING

Envisioning is the process by which individuals or groups develop a vision or dream of a future state for themselves or their organizations that is both sufficiently clear and powerful to arouse and sustain the actions necessary for that dream or vision to become a reality. The above quotation from Martin Luther King's 1963 speech on the steps of the Lincoln Memorial in Washington, D.C., is but one example of that kind of dream—a dream that helped shape and sustain the American civil rights movement and that has changed the very nature of American society.

However, the point of this book is not to understand the process of reshaping a society, but the role of envisioning in shaping or reshaping an organization. Are there visions that have had a similar profound effect on organizations? The answer to this question is an unequivocal "yes." For example, the Bennis and Nanus (1985) research report on interviews with ninety leaders of organizations as different as Lever Brothers, Polaroid, a major metropolitan newspaper, a major symphony orchestra, a championship college basketball team, and so on, supports the conclusion that one characteristic that all these leaders had in common was having a vision of the organization that focused the attention of the members of that organization and shaped its development in unique, successful ways. The dream that these leaders were able to share with their followers enabled those followers to believe that extraordinary feats were possible and that, through these feats, a uniquely successful organization would emerge.

"Dreams" and "visions" can appear to be soft and nonmanagerial. Because of this, having a dream or a vision for an organization sometimes can bring discomfort both to the visionary or visionaries and those the vision impacts. Nevertheless, regardless of what it is called—a purpose, a goal, a personal agenda, a legacy, or a vision or dream—the positive consequences of having one is clear. It provides members of the organization with a view of the future that can be shared, a clear sense of direction, a mobilization of energy, and a sense of being engaged in something important. A *vision,* which is our preference for how it should be identified, provides an organization with a forward-looking, idealized image of itself and its uniqueness (Kouzes and Posner, 1987).

Such visions provide organizations with a sense of how things can be—what the promised land looks like—and a sense that it really is possible to arrive safely in that promised land. It gives members of the organization a sense of pride and purpose—a sense of uniqueness that instills an esprit and a level of motivation that allows the organization to function at a higher level than was previously thought possible.

Steven Jobs, founder of Apple Computer, provides a clear example of such a vision when he said, "There's something going on here ... something that is changing the world and this is the epicenter" (Jobs, 1984, p. 18). Who would not want to be a part of the epicenter of a world change? James D. Robinson III, president of American Express, had a similar vision when he argued that AmEx must become a total financial service organization—one that dominated the services to travelers. Similar examples of such visionary goals can be provided for every imaginable type of organization (Davis and Davidson, 1991).

The well-known futurist, Joel Barker (1990) has developed an educational video that highlights the importance of dreaming in determining the success of both individuals and organizations. On the organizational level, Barker shows that success is a function of having a dream of future success and that the role of the organizational leadership is to develop and share that dream. It is important that this vision be positive and inspiring to give the members of the organization the clear sense that striving for the vision is worth the effort. While leaders need to listen to the reactions of followers, it is the leader's responsibility to synthesize these reactions into a final vision. The acceptance of that final, synthesized dream by the rank and file of the organization almost invariably leads to success. Barker goes on to point out that the final dream must be both comprehensive and detailed. A vision of an organization as "world class" or as "the industry leader" lacks the specificity that triggers these aspirations in ways that energize actions.

Barker's presentation ends with the observation that vision without action is merely a dream, that action without vision merely passes the time, but vision with action can change the world.

REASONS FOR ENVISIONING

While the reasons for envisioning are clear to some, others may still need convincing. Tregoe, Zimmerman, Smith, and Tobia (1990) analyzed the motivations of a highly mixed group of executives to develop a vision for their nineteen extremely different organizations and identified seven major motives. These are listed below (but *not* in the order presented by Tregoe, et al.):

1. A perceived need for a common vision and a sense of teamwork;
2. An experienced desire to control the organization's destiny;
3. A wish to obtain more resources for the operation;

Vision Without Action Is Merely a Dream

4. A realization that the organization's current operational success was no guarantee for the future;
5. The need to get out of trouble;
6. An opportunity to exploit a new opportunity or deal with a new threat; and
7. The need to pass the torch and carry it.

Let us briefly examine each of these in turn. The first of these motives is found in organizations with a growing awareness that the members of the organization are *not* working toward a common goal. One of our clients began to recognize that some segments of the organization were taking the organization's quality policy seriously and managing their operations accordingly while other segments were still operating under the more traditional "we always meet our shipping schedules" approach. The development of a shared vision that highlighted the exceptional quality of the organization's competitive products did much to alleviate that situation.

Second, continual "future shocks"—as well as the rise of unanticipated competitors—have led many organizations to recognize that they are not automatically in control of their own destiny. Rather, they see themselves as buffeted by circumstances that they do not understand. The development of an organizational vision—and completing the Applied Strategic Planning process—provides a vehicle to begin to change from a perception of lack of control to one of being in control over one's destiny.

Third, organizations require additional resources to support their growth. Be they segments of large organizations requiring support from headquarters or small, less-complex ones needing funding from their own board of directors, or government agencies, etc., the organization needs to have an integrated, coherent vision of the future and how these additional resources will facilitate the achievement of that future. The development of visions frequently is mandated under these circumstances.

Fourth, as conditions affecting an organization change ever more rapidly, the executives of that organization may come to the realization that "business as usual" simply is no longer an adequate prescription for the future, even in organizations that are currently successful. As these executives begin to think seriously about the future, they come to the realization that, in order to achieve success again, they must develop their own dreams of what the future should be and begin to work toward implementing those dreams.

Fifth, organizations that are having serious operational problems, that are not successful, begin to understand that developing a dream of a better tomorrow is one of the few ways of refocusing the energy of the organization and of developing hope.

Sixth, as organizations confront the changes around them, they identify new opportunities (the markets in Eastern and Central Europe open up or a new technology becomes available) and new threats (the fuller development of the European Common Market or the emergence of a new competitor). These opportunities and threats push the executives of an organization into the realization that they need an overriding vision or, at the very least, a set of visionary goals to provide an overall sense of direction, a set of guidelines to making decisions about the future.

Lastly, organizations are continually undergoing transitions in leadership. As the old leader leaves and the new leader comes in, the need for an overall picture—for a vision—becomes more apparent, not only in passing the torch but in carrying it into the future.

Any or all of these reasons, or any combination of them, are sufficient to instigate the development of a vision. Nevertheless, whatever the motivation, it should be clear that the envisioning process and its product—a clear vision of the organization and its desired future—are necessary for organizational survival and vitality.

THE ENVISIONING PROCESS

The process of envisioning is poorly understood at this time. It is clear that envisioning is a creative act, one that is unsuitable for formalization (Calingo, 1989). Rather, visions or visionary goals are developed more like dramas (Westley and Mintzberg, 1989), wherein an idea initiates the development of a vision, a more complete representation of that idea. The vision then becomes more and more elaborated, much like the playwright's script becomes more and more developed over time as the details of the plot emerge from the playwright's imagination.

The fact that vision involves a process of *seeing* is an important consideration in communicating the vision, as "seeing" the future state helps mobilize support for its adoption. The vision needs to be communicated by leaders to followers in a repetitive fashion, in a way that the followers understand that the leader himself or herself truly believes in the vision and regards it as an achievable goal, although clearly one that involves a personal and organizational "stretch."   Indeed, Hamel and Prahalad (1989) argue that those companies that have assumed global leadership during the last twenty years are those with ambitions that were out of all proportion to their resources and capabilities.

Some of the current literature on leadership suggests that such visions should emerge fully developed from the head of the leader, typically after a monastic retreat on the mountaintop. This pattern is offered as one important characteristic, if not the most important characteristic, of the truly charismatic leader. However, most of us do not function this way and the demands of our daily lives preclude such retreats. If this approach is not available, how then can we develop such visions?

These strategic perceptions can emerge in more ordinary ways in an organization or industry, with the notion or idea of a product, a market, or a technology. What is necessary is to be allowed to expand that notion or idea into a consideration of how things can be different, how things could be truly better, how to be innovative, how to apply our natural creativity to our organization—to legitimize these natural tendencies that are typically inhibited or suppressed by the daily demands of our organizational life. The capacity for envisioning exists in almost all of us, and this capacity needs to be unleashed and supported as it emerges. Few of us have been well trained to think conceptually. There may be a need to learn how to think about what our ideal future could be and to nurture our leaders in this effort. This is exactly what the Applied Strategic Planning process does.

But having the vision or setting the visionary goals is not enough. The vision must be shared; the vision comes alive only when it is

A Monastic Retreat Is Not Always Needed

shared. The vision must directly involve the followers and empower them. Consider the impact of Martin Luther King's speech excerpted at the beginning of this chapter. It involved the audience with its vision of a better tomorrow, just as the visions of Jobs and Robinson did. The images provided in such visionary goals involve a dynamic interaction between the leaders and their audience, rather than a unidirectional flow. The excitement engendered by the vision in turn excites the leader, whose own excitement further excites the audience, and so on. The reiterative process occurs at the moment of sharing the vision, as well as throughout the process of implementing the vision.

What we are suggesting is that envisioning can occur through solitary introspection by a leader, it can occur through the interaction of a group that shares leadership, and it can occur through interaction between a leader and a group of followers or through any combination of these. It can emerge suddenly and holistically, it can emerge slowly and incrementally through interactions among group members, it can be inductive or deductive, or it can be fixed or shift over time, but it always is future focused, involves a high degree of success, is relatively stable over time, and is inspirational.

Envisioning concentrates on the end goal (the desired future state), not the means to reach the goal. Indeed, one way for followers to develop a sense of ownership for the vision is to develop the mission, the means by which the vision will be fulfilled. Leaders who attempt to both develop the desired future state *and* prescribe the means for reaching that state may find themselves without followers!

ORGANIZATIONAL TRANSFORMATION

Envisioning assumes that the organization has or is experiencing a need for *transformation;* that is, the organization now understands—at least on some level—that its future must be discontinuous from its past and present. There are many ways by which this realization can occur. The organization's mandate may be challenged in some fundamental way. For example, the development of the Salk vaccine practically eliminated polio in the Western world. The March of Dimes organization had been founded to help eliminate polio and, once the vaccine was developed, was faced with the question of its future. One alternative was to "go out of business," because its mission had been accomplished; another was to develop a new mission, which was the chosen alternative. The March of Dimes—now an organization dedicated to the elimination of birth defects—experienced a discontinuous future; and it is extremely unlikely that this new, broader goal will ever be achieved, certainly not to the degree that polio has been eliminated.

An example of the yet-unmet need for a discontinuous future can be found in the case of the major American automobile manufacturers, whose mandate to be the primary supplier of reasonably priced, high-quality personal transportation to the United States has been dramatically challenged. General Motors, which less than twenty years ago had over 50 percent of the U.S. market, had less than 30 percent in 1990, with the Japanese manufacturers picking up the difference. A similar state of affairs exists for the rest of the industry. Despite the obvious danger inherent in ignoring this trend, the now-no-longer-so-Big Three American car makers have found it difficult to give up their traditional ways of doing business and focus on a discontinuous future. We will return to this example several times later in this book.

Of course, there are other, more subtle ways in which this realization can develop. For example, the board of directors or some other governing body might issue a mandate—a frequent occurrence in the public sector—based on demographic or other changes; a new chief executive may come in with very different ideas from his or her predecessor; or a new invention or product line may require a reconceptualization of the organization's mission. The important point to underscore at this juncture is that Applied Strategic Planning assumes that a transformational change is necessary or that, at the very least, the option of a transformational change needs to be seriously considered.

Long-Range Versus Transformational Planning

The alternative to organizational transformation is long-range planning, in which the assumption is one of a continuous future and there is *not* a need to regard the future state of the organization as substantially different from its past and present state. This situation can and does occur, and such organizations need not engage in the kind of Applied Strategic Planning that is the subject of this book. The time and energy involved would likely be unjustified. Our experience, however, in a wide range of organizations—profit and not-for-profit, public and private, large and small, in all sorts of industries, and offering every conceivable kind of product and service—suggests that organizations that can manage in today's environment with such long-range planning are few and far between. The changes in our society impinging on organizations almost on a daily basis are so widely understood that it would be redundant to discuss them here, and it is widely agreed that the pace of these changes is rapidly increasing. Organizations that fail to examine systematically the full impact of these changes on their future success are likely to have that success elude them, regardless of their past success.

FOUR APPROACHES TO PLANNING

Ackoff's (1981) typology of planning provides a provocative and useful way of understanding the planning process and why it often is difficult for organizations to understand their own needs for transformation. Ackoff suggests that there are four different approaches to planning:

1. Reactive, or planning through the rear-view mirror;
2. Inactive, or "going with the flow";
3. Preactive, or preparing for the future; and
4. Proactive, or designing the future and making it happen—our preferred approach.

Reactive planning occurs in historically static environments where well-established, conservative, traditional organizations have a long history of successes behind them. They tend to focus on the past, rather than the future, resisting and resenting the demands of the new, dynamic environment. They eagerly await the return of their "golden yesterdays," and most of their planning is aimed at preventing the changes that they see occurring around them or, at least, slowing them up.

American railroads, by and large, offer a good example of such an approach. For more than two-thirds of a century, they have resisted the changes in the pattern of surface transportation in the United States, especially the development of the trucking industry. They regularly lobby against highway construction, increased deregulation of trucking, increasing the size of trucks, and so on. They function as though they believe their actions can lead to the disappearance of trucking as a significant competitive force and that this in turn would lead to a return of their ascendancy in the transportation industry. In contrast, they could have seen the development of trucking as a given and planned how to use trucking as an opportunity to develop and strengthen their own industry. Piggyback transportation, in which truck trailers are transported by rail for most of the journey and then rehitched to a cab for final delivery, was long resisted by the railroads, even though it now accounts for a substantial percentage of their revenue.

The second approach to planning is simply to ignore the need for planning and count on muddling through. While this is how most people manage their personal affairs and may work well for very small, simply structured businesses, it involves a high degree of risk. Avoiding planning most frequently is a bet-your-business approach and one that is unlikely to pay off in the long run. The neighborhood strip mall or regional shopping center, with its high turnover rate of small shops that bravely entered the market without adequate planning and quickly failed, should provide strong evidence of the risks inherent in the avoidance of planning.

Most organizations utilize the third model of planning—preactive planning. This dominant model of organizational planning involves having the organization figure out, as well as it can, the shape of the future as it will affect its operations and then preparing for that set of events. For example, given the "graying of America," consumer-product manufacturers are turning their attention to penetrating this large, new, and unfamiliar market; given the "greening of America," these same organizations set about developing products that are environmentally safe. Organizations operating in this mode implicitly assume that the future is a given and their best strategy is to figure out the shape of that future and prepare for it. Hamel and Prahalad (1989) term this approach "maintaining the strategic fit," which involves focusing on the question of how things will be different in the future.

The most challenging and the most demanding type of planning is proactive or interactive planning whereby the organization believes that its own actions can shape its future. Applied Strategic Planning essentially involves proactive planning. Proactive planning is based on the belief that the future is not preordained or fixed and that organizations can shape their own future. Hamel and Prahalad (1989) term this approach "leveraging resources," which involves focusing on the question of what the organization must do differently in the future. We believe that—although an organization will need to respond to opportunities and threats beyond its control—shaping its future can be an interactive effort and allows the organization to proactively shape its best possible future.

To offer a dramatic example, consider the case of Procter & Gamble, a well-established and well-known consumer-product business. For years it has prided itself on its market research, and much of its success is due to reading the needs of the market and developing products to meet those needs. For decades, its market research had revealed that the major discontent of young mothers was soiled diapers. Diapers were regarded as unpleasant and difficult to manage. On the basis of the research, Procter & Gamble charged its product-development staff to come up with a product to reduce this source of discontent. After many years of experimentation, Procter & Gamble developed and brought to market Pampers, the disposable diaper. Today, the disposable diaper business is over three billion dollars world-wide. Procter & Gamble had not passively read the future and prepared for it, but instead was able to develop and market a new product that significantly affected its business future.

The kind of vision implicit in the Procter & Gamble story—that of meeting unmet consumer needs—involves exactly the kind of proactive planning that most organizations are capable of. However, developing that kind of vision is not a simple process; it requires developing, at least temporarily, a different kind of mind-set than is typically involved in solving the day-to-day operational problems involved in running an organization.

A very similar position was taken by John Scully, CEO of Apple Computer, when he stated, "More than anything, we believe the best way to predict the future is to invent it. We feel the confidence to shape our destiny" (Scully & Byrne, 1987, p. 297). Who could say it better?

Resistance to Envisioning

The notion of envisioning the future often inspires resistance. Since the envisioning of a discontinuous future involves change, all the usual resistances to change are present. However, Barker (1989) suggests that *paradigms* are another important reason why people do not accept new ideas. Paradigms are well-accepted sets of rules that lay the boundaries for our thinking and provide a set of guidelines for problem solving within those boundaries. The creativity required for envisioning is illustrated in the solution to the well-known nine-dot problem (Figure 2-1); to solve this problem one must break the paradigm. People must go outside the nine dots to find the solution, and they generally assume that the rules preclude moving outside the nine dots. Indeed, when we use the nine-dot problem to illustrate this point as part of the Applied Strategic Planning process, participants in the process sometimes object that we did not "tell" them that it was possible to work outside the nine dots. Envisioning involves a willingness to test the paradigm and move outside one's usual assumptions; and, most of the time, this is not easy for most of us.

Our paradigms serve as filters, preventing us from taking in information and experiences that are contrary to "prevailing wisdom." The American automobile manufacturers still believe, at least on some level, that the Americans' love affair with the mediocre-quality, gas-guzzling, big car is still not over and that our new love affair with their Japanese rival—the high-quality, energy-efficient, small car—will soon be over. Like most of us, they have great difficulty in seriously considering data that does not match their existing paradigm. Such data is overlooked, modified, or challenged. Barker calls this "the paradigm effect."

Successful envisioning breaks the existing paradigm by asking questions such as "What should you be doing in your organization that you aren't doing today?" The tremendous success of Xerox in eventually responding to the challenge of the Japanese copy-machine manufacturers is a case in point (Hamel and Prahalad, 1989). Xerox's initial success came from the manufacturing and distribution of high-end copiers, which were leased from Xerox together with a service contract. The service contract was necessary because the machines were complex and difficult to repair.

Canon developed smaller, simpler machines that allowed distributed copying (i.e., every small office could have its own copier) and that required little or no service. For several years—as it continued to operate under the old paradigm—Xerox was unable to meet the Japanese challenge. Xerox's leadership eventually took the Japanese challenge seriously and redesigned the machines so they did everything that Canon and the others did—and at a lower price. This paradigm shift has resulted in a resurgence of Xerox as a market leader in the copier industry, a feat that would not have occurred without this paradigm shift.

The function of envisioning in the strategic planning process is to enable the leaders of the organization to make a paradigm shift where

The task is to connect these nine dots with a pen or pencil with four straight lines *and* without lifting the pen or pencil from the paper.

Figure 2-1a. The Nine-Dot Problem

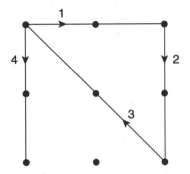

Figure 2-1b. The Nine-Dot Problem: A Typical Incorrect Attempt

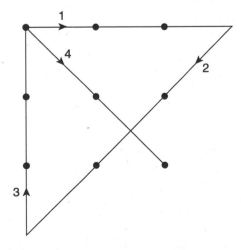

Figure 2-1c. The Nine-Dot Problem: A Correct Solution

necessary, to develop an openness to new ideas, and to understand and accept the need and opportunity for change.

Expect Resistance

The Positioning of Envisioning in Applied Strategic Planning

Given the central and important role of envisioning in the Applied Strategic Planning process, the reader may question exactly where this envisioning occurs. This question is particularly important because there is no element of the model specifically labeled as envisioning. The answer to this apparent paradox is a rather simple one.

The process of envisioning can occur in a number of places in the process. Sometimes an individual (frequently the CEO) or a group of individuals develops such a vision, and the individual's interest in strategic planning stems from the desire to develop a process to share and implement that vision. This is especially likely to be the case when the founders of the organization are still active in its management. When those in the power structure have such a vision, it needs to be made explicit as soon as possible; and members of the planning group need to test the relevance and power of that pre-existing vision and how they can impact it, if at all.

This, however, is often not the case, and there are a number of places in the Applied Strategic Planning model where envisioning can occur. One clearly is in the process of mission formulation; what business the organization will be in, who its customers will be, how it will go about its business as an organization, and what the organization's *raison d'etre* is are all questions that should involve a vision of the desired future state.

Similarly, the development of strategic business models—the process of deciding which lines of business the organization will develop and focus on and sorting out which strategic thrusts are necessary, as well as thinking through the necessary future culture of the organization—involves visionary processes. Indeed, since envisioning is so central to the model and so all-pervasive, it cannot be confined to a single element of the model.

The vision of the future must be developed prior to moving from strategic business modeling to the performance audit and gap analysis. The planning team must have explicated their ideal future, for it is that future that will be tested as the team moves into the next steps in the process. This vision must serve to energize both the planning process and its implementation. Without such a vision, the strategic planning process turns into an academic exercise rather than a template for proactive management.

As we have indicated, we believe the envisioning process to be at the core of strategic planning. We believe that managing strategically means systematically moving the organization toward achieving a vision of that organization's ideal future. For this reason, there must be no effort spared in creating and clarifying that vision of the future. The future success of the organization depends on it.

SUMMARY

Envisioning is the process by which individuals or groups develop a vision or dream of a future state for themselves or their organizations that is clear and powerful enough to arouse and sustain the actions necessary for that dream or vision to become a reality. Visions provide organizations with a sense of how things can be—what the promised land looks like—and a belief that it is possible to arrive safely in that promised land. The major reasons for a vision include (1) a perceived need for a common vision, (2) a desire to control the organization's destiny, (3) a wish to obtain more resources, (4) realization that the organization's success does not guarantee the future, (5) the need to get out of trouble, (6) a chance to deal with new opportunities and threats, and (7) the need to pass along the torch. Envisioning is a creative act and needs to be communicated in a way that will allow the followers to understand that the leader believes in the vision and regards it as an achievable goal. The most challenging type of planning is proactive planning, in which the organization believes that its own actions can shape its future. The envisioning process is at the core of Applied Strategic Planning. It is so central to the model and so all-pervasive, it cannot be confined to a single phase of the model. However, it must be developed prior to moving from strategic business modeling to the performance audit and gap analysis.

REFERENCES

Ackoff, R. (1981). *Creating the corporate future.* New York: John Wiley.

Barker, J.A. (1989). *Discovering the future: The business of paradigms* (2nd ed.) (Videocassette). Burnside, MN: Charthouse Learning Corporation.

Barker, J.A. (1990). *The power of vision* (Videocassette). Burnside, MN: Charthouse Learning Corporation.

Bennis, W.G., & Nanus, B. (1985). *Leaders: The strategies for taking charge.* New York: Harper & Row.

Bishop, J. (1971). *The Days of Martin Luther King, Jr.* New York: G.P. Putman's Sons.

Calingo, L.M.R. (1989). Achieving excellence in strategic planning systems. *SAM Advanced Management Journal, 54,* 21-23. Reprinted in J.W. Pfeiffer (Ed.). (1991). *Strategic planning: Selected readings* (rev. ed.). San Diego, CA: Pfeiffer & Company.

Davis, S., & Davidson, B. (1991). *2020 vision.* New York: Simon & Schuster.

Hamel, G., & Prahalad, C.K. (1989, May-June). Strategic intent. *Harvard Business Review,* 63-76. Reprinted in J.W. Pfeiffer (Ed.). (1991). *Strategic planning: Selected readings* (rev. ed.). San Diego, CA: Pfeiffer & Company.

Jobs, S. (1984, September 3). What I did for love. *Advertising Age,* p. 18.

Kouzes, J.M., & Posner, B.Z. (1987). *The leadership challenge: How to get extraordinary things done in organizations.* San Francisco: Jossey-Bass. Available from Pfeiffer & Company.

Scully, J., & Byrne, J.A. (1987). *Odyssey: Pepsi to Apple.* New York: Harper & Row.

Trego, B.B., Zimmerman, J.W., Smith, R.A., Tobia, P.M. (1990). *Vision in action: How to integrate your company's strategy into day-to-day management decisions.* New York: Simon & Schuster.

Westley, F., & Mintzberg, H. (1989). Visionary leadership and strategic management. *Strategic Management Journal, 10,* 17-32. Reprinted in J. W. Pfeiffer (Ed.). (1991). *Strategic planning: Selected readings* (rev. ed.). San Diego, CA: Pfeiffer & Company.

Chapter Three

Culture and Applied Strategic Planning

In order to make British Airways the world's favourite airline, we've got to change the culture of the airline.

Sir Colin Marshall
Chief Executive Officer
British Airways
(See Labich, 1988.)

In Chapter 2, we pointed out the central role of envisioning in the strategic planning process. This chapter is concerned with the organizational culture as the context within which any strategic planning must occur. One clear example of the critical interplay between strategic planning and organizational culture is found is the dramatic changes in British Airways (Goodstein and Burke, 1991).

THE CHANGE AT BRITISH AIRWAYS

In 1983 when Colin Marshall, now Sir Colin, was appointed CEO of British Airways (BA), the popular quip was that BA stood for "Bloody Awful." In 1982 BA had lost 900 million (U.S.) dollars, was losing market share, and was noted for unreliable and generally poor-quality service. During that year, the Thatcher government had decreed that BA would become a publicly owned company with shares sold on the London stock exchange. Marshall was hired to turn BA around and make it sufficiently profitable for the shares to be salable. Should that happen, Marshall would be assured of a successful career at BA and a knighthood.

Marshall, coming from a marketing and advertising background, understood that a vision was necessary if BA was to survive and prosper—a vision that rank-and-file members of the organization would understand and endorse. Marshall's vision was and is to make British Airways "the world's favorite airline," a straightforward but elegant view of the future. In the fiercely competitive world of international aviation, however, the quality of service is the primary determinant of consumer opinion and choice, especially with business-class passengers—the mainstay of the industry. British Airways had a long way to go in this regard.

The quality of service, in turn, is driven by the culture of the organization. Soon after Marshall arrived, he commissioned an independent study of the existing culture at BA. The study revealed that the then-existing culture at BA was seen by BA staff to be "bureaucratic," "militaristic," and "nonresponsive to customers."

Marshall quickly recognized that his vision could be achieved only by a dramatic shift in the BA culture, changing it to a service-oriented, market-driven one. This culture change was achieved through a variety of approaches, including training courses, a totally revamped personnel system, and changing a number of the players. Cultural change in an organization, especially cultural change of this magnitude, invariably involves the replacement of people. Rarely can a successful organizational cultural change occur without placing in key organizational roles

**Cultural Change Can Be Achieved
Through a Variety of Approaches**

a significant number of new members—people who have very different basic assumptions about how things work.

A noteworthy element of the culture change (see Goodstein & Burke, 1991) was that Marshall, himself, for a number of years regularly and systematically spoke and wrote about the need for this change and its importance in the successful execution of BA's strategy. Without that kind of focused support, it is rather unlikely that any significant changes in the BA culture would have occurred.

Significant changes did occur in the BA culture—it is far more market driven and service oriented than was ever the case—and BA is once again a highly successful organization, primarily because of these changes in its culture. Passengers regularly note their satisfaction with the high levels of service they received. British Airways successfully marketed its shares on the London stock exchange in February 1987; and, despite the usual fluctuations in share price, shares continually have sold for more than the initial offering price, and a reasonable dividend is paid to shareholders semiannually. It has become the dominant carrier between the United States and Great Britain and has ambitious plans for increasing its market share world-wide. While BA may not yet be the world's favorite airline, it continues to pursue that vision, and no one continues to call it "Bloody Awful." Without a successful culture change, Marshall's vision would never have been realized, and it is difficult to know what kind of future would have ensued. The BA story is but one example of the critical importance of organizational culture in both developing and implementing a strategic plan.

ORGANIZATIONAL CULTURE DEFINED

The past ten years have seen an upsurge of interest in corporate culture among both managers and organization consultants. Despite this interest, the field lacks an in-depth understanding of the concept of organizational culture (Schein, 1990). The most widely known definition is that of Deal and Kennedy (1982): "the way we do things around here," but that working definition focuses only on one set of observable data and ignores other data. Even more importantly, it avoids the critical issue of why and how such norms develop in an organization.

Schein (1985, 1990) provides a more comprehensive definition of culture as (a) a pattern of basic assumptions, (b) invented, discovered, or developed by a given group, (c) as it learns to cope with its problems of external adaptation and internal integration, (d) that has worked well enough to be considered valid and, therefore, (e) is taught to new members as the (f) correct way to perceive, think, and feel. In other words, an organization's culture is a social system based on a central set of beliefs and values. This social system was developed or learned as a consequence of the organization's efforts over time to cope with its environment. Its success in coping leads the organization's members to regard their ways of doing things as the best way to cope with its environment in the future.

Schein further points out that there are three levels on which one can understand an organization's culture: (a) the level of observable artifacts, including behavior; (b) the level of values; and (c) the level of basic underlying assumptions. Of these only the first—the artifactual—can be directly observed. The other two levels—most of which are unconscious—can only be inferred from the observables, including values that can be only indirectly assessed.

While there is considerable overt evidence about the organization's culture almost everywhere in its environment—in its physical structure and sites, in how it responds to visitors, in its annual and other reports, in its attempts to handle its relationships with various publics, in its "war stories" told about both the good and bad old days, in whom it regards as its heroes and villains, in its rites and rituals, and so on. But all this data must be decoded. What do these overt artifacts of the culture tell about the deeper values and the even deeper assumptions that the organization makes about the world in which it operates? This often frustrating and difficult question needs to be answered in order to test the culture's alignment with the organization's dream of the future (see Schwartz & Davis, 1984). When there is a lack of alignment—as was the case with BA—then either the dream or the culture needs to be modified. And—the BA experience notwithstanding—dreams are easier to "fix" than cultures.

CULTURAL MISALIGNMENT: THE CASE OF BROWNING-FERRIS

Consider another case of misalignment between culture and vision—one without a happy ending, as least as yet. Browning-Ferris, a waste-management corporation, was founded in 1969 by Tom J. Fatjo, a Texas deal maker with no prior experience in waste management. Within a few years it was the largest waste-management company in the United States, primarily through its acquisition of hundreds of smaller companies throughout the country. The Browning-Ferris motto became, "The company that built an industry." The culture of the company was clearly focused on acquisitions with little attention to either management or governmental regulations.

In 1976 the lack of industry knowledge began to hurt, and there were fewer and fewer small companies to acquire. In 1976, Fatjo turned the control of Browning-Ferris to Harry Phillips, an experienced waste-management executive. While the company's revenues and profits grew rapidly over the next twelve years, so did its difficulties with regulators. By 1988, as more and more regulatory controls began to impact the industry and the company, the growth culture of Browning-Ferris came into sharp conflict with those increasing pressures. In 1987, William J. Ruckelshaus, the former director of the U.S. Environmental Protection Agency (EPA), was brought in as CEO with a mandate to solve the company's problems with the several regulatory agencies.

Ruckelshaus was an accomplished bureaucrat with experience in both the EPA—he was twice its director—and the U.S. Department of Justice and had some business experience as a vice president of Weyerhauser, the timber company. He, however, had no "hands-on" business-management experience and knew very little about the ins and outs of running a giant waste-management company. Apparently Ruckelshaus had spent his time and energy handling directly the regulatory problems the company faced and serving as a spokesman for the company. The day-to-day management of the company was largely neglected and the company's problems began to escalate. The company's culture developed in an era of rapid growth, endless acquisitions, and a permissive regulatory environment. Neither cost consciousness and tight management controls nor attention to environmental regulations was part of the Browning-Ferris culture. Today's environment is quite different, so an organization needs a different culture to be successful in this new environment. It remains to be seen whether Browning-Ferris and its management are willing and able to address this challenge directly.

An organization's culture provides the social context in and through which an organization performs its work. It guides the organization's members in decision making, in determining how time and energy are invested, in choosing which facts are examined with care and which are summarily rejected, in deciding which options are looked on favorably from the start and which types of people are selected to work for the organization, and in practically everything else that is done in the organization. The changing environment in which Browning-Ferris now finds itself suggests that much of its prevalent culture of ignoring or fighting the regulators and paying little attention to sound business-management practices is interfering with rather than facilitating its pursuit of viability and success.

CULTURE AND VALUES

Culture is a pattern of beliefs and expectations deeply held in common by members of an organization. These beliefs in turn give rise to values, the end state of being, that are cherished by the organization and its members. These values, in turn, give rise to situational norms ("the way we do things around here") that are evidenced in observable behavior. This normative behavior, in turn, becomes the basis for the validation of the beliefs and values from which the norms originated.

This closed circuit of beliefs-values-norms-beliefs is the process of cultural development and accounts for the tenacity that cultures exhibit. Members who violate organizational norms are initially pressured to conform. If pressure does not produce the desired conformity, then ostracism or other severe sanctions are brought to bear on the deviant member. Harshbarger (1975) differentiates between deviants and heretics. Deviants are those who simply violate norms, either offhandedly or seriously, to test the system. Heretics, in contrast, challenge the basic assumptions and beliefs of the system and thus are far more dangerous to the established order. It is for the heretics who refuse to repent that the most severe sanctions are reserved.

Large-scale cultural change, however, requires heretical challenges that can precipitate the emergence of a new order. Mere behavioral deviance is insufficient to produce that degree of change. Heretical behavior is far less risky to those at the top of the organization than those at lower levels, whose careers can be sacrificed on the altar of organizational change. This helps explain the critical need for overt top-management commitment to any serious cultural-change effort.

The role of culture in the development and maintenance of values is clearly demonstrated by Schein's (1985, 1990) analysis of two organizations—the Action Company and the Multi Company. Even the most casual observer would note the differences in the behavioral norms of the two organizations, both of which are known to us despite their pseudonyms. At Action, the atmosphere is very informal and people are open, argumentative, and casual in their interactions; whereas at Multi, the atmosphere is formal and polite, and people are very deliberate in how they express themselves.

Schein's analysis explicates the basic assumptions that undergird these norms. Action's basic belief is that the individual is the source of good ideas. This belief leads to a value of openness whereby, through direct discourse—often to the point of argumentation—truth will emerge; thus, the norms of informality and casualness. Multi has a very different basic assumption, namely, that truth and wisdom reside in those with the most education and experience. This basic belief then leads to the values of subservience—to one's betters and elders—and these, in turn, lead to the norms of formality, politeness, and deliberateness.

Without understanding this causal chain of events, it is exceedingly difficult to make sense of why certain values are held. Values are an integral part of the matrix that is organizational culture. We will return to a more detailed analysis of values—both individual and organizational—and their role in the strategic planning process in Chapter 7.

MODELS OF ORGANIZATIONAL CULTURE

The level of analysis that Schein used with Action and Multi requires more information, time, and involvement than is ordinarily available in the strategic planning process. Models of organizational culture provide helpful mechanisms that can be used more easily to decode the available data.

The earliest of these models was developed by Deal and Kennedy (1982) and proposed the following four generic organizational cultures:

1. The Tough-Guy, Macho Culture. In this individualistic culture, high risks are taken but the environment provides quick feedback on whether the actions were right or wrong. The entertainment industry,

Some Cultures Are Formal

especially motion-picture production, is a prime example of this culture, as is advertising.

2. The Work-Hard/Play-Hard Culture. Fun and action are the rule in this culture. Employees take few risks, and even those few provide quick feedback; to succeed, employees must maintain a high level of relatively low-risk activities. Sales-driven organizations, especially retail-sales organizations specializing in door-to-door selling, are outstanding examples of this culture.

3. The Bet-Your-Company Culture. This culture calls for big-stake decisions with years passing before the environment provides clear feedback on whether or not the decision was correct. This is a high-risk, slow-feedback culture. Many high-tech organizations, especially in aerospace, are prime examples of the bet-your-company culture.

4. The Process Culture. Little or no feedback is provided in this culture, and employees find it difficult to measure what they do. Instead, they concentrate on *how* their work is done. Most highly regulated organizations, including most governmental agencies, are common examples of the process culture.

This early model by Deal and Kennedy contributed greatly to bringing attention to this issue—and to shaping the ensuing discussion. Their typology of organizational cultures, however, is not all-inclusive, and the criteria for classifying organizations into one of the categories is difficult to apply. An alternative model is offered by Harrison and Stokes (1990), which also involves four generic types of organizational cultures. These are as follows:

1. The Power Culture. This culture is based on the assumption that an inequality of resources is a naturally occurring phenomenon; that is, life is a zero-sum game with clear-cut winners and losers. Among the resources that will be unequally distributed are money, privilege, security, and the overall quality of life. Strong leaders are necessary to manage these inequalities and maintain the overall balance of the system. In organizations with a strong power culture that works well, leaders are firm but fair and generous to their loyal followers. There is an acceptance of the hierarchical structure of the organization. Badly managed power cultures, on the other hand, are ruled by fear, with power abused for personal advantage for the leaders and their followers, often with much political intrigue and infighting. Power cultures are best suited for entrepreneurial and start-up organizations where the leaders are the ones that have the vision and drive to develop the organization. However, as the organization grows and becomes more complex, the demands on leaders for multiple decisions usually make a power culture ineffective. There arises a need for functional systems and structures to help with getting work done.

2. *The Role Culture.* The role culture substitutes rationally derived structures and systems for naked power. The basic assumption is that work is best accomplished through the rule of law. Roles are developed that spell out each person's responsibilities and potential rewards, and systems are installed to make certain that this is done fairly. Control is remote, through a system of delegation rather than through personal power of top leadership. Well-managed role cultures provide stability, justice, and efficiency. People are protected from arbitrary decisions from the top and thus can devote their energies to tasks rather than self-protection. In stable environments, role-oriented organizations (bureaucracies) can be very efficient, because work is routine and can be managed by a series of impersonal rules with checks and balances. When new problems emerge, as they occasionally will, systemic solutions are developed and incorporated into the standard operating procedures (SOPs). The weakness, however, of the role organization is in the reliance on these impersonal SOPs. They tend to stifle creativity and innovation and are rather inflexible, which is dangerous to organizational vitality in rapidly changing environments. Although these attributes are not necessary characteristics of role cultures, unfortunately they tend to be typical of most bureaucracies.

3. *The Achievement Culture.* The basic assumption of the achievement culture is that all people want to make meaningful contributions to their work and to society and enjoy their interaction with both customers and co-workers. Satisfaction for a job well done and from meaningful interactions with others in the workplace are the really important rewards for people, and work should be organized to allow both intrinsic rewards and satisfying interactions. Neither the power culture nor the role culture allows for these to occur. The role of management in such cultures is to develop work situations that seriously engage people, that help people feel that they are contributing to some higher goal that is articulated in a clear mission statement, that allow for people to supervise themselves in self-directed work teams with managers available to provide support and technical assistance when necessary, where there is open communication—upward, downward, and laterally—and where people have an opportunity to learn and grow on the job. Although an achievement organization has rules and structures—as do role organizations—they work to serve the system rather than becoming an end in themselves. The power in the achievement culture is focused on creating

the mission and then monitoring its achievement. The down side of the achievement culture is the difficulty in sustaining the energy and enthusiasm found in the early development of the achievement organization. Such organizations often do not pay sufficient attention to the development of useful systems and structures, overdepending on the common vision to organize work.

4. The Support Culture. The support culture's basic assumption is that mutual trust and support must be the primary basis of the relationship between the person and the organization. People must be valued as human beings, not just as contributors to work or occupiers of organizational roles. People are seen as basically good and they are expected to blossom in this nurturing environment. Support organizations foster warmth, and even love, between organizational members, but not driving enthusiasm. People work in support organizations because they deeply care about the people with whom they work. Because of this caring, they form closer, warmer relationships with their customers and others with whom they deal at work. Communication among people in such organizations is extremely open and supportive, and relationships are extremely close. Harmony is an important value, and confrontations that can disturb this harmony are avoided. In most organizations in the Western world, the support culture is the least typical, especially in its pure form and certainly in organizations with tasks to accomplish. The normative behaviors of this culture are simply not valued in the other three more-prevalent cultures. Whereas the weakness of the support organization is in its internal commitment to its own members rather than in a commitment to external task accomplishment, its strengths are in its nurturing and development of its members. The support culture clearly meets some important human needs that are all too often ignored by organizations.

The Harrison and Stokes model does not require sorting an organization into one of the four categories. Rather, the question is to what extent are elements of each of the four cultures represented in an organization. Organizations thus have a profile based on their relative dependence on each of the four categories. Furthermore, we find that the Harrison and Stokes model is more closely related to the reality of the organizations that we have encountered and also provides an instrument with which to begin the process of understanding the culture of a particular organization.

Neither of these models—nor any other model with which we are familiar—will fit any organization exactly. They are useful, however, in formulating ideas about how to think about the culture of an organization and can help to bring that culture into focus as part of the strategic planning process. The members of any organization involved in strategic planning must examine the culture of their own organization, understand it, and find ways to integrate that understanding into their vision of the organization's future.

EFFECTS OF CULTURE ON PLANNING

The impact of organizational culture on both the process of planning and the resultant strategic plan is considerable. These effects can be either direct or indirect, but in either case they need to be both understood and managed in order to conduct a successful planning process and to ensure that a useful plan emerges from that process.

First, and perhaps most importantly, there is the question of whether or not the organization will even seriously consider engaging in strategic planning. Organizations that have a strong "tough-guy, macho" culture in Deal and Kennedy's (1982) typology, a culture typified by a belief that the organization is tough enough to survive whatever the environment can dish out and flourish despite such adversity, are usually unwilling to even begin a serious planning process. They take the extreme view that planning is for "wimps" and they will tough it out. When such organizations are forced by circumstances to enter into such

The Team Must Integrate the Culture into the Vision

a process—typically through pressure from some superordinate corporate body or from the organization's financial supporters—they simply do not take the activity seriously.

A second influence of the corporate culture on the planning process relates to the realism implicit in the process. Organizations with a culture that ordinarily avoids confronting harsh realities will find the need for objective soul-searching in the performance audit and gap analysis phases of the process difficult, if not impossible, to achieve. Such organizations blithely assume that things are better than they are, that obstacles can always be overcome, and that reality can be conveniently reconstructed. One common error that such organizations make is the belief that their own culture can be adjusted to the strategy (Schein, 1991), rather than the other way around. As previously noted, strategy typically is limited by and adjusts to the existing culture.

Third, organizations with experience in dealing with their environment will have assumptions about the following:

1. Their basic mission;
2. The specific operational goals that are derived from that mission;
3. The means by which their mission can be achieved;
4. The appropriate ways of evaluating the success of the organization in mission accomplishment; and
5. How best to develop mid-course corrections in their plans.

The Browning-Ferris organization, for example, clearly but implicitly assumed that its primary mission was growth through acquisition, that the operational details would look after themselves, that growth in revenues and earnings was the only measure of success, and that circumventing regulations was an important and necessary tactic for achieving success. When it experienced problems in continuing to implement this strategy, its strong culture apparently prevented the company from taking the necessary mid-course corrections.

Fourth, in terms of internal processes, organizations will have assumptions about the following:

1. The best communications systems to use in disseminating both the nature of the planning process and the plan itself, as well as the conceptual framework in which to embed those communications;
2. The criteria about who should and should not be included in the planning process;
3. The control system that will manage the planning process;
4. The nature of the interpersonal relationships of the planning group;

5. How rewards and sanctions for participation and nonparticipation will be administered; and

6. How the unexpected will be managed (Schein, 1985, 1990).

All of us can examine our own organizational culture to find the necessary examples to illustrate these six points, even if the organization has never attempted strategic planning.

The organizational culture—with all these ramifications—is omnipresent and needs to be both understood and confronted during the Applied Strategic Planning process. Facilitating this confrontation is one of the most important tasks of the strategic planning consultant. Indeed, since internal consultants are frequently not only involved in the culture of their organization, but, in their most common role as human resource specialists, serve as culture carriers and disseminators, they often have difficulty in seeing and transcending their own culture. This observation strongly supports the usefulness of external consultants who bring "fresh eyes" to the process, eyes that can see the all-pervasive role of these cultural assumptions.

The role of the consultant, especially the external consultant, is to make certain that plans that are countercultural (that is, inconsistent with the prevailing wisdom of the organization) are considered and that the role of the culture (in either facilitating or interfering with the adoption and implementation of these plans) is carefully thought through, especially as it impacts the implementation phase. There are all too many examples of organizational mergers and acquisitions that appeared brilliant beforehand but resulted in failure because the cultures of the two organizations were incompatible.

In other words, the central role of culture in organizational life cannot be overemphasized. One of our clients, for example, has been a low-cost producer. In order to protect and even expand its market share, it has been a ruthless cost-cutter, reluctant to hire staff and tolerant of mediocre quality. "After all," the company reasoned, "you get what you pay for; and what can you expect from the low-cost producer?" Over the past few years, however, it has met some resistance from its customers whose quality requirements have been raised by heightened end-user expectations. Based on these new quality requirements, our client began to strategize about improving the quality of its product, assuming that a few modest changes in the manufacturing processes would accomplish this end. The idea that it would need a quality-oriented culture to supplant its cost-cutting culture only emerged when the initial effort at quality improvement failed and it began to understand what would be involved in producing higher-quality products. Once this understanding was reached, the organization could decide whether or not it had the resources and the desire to make the necessary changes or whether there were other strategies that were more in alignment with its culture.

While the strategic planning process can change parts of the culture, this is a process that takes time and effort. The successful change effort at BA took five years, and an ongoing process to maintain the new culture continues. Many millions of dollars in direct costs were expended in this effort and the indirect costs are incalculable. Since few organizations can or will devote this level of resources to changing the organizational culture (and so few organizations even know how to approach such an awesome task), most cultural-change efforts are far more modest and, perforce, yield more modest results. One of the central issues in the gap analysis phase of Applied Strategic Planning is determining how to close the gap between the organization's existing culture and the culture necessary to achieve the organization's success. As we noted above, the willingness to admit that such a gap can and does exist is itself a cultural issue.

ORGANIZATIONAL CULTURE
AND ORGANIZATIONAL EFFECTIVENESS

Organizational culture, however, impacts far more than the process and outcomes of strategic planning. Its consequences for overall organizational effectiveness are even more profound. Denison (1990) provides data on these relationships in his comprehensive quantitative analyses of the cultures of thirty-four different organizations, as measured by two different and extensive questionnaires. Over forty thousand people completed the Survey of Organizations (SOO) and the Organization Survey Profile (OSP). The relative success of the thirty-four organizations was measured over a five-year period by two important financial ratios: return on sales and return on investment. In addition, Denison illustrates the relationships between organizational culture and success through in-depth qualitative case studies of five of these organizations: Medtronics, People Express Airlines, Detroit Edison, Procter & Gamble, and Texas Commerce Bancshares.

Based on his analyses of extensive quantitative and qualitative data of these companies, Denison concluded that differences in organizational culture have a strong impact on organizational effectiveness. Those organizations with cultures that provided for high employee involvement (through vehicles such as self-managed work teams, employee stock ownership, and profit sharing) and that carefully monitored their external environment and then promptly responded to changes in that environment (especially with respect to markets and stakeholders) were clearly the most effective, both immediately and in the longer run. Another feature of the cultures of the more effective organizations is a clear sense of mission. Denison's work seems to provide sufficient evidence to impress even those skeptics who have regarded the current interest in organizational culture as just another "one of those management fads."

The conclusion from this chapter seems inescapable. Organizational culture is a critical factor in both strategic planning and overall organizational success. One of the central roles of organizational management, especially top management, is to understand, shape, and manage that organization's culture. The costs of not attending to organizational culture are far too high.

SUMMARY

An organization's culture is a social system based on a central set of beliefs and values. When there is misalignment between culture and vision, then either the dream or the culture needs to be modified. An example of a change in the culture of an organization and the resulting success is found in British Airways. This was done under the leadership of Colin Marshall. Culture gives rise to values, and these values—in turn—give rise to situational norms, which—in turn—become the basis for the validation of the beliefs and values from which the norms originated. This closed circuit of beliefs-values-norms-beliefs is the process of cultural development and accounts for the tenacity that cultures exhibit. Large-scale cultural change requires heretical challenges that precipitate the emergence of a new order. The Deal and Kennedy model of organizational culture proposed the following four categories: tough-guy, macho culture; work-hard/play-hard culture; bet-your-company culture; and process culture. Harrison and Stokes offer these categories: power, role, achievement, and support cultures. The organizational culture must be understood and managed in order to conduct a successful strategic planning process and to ensure that a useful plan emerges from the process.

REFERENCES

Deal, T., & Kennedy, A. (1982). *Corporate culture: The rites and rituals of corporate life.* Reading, MA: Addison-Wesley.

Denison, D.R. (1990). *Corporate culture and organizational effectiveness.* New York: John Wiley.

Goodstein, L.D., & Burke, W.W. (1991). Creating successful organizational change. *Organizational dynamics, 19*(4), 5-17.

Harrison, R., & Stokes, H. (1990). *Diagnosing organization culture.* Mountain View, CA: Harrison Associates.

Harshbarger, D. (1975). The individual and the social order: Notes on the management of heresy and deviance in complex organizations. *Human Relations, 26,* 251-269.

Labich, K. (1988, December 5). The big comeback at British Airways. *Fortune,* pp. 163-174.

Schein, E.H. (1985). *Organizational culture and leadership.* San Francisco: Jossey-Bass.

Schein, E.H. (1990). Organizational culture. *American Psychologist, 34,* 109-119.

Schein, E.H. (1991). The role of process consultation in the creation and implementation of strategy. *Consulting Psychology Bulletin, 43,* 16-18.

Schwartz, H., and Davis, S.M. (1984). Matching corporate culture and business strategy. *Organizational Dynamics, 14,* 30-48. Reprinted in J.W. Pfeiffer (Ed.). (1991). *Strategic planning: Selected readings* (rev. ed.). San Diego, CA: Pfeiffer & Company.

Chapter Four
Potential Roles of the Consultant

It is unwise to be heedless ourselves while we are giving advice to others.

Phaedrus,
c. A.D. 8
Book I. Fable 9

This chapter, as the title implies, addresses the several roles that consultants—both external consultants and internal human resource development (HRD) professionals—can play in Applied Strategic Planning. Both external and internal consultants have important roles in this process, sometimes different and sometimes overlapping. Our general position is that the process of strategic planning is best managed when *both* external and internal consultants are involved. Our position will become clear as we re-examine the Applied Strategic Planning process from the consultants' viewpoints.

MAJOR STAGES AND ROLES

After the decision to initiate strategic planning has been made, the Applied Strategic Planning process breaks down into the following three major stages, each of which requires different consulting strategies and skills (see Figure 4-1).

1. *Setting the Stage for Planning.* This involves helping participants understand the planning process and how it works, as well as their roles in the process. This stage is essentially covered by the first eight chapters of this book and includes the first three phases of the Applied Strategic Planning model (planning to plan, the values scan, and mission formulation).

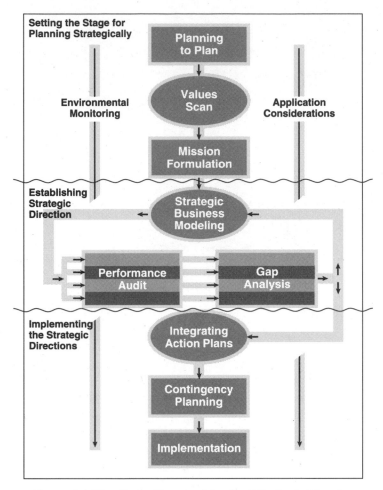

Figure 4-1. The Three Stages of Applied Strategic Planning

2. *Setting Strategic Directions.* This stage involves strategic business modeling, performance audit, and gap analysis (Chapters 9 through 11).

3. *Implementation.* This stage involves integrating action plans, contingency planning, and implementation (Chapters 12 through 14).

Each of these stages poses different challenges to consultants and requires different roles to be filled. Among the possible roles that consultants need to play—sometimes simultaneously, sometimes sequentially, and sometimes alternately—are (1) the advocate or champion, (2) the stakeholder, (3) the trainer, (4) the facilitator, (5) the coach or content expert, and (6) the strategist. We will describe each of these roles and explain how the needs for these various roles change during the planning process.

Advocate or Champion

Chapter 1 addressed the question of why an organization should do strategic planning. Usually the precipitant is a growing awareness of some organizational "pain." That is, there is more and more evidence that the ship is adrift, rudderless, and without clear direction. This includes everything from declining earnings, loss of market share, and other "hard" business considerations to "softer" indices like turnover, especially of key personnel, lowered morale, and reduced quality.

However, the awareness of an organization's pain and the realization that this pain can best be reduced by strategic planning often emerge slowly. Consultants can highlight this emerging problem and its potential solution in dealing with top management. Thus, one consultant role is to advocate or sell the process to the organization. This role needs to be fulfilled prior to the initiation of the three major stages of the actual strategic planning process.

Of all the senior managers in an organization, it is often the HRD manager who has the required distance and objectivity, together with the appropriate process-analytical skills, to recognize the need for strategic planning and to press for the initiation of that process. The internal HRD professional is thus in a unique position to recognize that an organization is floundering: that it goes from crisis to crisis, that there is no overarching sense of purpose or direction, and that it is run tactically rather than strategically.

One of the most striking bits of direct evidence that no strategic plan is in place is the lack of any clear-cut guidelines for deploying an organization's resources, especially human resources. Such guidelines are a necessary outcome of a strategic planning process. Without them, each resource-allocation decision must be made in a vacuum, greatly stressing the system and all its members, because decisions will be contradictory, unpatterned, and disruptive to a smooth flow of operations.

If these guidelines are not directly available to the HRD professional, then the need for a strategic plan is quickly apparent from indirect sources—exit interviews with departing employees, performance-appraisal reports, climate-survey data, and many sorts of informal discussions within the organization. Because of their unique role in organizations, HRD professionals are more likely to be privy to such indirect information; and how they make use of these data is often critical to the organization's success, especially in the strategic planning process. This information needs to be interpreted to the top managers of the organization to alert them about the risks to which the organization is exposed. As discussed in Chapters 10 and 13 and referred to by the acronym SWOT, an organization must look at its *strengths, weaknesses, opportunities,* and *threats.* The internal HRD professional can be invaluable in contributing to this analysis.

Obviously we are not suggesting that HRD professionals violate individual or group confidentiality, but rather that they serve as an early warning system to the organization about how emerging HRD issues may portend serious organizational problems stemming from a lack of strategic planning. One important positive consequence of sharing this awareness will be to help dispel the perceived distinction between the HRD professionals and the rest of the organization, especially at the managerial level. The HRD manager's responsibilities can then be seen as extending beyond simply managing human resources to include sharing with peers the responsibility for the future direction and vitality of the entire organization (Goodstein and Pfeiffer, 1984).

Once the need for strategic planning has been identified, then the internal HRD professional can carefully begin to orchestrate a campaign for such a process. The HRD professional needs to understand what is involved in such a process, how it can benefit the organization, what it will cost the organization, and how to proceed. The importance of this advocacy role for the internal HRD professional as an individual and for the HRD component of the organization can hardly be overemphasized. This advocacy role helps to blur the boundaries between the HRD group and the rest of the organization, especially at the managerial level. This blurring has positive consequences for the effectiveness of the organization and for the status and power of the HRD function in the organization. Strong support for this idea is found in a research report (A.T. Kearney, Inc., 1983) that contrasts the human resource function in sixteen highly productive businesses in eleven industries with twenty-four less-productive organizations in the same industries by using financial data to define the two groups. The key difference is that the HRD groups in the highly productive organizations were more often involved in implementing organizational strategies and making business decisions.

The HRD groups in the more productive organizations also are more likely to use their current resources and programs to solve important company problems. New HRD programs are added in these companies only to give them a competitive edge, either in productivity or in attracting or retaining personnel. In the leading organizations, the HRD unit is twice as likely to be proactive in its programming, whereas in the less-productive organizations, the HRD group is reactive, primarily to line requests. Most importantly, in the leading companies, the HRD group is three times more likely to share responsibility for developing and administering programs such as succession planning and incentive-compensation programs with line managers. It seems obvious from these data that in more productive organizations the HRD function is more like a line organization and less like a traditional staff organization. These boundaries tend to be especially blurred around the strategic planning function.

In response to a request from one of our key client systems, the authors performed an analysis of HRD functions across a wide variety of western corporations. This analysis indicated that there was a direct relationship between the impact of HRD functions on the organization and how closely the HRD functions were tied to the strategic planning process.

The HRD Professional Can Orchestrate the Campaign

In a *Wall Street Journal* article, Andrew Grove (1985), president of Intel, makes a strong case for involving the HRD professional, but he also draws attention to some common shortcomings of these individuals. For example, Grove states, "We [CEOs] don't like to set objectives that won't please our own bosses, so we set unrealistic ones that look good but also set up our employees for failure. Our human-resource organizations—which should be our conscience—allow us to do this, although they usually know better." He ends the article by stating, "Our organizations are—and will always be—peopled by imperfect managers who need the contributions of the human-resource profession. But we will only truly enjoy the ensuing benefits when our human-resource colleagues accept the inherent element of risk involved in making those contributions and overcome their own fear of that risk."

This discussion of the advocate or champion role has concentrated on the internal HRD professional, but this role can also be filled by an external consultant, particularly one who has had an ongoing relationship with the organization, understands its dynamics, and has both the confidence and ear of the organization's top management. The focus on the internal HRD profession is a reflection of the fact that the advocate or champion role is *usually*, but not necessarily, filled by an internal rather than an external resource.

Stakeholder

In addition to serving as a champion for strategic planning, the internal HRD professional can play several other roles. One of these is as a stakeholder in the planning process. As stakeholder, the HRD professional has the important responsibility of linking the organization's overall strategic plan to its human resources. To do this, he or she must understand the nature of overall strategic planning and be willing to work within such a context. More than anything else, the HRD professional must understand that strategic planning is the process through which the senior management of the organization clarifies what it intends the organization to become and what its goals are, both financial and nonfinancial. The process by which such a set of decisions is made requires a high degree of problem-solving skills, and the HRD professional is expected to be a model for such skills.

The HRD professional also must be clear about his or her role in this process. As a stakeholder, the HRD professional must assure that human resources necessary for achieving the goals that are the outcomes of the planning process are correctly identified. The gap between the organization's present resources and future human resource requirements must also be clearly identified together with an action plan to close that gap in accordance with the other dimensions of the strategic plan. The success of the organization's basic strategy depends on how its two most precious resources, people and money, are utilized.

There usually is no one other than the HRD professional to address the first of these two.

Most strategic planning decisions have direct human resource consequences; that is, more or fewer people are needed, new skills are necessary in the work force, new obstacles need to be overcome, and so on. The HRD professional needs to be involved in these strategic discussions to help determine how many people are going to be needed, what kind of training needs to be provided, what types of people need to be recruited, and what the impact of these decisions will be on the organization's culture. It is critical that the HRD professional both surface these issues and be able to assist the other senior managers in the organization in exploring such issues and in answering the questions raised by each of these considerations. Since these questions are raised throughout the strategic planning process—especially during the implementation stage and, to a lesser degree, while setting the strategic direction—this stakeholder responsibility must be met in a decisive manner.

For many HRD professionals, this represents a sharp role change—from a rather traditional personnel function to that of truly representing the organization's human resource concerns. As Kathryn Conners, vice president of human resources at Liz Claiborne, put it:

> Human resources is part of the strategic (business) planning process. It's part of policy development, line extension planning and the merger and acquisition process. Little is done in the company that doesn't involve us in the planning, policy or finalization stages of any deal. (cited in Jackson & Schuler, 1990, p. 223)

This involvement, however, invariably requires moderate to high degrees of expertise in areas outside the human resources field, including a working understanding of finance and financial analysis, legal considerations, the competitive environment, the long-term trends in the industry, the market potential for the organization's goods or services, and the threats and opportunities facing the organization. Although the focus of the HRD professional's concern should be the proper planning for and utilization of human resources, these concerns need to be expressed within a total organizational context, and each HRD professional must be able to hold his or her own in the general give-and-take of the strategic planning process.

The role of stakeholder is perhaps the only one of these consultant roles that is unique to the internal HRD professional. Representing the internal interests and needs of the human resources function can be best fulfilled by a person internal to that organization, someone who has cast his or her lot with the organization and whose personal future and career largely depend on the success or failure in that organization.

Taking on the stakeholder role, however, severely limits the degree to which the internal HRD professional can play any of the other roles, especially that of the facilitator. It is difficult, if not impossible, for most people to strongly hold a stakeholder position and also be an impartial and objective facilitator of the group process: it is hard for most of us to be both players and referees. To the degree that internal consultants are participants in the strategic planning process, their commitment needs to be one of representing their stakeholder interests. Although it may be possible for one person to fill both roles if all the other members of the planning group in question are skilled in group process and have a high, shared commitment to using those skills, most internal HRD professionals should assume that these conditions are unlikely to exist in their circumstances.

Therefore, the two roles of being a stakeholding member of the strategic planning team and being the facilitator of that process are incompatible and should be avoided. Although an HRD professional can be a champion of strategic planning and also fill some of the other consultant roles, few people can be sufficiently objective and alert to facilitate group processes when they are strongly advocating a particular position. Indeed, even if the HRD professional did have such a high level of skills and such a dispassionate nature, one would still wonder about the degree to which such a performance would be credible with the other members of the strategic planning team. Consequently, internal HRD professionals, especially senior HRD managers, must choose which of these roles they are going to fill.

Furthermore, it is critical to the success of the organization's strategic planning process for the internal HRD professional to fill the role of player in that process rather than referee. Having such a player at the planning table is the best way to assure that human resource considerations will be taken into account in the general strategic planning process and that human resource issues will be seriously addressed and given adequate weight in the emerging strategic plan. It is extremely unlikely that anyone external to the organization will represent this position as well as the most senior internal HRD professional. However, it is possible to identify and engage competent external consultants to fill the other consultant roles in the planning process; they may be found in the rapidly emerging OD (organization development) subspecialty of strategic planning.

Occasionally someone suggests that a junior HRD person play the facilitative role while the most senior HRD manager plays the stake-

A Stakeholder Should Not Be the Referee

holder or protagonist role. Although the skills might be appropriate for the situation, we are concerned about the objectivity of such a facilitator, as well as the strong inherent conflict of interest involved. We would wonder whether such a person could genuinely be objective when his or her supervisor was a member of the planning team and whether the necessary interventions would be attempted in the face of the perceived risks. We would also wonder what would happen to the credibility of the entire process under these circumstances. It is far more appropriate, given these concerns, to recruit a more neutral, outside person to play this critically important role.

In large, complex organizations, a seasoned HRD professional may be available from corporate headquarters to serve in a facilitative capacity for subsidiaries, or regional planning teams may be able to furnish facilitators to their not-for-profit community organizations. However, the decision to use such resources should depend on the level of their skills, their capacity to be objective, and the political implications of bringing them in or excluding them. The need for a highly skilled facilitator is clear, and the question of where to find this person is open; but the answer to the question typically does not include the internal HRD professionals of the organization unless they are prepared to abandon their natural—and necessary—places at the planning table.

When internal HRD professionals opt for the stakeholder role—as they should—one of their responsibilities is to identify how the other consultant roles in the strategic planning process will be filled. It is most often the internal HRD professional who needs to raise this issue and make certain that adequate answers are developed by the planning team.

Trainer

Although the Applied Strategic Planning model is straightforward and rather easy to understand, it needs to be understood by the members of the strategic planning team at a very high level of comprehension. Since it serves as a template for the planning team's activities over a period of time, a casual level of understanding is inadequate for effective implementation. Therefore, another important consultant role is that of trainer—training the strategic planning team in understanding and using the Applied Strategic Planning model. Although *Applied Strategic Planning: An Abridged Guide* (Goodstein, Nolan, & Pfeiffer, 1992) provides a useful overview of the model, it is best regarded as an adjunct to a formal training process that allows the planning team to fully explore the model as it applies to them and their organization.

There are also important training needs beyond those of the strategic planning team. One of the significant ways in which the Applied Strategic Planning model differs from other planning models is its insistence on organization-wide understanding of and involvement in the process, including the development of structured mechanisms for broad-scale input into the process. There needs to be total awareness throughout the organization that strategic planning is underway; also who is involved in the process, why such planning is being conducted, the timetable for the process, and the expected results should be announced. Since such a planning process ordinarily has organization-wide implications and requires the understanding, involvement, and commitment of rank-and-file members of the organization, there is a clear necessity to brief them early and often about what is going on. Although it is not necessary for the consultant to be personally involved in all these briefings, it is part of the consultant's role as trainer to educate those who do the briefings, to supervise the briefing process, and to ensure that it occurs.

As the strategic planning process unfolds, there are frequent needs for brief theory inputs—for example, what culture is, how culture and values are related, whether public-sector organizations can have lines of business, and where vision fits into the model. It is at these junctures that the consultant needs to suggest time out to offer a brief theory input to answer, illuminate, and clarify the issues that are being raised. There also are a number of opportunities to provide theory inputs to the planning group around the various issues of group dynamics that arise during the planning process. Whether these interventions are better regarded as part of the trainer or facilitator role, which is discussed next, is far less important than making sure they are provided where needed. Since there are continual opportunities for training throughout the planning process, the trainer role is a continual one; however, it is especially important during stage 1 (setting the stage), when learning the model is critical.

The training-teaching function is a very important one. One of the critical by-products of the Applied Strategic Planning process is a learning, adaptive organization, one that has moved from single- to double-loop learning (Argyris and Schön, 1978). Single-loop learning simply involves learning how to solve the immediate problem that confronts us or the organization. Double-loop learning provides not only a solution to the immediate problem, but also how to solve the same or similar problems that will arise in the future. The Applied Strategic Planning model leads to double-loop learning; it not only produces a useful strategic plan, but it also develops the ability to plan again. As the future is always just beyond our reach, strategic planning is always a reiterative process. In assuming the trainer role, the consultant accepts the challenge to make certain that double-loop learning occurs.

Facilitator

Another critical role is that of facilitator. In strategic planning, this is an *enabling* role. The facilitator helps the planning team deal with the small-group process issues that are vital to a successful planning process. Facilitators help the group deal with issues that otherwise might be avoided, overlooked, or swept under the rug. A facilitator can also serve to ensure that reluctant participants are involved in the process, that consensus rather than compromise is the primary method of decision making, that the necessary group norms of openness and confrontation develop, and that the group process enhances rather than blocks the development of a functional strategic plan that will provide the vision for directing the organization's future.

The Applied Strategic Planning process requires that the members of the planning team directly confront their most fundamental beliefs about organizational life and the future of the organization. This is especially true in the values scan and performance audit. Engaging in such a values-based planning process is difficult and painful for most groups, especially those with little or no experience in team building, values clarification, or the other processes integral to an OD effort. The honesty and openness needed for a valid performance audit will require similar efforts. Such teams will need a skilled facilitator. The cultural analyses, values clarification, and performance audit discussed in Chapters 3, 7, and 10 will be helpful in training such planning teams.

Planning teams experience a number of common problems that result from natural human tendencies. If these frequently encountered difficulties are not properly identified and managed, they can dramatically interfere with a successful outcome of the strategic planning process. One of the most common such tendencies is the unwillingness of the planning team to face important organizational issues—especially if these issues have never before been directly addressed—such as declining markets, a preponderance of mature products or services, a lack of resources for growth, complacency among senior managers, or strong conflict or competition among organizational segments.

A closely related difficulty is the reluctance of many planning teams to make hard choices, especially if these choices directly affect the careers or jobs of members of the planning teams. For example, how can they decide to develop product X and not product Y when John, who has been the leading champion of product Y, is a member of the planning team? Rather than make such a tough decision, planning teams often avoid the choice, deciding not to differentiate resource allocations that would demonstrate their commitment to one product or another. Instead, they attempt to increase both products, a popular but unwise decision. Another way of hiding or avoiding such a problem is to define strategies and objectives broadly enough to allow a variety of alternative action plans, rather than forcing the planning team to identify a clear, unambiguous direction.

Under such circumstances, planning teams often spend their time dealing with other issues—those that are interesting but noncritical; for example, attempting to resolve a particular, difficult personnel problem rather than addressing the adequacy of personnel policies for the execution of the emerging strategic plan. The intrinsic interest in such topics helps the group to delude itself into believing that it is engaged in the critical work of strategic planning rather than avoiding it.

Applied Strategic Planning is concerned with *what* the organization will do, not the details of how the plans will be implemented. The senior managers who comprise the planning team probably became senior managers because they excelled at *how* to do things. They need to learn to think in terms of *what* should be done. An important role of the facilitator is to teach the planning team to think in terms of "what" rather than "how." Although openness and honesty are needed throughout the strategic planning process, it is critical during stage setting. Therefore, early in the process facilitation is needed to enhance openness and honesty.

Facilitators should recognize and identify for the group its natural human tendency to be unrealistic about the future. The group may be overly optimistic; indeed, one might argue that the group's unwillingness to face tough issues is simply a special case of optimism. Typically, planning teams are overly optimistic about their revenue projections for the future, simply insisting that "things are bound to be better." Groups all too often project substantially improved organizational performance without adequate reasons for such a projection. The underlying assumption is "The future will be better because we want it to be better." But the future must be created, not simply wished for.

Conversely, in organizations in which the prevailing cultural climate is negative and there is a prevailing set of beliefs that "all is lost" and that "nothing can be done," the facilitator needs to challenge such verbalizations and help the group address the realities of the situation. Certainly, if nothing is attempted, then truly nothing can be done.

Undue optimism can lead to the group's overlooking the external environment, especially the competition. The planning team usually finds it difficult to anticipate any counterstrategy from the competition, especially a strong move that might seriously interfere with the implementation of its own plan. This type of optimism seriously hampers down-board thinking. The planning team may also be overly optimistic about the future environment, neglecting signs that the marketplace may be shifting in ways that could significantly dislocate the planning team's developing strategy. In the computer industry, for example, Apple's failure to understand the necessity for a business-based distribution system led to an unrealistic initial expectation about the significance of the Macintosh microcomputer in the business marketplace.

Planning teams often have trouble in maintaining the long-term time frame that may be required in strategic planning, even though there is clear agreement about the necessity for doing so. The future is uncertain and hard to read. It is much easier to consider short-term performance and plan for tomorrow and not for the more nebulous future. Perhaps the hardest work a planning team can do, with the exception of the values scan, is to consider an uncertain future seriously and develop alternative scenarios for different futures. Most managers are too pragmatic, too limited in their scope, and too uneasy about uncertainty to tackle such a task with enthusiasm, especially the first time.

Another frequent and important tendency that must be avoided in the planning process is the tendency to minimize the difficulty of producing and sustaining change in an organization. Efforts to produce organizational change will always arouse resistance to that change. Resistance to change is another of those natural, common, human tendencies that is often neglected in the planning process. Usually there is a high degree of acceptance in the organization's present way of operating (otherwise it would have already changed), regardless of how awkward or ineffective it appears; and there are all sorts of people who have a strong vested interest in the status quo. Strategic planning invariably will involve change; and the planning team needs to recognize that the changes required to implement the plan will encounter resistance, especially internal resistance, and should develop plans to manage and reduce such resistance.

This brief survey of the common human problems that are encountered in strategic planning should surprise few, if any, internal HRD professionals or organizational consultants. Dealing with such human foibles is part of their daily work. This list is intended simply to provide some support for the need to have professional facilitation of the strategic planning process. Clearly one role for the consultant is that of a process facilitator to the planning team.

Coach or Content Expert

Another important role for a consultant to play is that of coach or expert in strategic planning. Teaching the Applied Strategic Planning model was discussed above as one aspect of the consultant's role as trainer. The external consultant is brought into the strategic planning process as an expert in the process of strategic planning. The consultant needs to counsel the planning group on the best practices in strategic planning. This often means that the consultant is expected to lead the planning team through the many planning sessions, to help the members of the team understand where they are and why, to make certain that they prepare for the next session by identifying what assignments need to be completed prior to the next group session, and to obtain volunteers to accept these assignments. These tasks regularly occur throughout the planning process, and the coaching role needs to be filled regularly.

For instance, it is important to have comprehensive notes taken at each strategic planning session, both as an accurate record of what was accomplished and also to serve as a record of the agreements made about who has accepted the many assignments for work to be done between sessions and the timetable for completing that work. Although it is not necessary for the consultant to write the notes, note taking is a critical task and the notes must be circulated for review and agreement.

Our preference is for this note-taking responsibility to be rotated among the members of the planning team, rather than asking one person to be saddled with that task for the entire process. However, making sure that the person assigned that responsibility for each meeting is ready, willing, and able to do the task is the consultant's responsibility in the coaching role.

Another important consideration for the person filling the coaching role is to make certain that the environmental monitoring process is in place and that mechanisms exist for the information acquired through that monitoring to be regularly fed into the strategic planning process. At each phase of the Applied Strategic Planning process there are clearly indicated implementation steps that need to be carried out. For example, following the mission formulation phase, the draft mission statement needs to be reviewed and responded to by the various stakeholders. Their feedback then should be received and reviewed by the planning team and, where appropriate, the necessary changes made. The revised draft should then be circulated. Making certain that all this occurs is again the responsibility of the consultant as coach.

It may be argued that this coaching or managing function should be a responsibility of a member of the planning team. However, members of the planning team ordinarily are too busy and involved in their stakeholder roles to take on such a management responsibility during the course of the actual planning session. Furthermore, most members of the team simply are not sufficiently aware of the model and what needs to be done to manage this function adequately.

One more element of this coaching function is to guide the team in establishing a realistic timetable for its work. Planning teams, like most other groups, are far too optimistic about how long things take. If a realistic timetable is not established and held, planning teams often become discouraged and the process can bog down. In each of the appropriate succeeding chapters we will share our experience of how long each phase of the Applied Strategic Planning process has taken, in order to provide a baseline for consultants new to this area.

Yet another aspect of the coaching role is to push strongly for some tangible product to be produced early in the process—a product that can be widely circulated through the organization and convince the rank-and-file members that something important and productive is really going on in this planning process. Among the products that can be considered are a values statement, a preliminary mission statement, a cultural analysis, and a philosophy of operations. However, regardless of what the product is and whatever the reaction to it, distributing such a product is almost invariably an important positive factor in increasing

The Content Expert Has an Important Role

the credibility of the planning process in the eyes of members of the organization.

Still another aspect of the coaching role involves how the strategic planning process gets started. One option is to begin with individual in-depth interviews of the CEO and his or her direct reports. These interviews focus on two separate but interlocking issues: strategic issues and teamwork issues. Among the strategic issues that typically are addressed in these interviews are growth, profitability, marketing direction, and competition. Included in the teamwork issues are conflict management, style differences, problem solving, and decision making. This strategic-team assessment provides the consultant with a good overview of the ongoing direction of the organization, surfaces different points of view, and provides insight into some of the differences among the top group that will have implications for the planning process. It also provides for some early relationship building. At the initial team meetings, the consultant feeds back the results of these interviews in an organized fashion, highlighting some of the issues and concerns that surfaced and how the strategic planning process might deal with them.

In general, the role of the consultant as a coach or content expert is one of trying to ensure the quality of both the strategic planning process and the actual plan by guiding and managing the planning team through the planning process, attempting at all times to keep the model in focus and moving the team systematically through the model.

Strategist

In the process of participating in Applied Strategic Planning as a consultant, one sometimes realizes that certain strategic issues are being overlooked. A frequent example is the group's inability to apply down-board thinking. In considering the launching of a new product to meet an emerging market need, one of our client organizations considered the competitors and their array of present products but never even raised the possibility that any of these competitors might also be developing a new product to meet this same need. After a decent period of time elapsed, we gently raised this issue. And after a period of stunned silence, we were asked how we had access to this information—how did we know what "they" were up to? We simply assured them that we had no such knowledge but that we did know, from regularly reading the business literature, that at least one of their competitors prided itself on being early to market with new products and had a well-established and highly regarded market-research group, as well as a successful product-development staff. Common sense, not insider information, led us to conclude that the competition, or at least one competitor, was not simply waiting for the future to happen but rather would help shape its future. In this case, we temporarily left our other roles as neutral, external consultants and became active strategists.

Most of the time, our knowledge of the industry, the markets, the competition, and so on, is such that we would be foolish to attempt to become actively involved as strategists. Nevertheless, we realize frequently that the planning team has failed to see the options that are open and to engage in down-board thinking. Therefore, we are able to make meaningful contributions in the relatively unusual role as strategist. As consultants, we have a responsibility to be current on the strategies available to the organization. This is a role that is most likely to arise during the second stage of the process (setting strategic direction), when the group is struggling to find that direction. In other words, where appropriate, one of the consultant's many roles is to contribute positively to strategy development, particularly by pointing out additional options that might not otherwise be considered.

We need to make clear that there are many strategy consultants whose contributions are to the actual formulation of strategy—specialists in marketing, finance, mergers and acquisitions, and so on. They regularly engage in making precisely these contributions. Our usual roles, and those for which we have contracted with the client, are those discussed above—advocate, stakeholder, trainer, facilitator, and coach. However, sometimes because of our business and consulting experience, we can make a strategic contribution. While we always make it with caution and offer caveats before doing so, we have become comfortable in this role when our knowledge and understanding makes it appropriate.

ROLE ISSUES

Typically, all the roles outlined above are necessary at various times in an organization's planning process. The strategic planning process needs a champion and advocate, the HRD function needs to be strongly represented at the planning table by a stakeholder, the process has clear-cut training requirements, and the planning team requires some expert facilitation as well as a guide through the process. It should be obvious from the above that it is virtually impossible for a single individual to fill all of these roles. This confirms our earlier position that at least two consultants should be involved in this process. Although the typical division is for one of them to play the stakeholder role while the other plays all of the remaining roles, this is not the only possible decision.

While the facilitator and stakeholder roles are clearly incompatible, the internal HRD professional may take on a trainer role, especially in developing and implementing processes to share what is happening throughout the organization. Obviously, it is also possible for the internal HRD professional to play the strategist role, especially around HRD issues. What is important here is clarity around roles and continual recontracting about these roles between the HRD professionals to ensure that this clarity is maintained.

EXTERNAL CONSULTANTS

On what basis can one choose an external strategic planning consultant? Clear-cut criteria for selecting an external consultant to facilitate the strategic planning process may be found in the characteristics of people in the subspecialty group of OD consultants who specialize in strategic planning, because they have high-level processing skills and a solid understanding of and commitment to the planning process. They also have a good understanding of organizational culture, of organizational behavior, and of both the hard and soft side of organizational management. Typically, they are risk takers, possess high personal integrity, and are willing to confront organizational issues when necessary; that is, while they do not seek controversy, neither do they shy away from it, particularly when direct confrontation is clearly the necessary course.

They frequently have had line-management responsibilities, either as part of their HRD careers or prior to that portion of their lives. Although they can be supportive and nurturing, they ordinarily have pragmatic and matter-of-fact styles. In general they tend to be problem solvers and planners rather than idealists or dreamers, but they also understand and support the importance of a vision of the survival of an organization, especially when that vision leads to action plans.

Professional Development

Becoming a competent strategic planning consultant, especially one who can compete successfully in the fiercely competitive world of external consultation, is an arduous task. To successfully apply the Applied Strategic Planning model, one needs a high level of the usual process consultation skills, a high degree of marketing savvy, an in-depth understanding of organizational dynamics and behavior, and a sophisticated level of contracting skills that typifies any highly successful external consultant. In addition, however, there is a further requirement that the consultant be familiar with the literature both of business and of strategic planning.

The world of business and how it operates is foreign territory for many consultants. Regular reading of business periodicals, such as *The Wall Street Journal, Forbes, Business Week,* and *Fortune,* will go a long way to familiarizing the relatively unsophisticated consultant with the world of business and is a necessity even for the knowledgeable ones as a way of keeping current with business thinking. For those consultants who choose to work in the public sector, there is a similar set of periodicals that merit serious attention.

Then there is the literature of strategic planning, both journals and books. Pfeiffer (1991) provides a comprehensive list of the available journals, an annotated bibliography of the current, relevant book literature, and a list of professional planning societies that provide a forum for sharing of ideas about strategic planning through professional meetings and journals. What is essential to understand from this overview of the field is that strategic planning is a serious undertaking and the field is becoming increasingly professionalized. To compete successfully in this field, a consultant has to develop and keep current his or her own level of professionalization.

A final area for professional development is imagination and creativity. Strategic planning involves operating in an area of high uncertainty, the future. What is thus required for effective strategic planning is imagination and creativity, not skills in operational management, the area from which most managers and consultants are drawn. Wheatley, Anthony, and Maddox (1991) conclude that effective strategic planning consultants need to be extraverted, so that they are in touch with the external world; intuitive, so that they see alternatives; feeling rather than thinking based; and perceptive, so that they are flexible. In the typology of the *Meyers-Briggs Type Indicator,* such people would be classified as ENFPs (Kroeger and Thuesen, 1988). They should be more comfortable in being marginal rather than central to an organization, and finally they should have an internal rather than an external locus of control. Wheatley, Anthony, and Maddox suggest that consultants who have rather different styles should involve themselves in a variety of training programs to enhance these aspects of their approach. Their viewpoint is interesting, but finding a consultant who has these personal characteristics in addition to the specific knowledge and skills discussed above poses an exceptional challenge for most organizations in search of a strategic planning consultant.

SUMMARY

Both external and internal consultants have important roles in the Applied Strategic Planning process. These roles include advocate or champion, stakeholder, trainer, facilitator, coach or content expert, and strategist. Sometimes these roles are separate and sometimes they overlap, but the same consultant should not attempt to fill both the role of stakeholder and that of facilitator. An OD consultant is typically the type of person who can fill the roles of the external consultant.

REFERENCES

Argyris, C. & Schön, D. (1978). *Organizational learning.* Reading, MA: Addison-Wesley.

A.T. Kearney, Inc. (1983). *Managing the human resources for strategic results.* Chicago: Author.

Goodstein, L.D., & Pfeiffer, J.W. (1984). Human resource development: Current status and future directions. In J.W. Pfeiffer and L.D. Goodstein (Eds.). *The 1984 annual: Developing human resources* (pp. 155-160). San Diego, CA: Pfeiffer & Company.

Goodstein, L.D., Nolan, T. M., & Pfeiffer, J.W. (1992). *Applied strategic planning: An Abridged guide* (rev. ed). San Diego, CA: Pfeiffer & Company. (In press.)

Grove, A.S. (1985, September 30). Manager's journal. *The Wall Street Journal.*

Jackson, S.E., & Schuler, R.E. (1990). Human resource planning: Challenges for industrial/organizational psychologists. *American Psychologist, 45,* 223-239.

Kroeger, O., & Thuesen, J.M. (1988). *Type talk: Or how to determine your personality type and change your life.* New York: Delacorte Press.

Pfeiffer, J.W. (Ed.). (1991). *Strategic planning: Selected readings* (rev. ed.). San Diego, CA: Pfeiffer & Company.

Wheatley, W.J., Anthony, W.B., & Maddox, E.N. (1991). Selecting and training strategic planners with imagination and creativity. *Journal of Creative Behavior., 25,* 52-60.

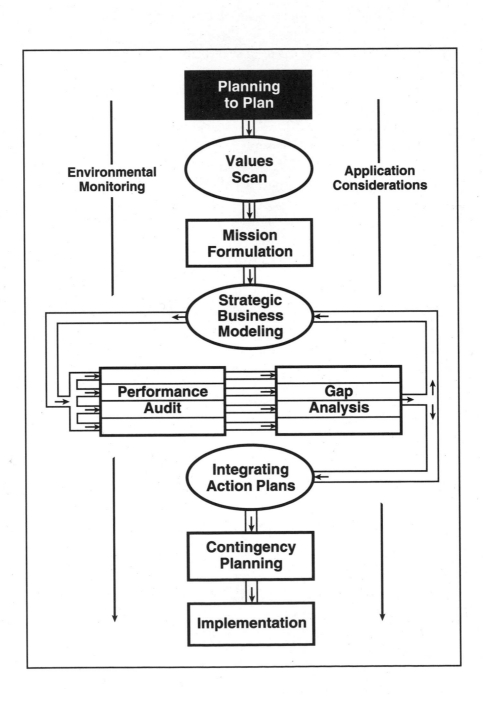

Chapter Five

Planning to Plan

We never know how high we are
Till we are called to rise
And then, if we are true to plan
Our statures touch the sky.

Emily Dickinson
c. 1890
The Collected Poems of Emily Dickinson

While virtually everyone understands the need to plan prior to beginning a large-scale, complex project, there is far less understanding of the need to plan how to plan. By planning to plan, we mean the in-depth consideration of how the planning itself will be conducted—who will be involved, what the timetable will be, what the anticipated consequences of this planning are (and what some of the unanticipated consequences could be), what resources are necessary, and so on. While planning to plan is ordinarily important in project management, it is absolutely critical to the success of Applied Strategic Planning.

In Applied Strategic Planning, *planning to plan* is the term applied to the prework that must be accomplished prior to the formal initiation of the strategic planning process. Individuals who are responsible for making key decisions will determine whether or not the organization is ready to engage in formal strategic planning. If the decision is positive, this phase will include the careful selection of the planning team and the establishment of methods to feed information back to nonplanning managers, rank-and-file members of the organization, and other key stakeholders.

Our view of the planning-to-plan phase includes the following six elements:

1. Determining organizational readiness for strategic planning;
2. Developing commitment, especially from the organization's chief executive officer (CEO) or executive director;
3. Identifying the members of the planning team;
4. Educating the entire organization, especially the planning team, about the process of strategic planning;
5. Determining which other organizational stakeholders need to be apprised and the methods of keeping them and other nonparticipants in the planning process informed; and,
6. Contracting for successful strategic planning.

The effective execution of these six steps is an important determinant of the overall success of strategic planning. By and large, the intent of the planning to plan phase is to clarify the expectations of the many organizational stakeholders about strategic planning and to gain their commitment to that process. Given the importance of these steps, this chapter reviews them in detail.

READINESS FOR STRATEGIC PLANNING

Strategic planning, if it is to be effective, involves a considerable expenditure of time and energy from the organization. The planning team will devote a substantial amount of its time to the actual process; others in the organization who are not directly involved will need to be informed on a regular basis of what is happening; data will need to be collected and processed, and so on. There are times when an organization is not ready for this level of activity.

Pfeiffer & Jones (1978) note an intriguing parallel between the concepts of readiness for organization development (OD) and reading readiness in children. Once an individual child is ready to read, there are differences in outcome among the different teaching methods, although they are slight. Conversely, when a child is not ready to learn to read, all strategies are relatively unsuccessful in teaching that child how to read. In an analogous way, if an organization is not ready to undertake a project of planned change, the most sophisticated techniques employed by the most competent and experienced consultants and managers are doomed to failure.

For example, one of the authors was a consultant for a small distributor of electronics equipment. Although the initial overtures were for "strategic planning," it quickly became apparent that what was really necessary was "survival planning," and a contract for such planning was established instead. The total resources of the organization were required for bailing out the lifeboat; determining a long-term direction was immaterial.

Once the seaworthiness of the craft was restored, other steps could be contemplated; but at the time, survival was the name of the game.

Applied Strategic Planning is, de facto, a project of planned change, and a simple, overarching principle applies. If, on one hand, an organization is not ready to plan and implement the plan simultaneously and, on the other hand, carry on the ordinary work of the organization, it makes little practical difference what planning processes are used or, in fact, what level of consultation skills are available. It is highly unlikely that any significant outcome will result.

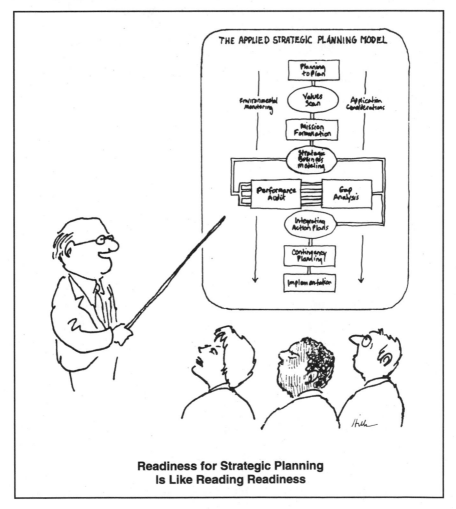

**Readiness for Strategic Planning
Is Like Reading Readiness**

In contrast to reading readiness, however, if an organization is ready for strategic planning, which methodology it selects does make a significant difference in the consequences of the plan for the organization. In contrast to some other planning methodologies, Applied Strategic Planning provides criteria for managers to make important day-to-day decisions that will drive the organization in the desired, predetermined direction and thus increase the probability that the organization's mission will be achieved.

Assessing the readiness of the organization for strategic planning is thus a critically important first step in planning to plan. A variety of factors need to be considered in determining planning readiness. These include the organization's fiscal viability, the vitality of its products and services, its culture, how thinly its resources are spread, and so on. Another readiness factor is the job security and expected job tenure of the CEO. When there is uncertainty in an organization about its future leadership, all its psychological energy focuses on that decision and strategic planning is contraindicated. All the consultant's skills in organizational assessment and diagnosis are necessary to make this important initial decision: How ready is this organization for Applied Strategic Planning? The single most important factor in determining this readiness is the interest in and commitment to strategic planning by the organization's chief executive.

THE CEO'S ROLE IN STRATEGIC PLANNING

Over the past several decades, organizational life and structures have become more complex, especially in the executive suite of large organizations. As a result, it sometimes is not clear who the CEO is. Steiner (1979) defines the CEO as the person or persons with the authority to manage the organization. He points out that the CEO can be the president, the president and the executive vice president, or some other combination of individuals. When the term "chief executive officer" does not necessarily refer to one individual, the term "chief-executive-officer function" is often used; for simplicity, in this book, we will use the term CEO to stand for that function, be it an individual or a group of individuals, regardless of the person's actual title. And, regardless of the title, the function is critically important in strategic planning, just as it is in all other important issues facing the organization.

The Importance of the CEO in Strategic Planning

There are several reasons for the importance of the CEO's interest in and commitment to strategic planning. Clearly, the CEO can simply abort the process at any juncture, but this rarely happens. Modern management theory and practice strongly endorse strategic planning as an organizational necessity. Actively canceling a planning process would be seen by most CEOs as a dangerous, if not a foolhardy, action. Rather, we find CEOs who verbally endorse the process but who are "too busy" to be involved personally and who will not actively support the implementation of the plan that emerges from the process. This reluctance to support the plan can represent myriad reasons; for example, an unwillingness to subject oneself to the discipline imposed by having a strategic plan, a reluctance to share information or power with others, a result of having contradictory visions (having a high rate of growth and a relaxed lifestyle), a lack of belief in the uses of planning, or a prior unfortunate experience with strategic planning. However, the *reasons* for CEO reluctance matter far less than the fact that it exists. This chapter will return to these issues and suggest some ways to manage them.

Assessing CEO Commitment

The importance of the CEO makes it imperative that he or she be personally interviewed by the consultant(s) to evaluate his or her level of commitment to planning. A useful way to begin the strategic planning process is to interview the CEO about his or her personal vision for the organization, as well as his or her willingness to risk bringing that vision to reality. If the CEO can be helped to understand that strategic planning is a way to surface, test, refine, gain support, and implement that vision, the strategic process is well begun. If, however, the CEO has no such vision or, even worse, is unwilling to accept the notion that vision has a place in creating the future of the organization, then the prospects for a successful planning process are slight.

If a vision and some willingness to work on that vision are present, then the CEO's direct reports can be interviewed about how the vision has been shared, their reactions to the vision, and what issues the vision has raised. In this case there is a danger that the planning process can be seen as merely a facile way of endorsing the CEO's vision, but there is also a danger in ignoring such a vision or in pretending that it does not exist and will not impact the planning process. It often is helpful to have each of these interviewees read a copy of the six-page explanation, *A Brief Introduction to Applied Strategic Planning* (Goodstein, Nolan, and Pfeiffer, 1992a) as a way of understanding the process that is being contemplated and thus to better prepare themselves for the interview.

A critical question to answer during this initial interviewing process is whether or not there is a well-functioning management team involved in the running of the organization. While the Applied Strategic Planning process will smooth out some problems that emerge during the course of planning, the model is predicated on the organization's having an intact, fairly well-operating management team. The initial interview may result in recommendations for an in-depth team-building process prior to initiating any planning.

This interview process also provides an opportunity to evaluate the degree of pain in the organization. As noted earlier, it is this organizational discomfort that often provides the primary motivation for the organization to invest in strategic planning, especially where transformational change is necessary. Although the experience of pain is certainly not a universal factor—organizations sometimes are seeking opportunity—it is a frequent occurrence and needs to be evaluated. The consultant needs to know the CEO's assessment of the health of the organization. In any case, the CEO's commitment to strategic planning must be tested; otherwise the process can be sabotaged, and the interview process is a useful way to begin that testing.

The CEO and Strategic Leadership

There is more to the importance of the CEO's role in strategic planning than having a vision that looks beyond the present to a desired future. The CEO must help set the goals to articulate that future and the processes to measure progress toward that goal. The CEO also must have the integrity to proceed in the right way and to know what is right, both in the planning process and in its implementation. He or she must have the courage to initiate change and start moving obstacles and, at the same time, the political skill to live and succeed in the real world where there are differing objectives and conflicting demands that must be resolved. To be a strategic leader, a CEO must have all of these characteristics.

CEOs must also know themselves, be able to use staff effectively, be courageous, be open to feedback, and be able to use it effectively. It is imperative that their staff members not be "yes men" or "yes women" but that they have both the knowledge and confidence to challenge the boss, where necessary. The evaluation of the CEO against these exceedingly high criteria is clearly part of the consultant's role as a coach or manager of the strategic planning process. Without understanding the CEO and his or her style, the consultant will encounter surprises that may impede the planning process.

Assessing the CEO

Ultimately the question that must be posed to the CEO is twofold:

1. Do you, as CEO, believe that you sufficiently understand the time and energy required for the proposed Applied Strategic Planning process?
2. Are you prepared to make a commitment to ascertain that the cycle is completed in a reasonably thorough manner?

In the absence of affirmative responses to these two questions, the planning process must stop until education can resolve the former and reinforce the latter. The educational process typically involves dealing directly with the issues of CEO resistance discussed above. For example, with respect to the issue of the discipline imposed by a strategic plan, commitment to its implementation is often difficult, especially in single-proprietorship organizations. The discipline and rigor required by the planning process simply do not fit the energy, vitality, and problem-solving styles of such individuals. As one such entrepreneur recently argued, "I make my best deals on airplanes, just by sitting next to a stranger. How are you going to plan for that?" The only answer is that one cannot plan for such unanticipated opportunities. The real question should be, "How will I be able to deal with such contingencies in this new framework?"

Single-Owner and Family Businesses

Single-owner and family businesses offer both a unique opportunity and a unique challenge to strategic planning. In organizations that are owned by a single individual or small family group, we recommend a one- or two-day preplanning-to-plan session with the individual(s), including, if appropriate, spouses. It is our belief that personal human needs must be explored in private so that they can be clearly articulated as nonnegotiable boundaries in the remainder of the process, especially in the values scan. In such a meeting it may be important to involve expert help from tax consultants and estate-planning specialists. The meeting would focus heavily on the personal needs and wants of the sole proprietor or of the individuals who in truth own the organization.

Among the questions to be explored are the following:

1. Is there a current will?
2. Is there a current inter vivos trust?
3. Is there an adequate plan to integrate individual and company tax obligations optimally?

Items of this nature will most certainly drive value discussions during the values scan. It is possible to create double binds if it is both inappropriate to discuss these issues with the planning team and also difficult for the planning team to understand the process by which some early decisions are made. The obvious down side of this scenario is that the owners will impose values that are feigned to be business-based when in fact they are simply perquisites of ownership. The consultant should push to identify such issues early and coach the owners to make them explicit, as givens in the process.

The most frequent example of this type of situation occurs when advancing age and increasing outside interests (grandchildren, golf, extended travel, etc.) combine with reasonably high levels of accumulated wealth to produce an organization in which there is no drive for growth at a time when technological or market conditions tell nonowner managers that a higher growth orientation is desirable. Another variation occurs when the outside interests mentioned above result in an inappropriate tolerance for inefficient practices, processes, or individuals.

With most executives, however, it is possible to use a developmental strategy and help them understand the advantages of creating an applied strategic plan. With the exception of the stereotypical entrepreneur, there is almost always some interest in the planning function, and the competent consultant needs to focus on that interest and nurture it. Without such a process of developing CEO commitment, when not already present, there is little likelihood of mounting a successful strategic planning process.

CEO Responsibilities in Strategic Planning

In addition to the key personal commitment detailed above, the CEO must be willing to transfer appropriate levels of responsibility and authority for the execution of the planning function to the planning team. This may require sharing data with people who have never before had access to such information. The CEO must also promote the acceptance of the participation of managers and nonmanagers who, although not a part of the formal planning team, will be responsible for the implementation of planning decisions. Without the commitment of appropriate managers (and other key staff) the planning process will not be implemented.

The CEO *must* provide overall direction and assume ultimate responsibility for the creation and execution of the strategic plan. The CEO must aggressively instill enthusiasm in key staff members while coaching (and, if necessary, cajoling) them through the appropriate use of rewards and sanctions. The consultant should work with the CEO and other members of the planning team to determine what types of decisions will be made during the planning process. *Command* decisions are those made by one person (the CEO) and accepted by the other members of the planning team; *consultative* decisions are made by one person after consulting with the other members; and *participative* decisions require the participation of the group and are made by the group.

Nevertheless, regardless of how the decisions are made, top management must be united and rally behind the strategy that is finally developed. Without such unity, there will be destructive internal conflict that will defeat even the best of strategies. Top-management unity and commitment is critical to successful implementation, and assuring such unity and commitment is one of the CEO's important responsibilities in the planning process. Another such responsibility is to make certain that the strategy is clear and easily understood; without such clarity, implementation becomes difficult.

Still another CEO responsibility is a commitment to make sure that the organization's new strategy, when it is developed, is articulated at every level of the total organization through its divisional and departmental structure, down to the smallest work unit and individual employee. The CEO also must believe this to be important for the applied strategic plan to be successful. Without that kind of intense dissemination, the strategic plan will not serve as a rallying point for organizational vitality. And, finally, the CEO is responsible for making certain that a rather complete system of bench marks and measurement (*critical success indicators*) are in place to track the progress of both the planning process and its implementation. If the CEO takes responsibility for these five requirements (overall direction, top-management unity, clarity, organization-wide articulation of the plan, and bench marks) and carries them out, the probabilities of success for strategic planning are enormously increased.

One way of evaluating the forces supporting and opposing the Applied Strategic Planning process and its execution is Lewin's (1975) force-field analysis (see Figure 5-1). It may be worthwhile to conduct such an analysis with the planning team to identify these forces and decide how the opposing forces can be reduced while the supporting forces are being increased.

IDENTIFICATION OF THE PLANNING TEAM

Once the full commitment of the CEO is secured, the next concern is to identify the most effective planning team. Selection for the planning

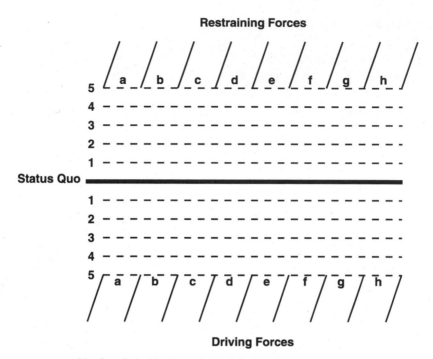

List forces in blanks a through h. Draw arrows toward
status quo line to indicate intensity of 1 through 5.

Figure 5-1. Diagram for Listing Forces in a Force-Field Analysis

process should be marketed as a prestigious opportunity to participate in the envisioning of the organization's future and not, as is often the case, a seemingly endless string of meetings that detract from other work assignments without producing any positive impact on how day-to-day decisions are made.

The planning team should have between five and twelve members. Significant amounts of research indicate that groups of five are typically the most effective in problem solving, and our experience tells us that groups larger than twelve are difficult to "read" in terms of group process; furthermore, a group larger than twelve limits each person's "air time" to the degree that it is difficult for every member to make appropriate contributions. Very often group progress is slowed and additional members make scheduling of meetings even more difficult than it usually is. Additionally, groups of more than twelve have a tendency to break down into two or more subgroups. All other things being equal (which they rarely are), the authors prefer to work with a group of seven to nine, the optimal balance between the need to represent stakeholder factions and the need to allow for productive dialog.

One of the consultant's responsibilities is to work with the CEO and other key managers to identify potential management and nonmanagement planning-team members. It is imperative that this process be given the attention and respect necessary to identify a good working team. In many organizations there will be individuals who feel that they "should" be included in such a process, regardless of their skills or potential contributions to the process. When these are people who can impact the implementation of the plan, the decision must be handled with tact. If such people are not included, a course we strongly recommend, they need to be "cooled out" and their potential negative consequences on the planning process needs to be neutralized. This can be done through a variety of creative efforts to have them involved—while not actually sitting at the planning-team table.

The Role of Staff Planners

In many settings it is fashionable for senior management to be over-committed, overextended, and overworked. This frenzied-chic approach to management is often in vogue among entrepreneurially oriented owners/managers, and in such cases there may be an attempt to transfer the responsibility for the planning function to a staff planner or a staff planning group. This approach categorically does not work! Although there has been a strong precedent for planning staffs in some large companies, most notably General Electric, there is little (if any) evidence to suggest that planning done by staff will be implemented by line managers.

There are, however, many important administrative functions that can be done by staff planners or by staff assigned to planning-support roles. They can play facilitative, research, and support functions, especially providing follow-through on the assignments made during the course of planning. It is often desirable, particularly in medium-sized companies, to assign a junior manager to be the planning-project liaison. (In smaller companies this task may be performed by the executive secretary.) Ideally, this role should be offered as a reward, that is, a unique opportunity to learn, firsthand, the essential strategic planning skills needed to become a successful senior manager in today's increasingly complex business environment.

This planning-coordination role can provide important support as the focal point for data collection and analysis, decision recording and dissemination, and management of clerical and logistic factors to ensure that formal planning sessions are optimally effective. Each planning session should close with an agenda setting for the next session. It is useful for the planning coordinator to assume the responsibility for circulating this agenda shortly before the next meeting as well as checking for the completion of assignments agreed to during the previous session.

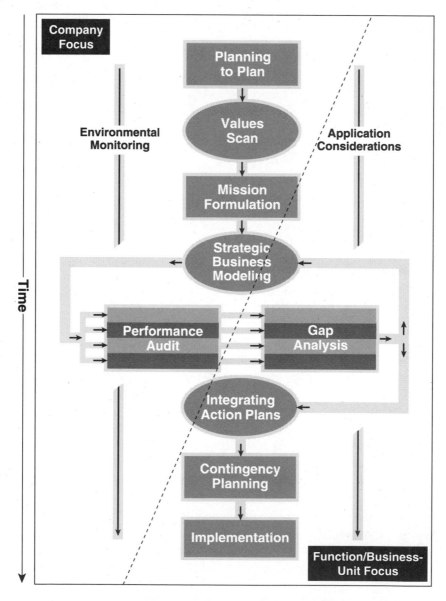

Figure 5-2. Constituency Ratio During Applied Strategic Planning

Shifting Focus in Strategic Planning

Figure 5-2 illustrates the degree to which planning-team members appropriately change their foci from the company to their own functions as strategic planning progresses. When they first join the planning team, their commitment is primarily focused on the organization. As the planning process continues and members begin to see what strategic planning means for their own functional areas, the focus begins to change. Each member becomes more and more concerned with the implications for his or her own department or division.

Another aspect of the shift in focus is that the early sessions of Applied Strategic Planning, especially the first one or two, are devoted to extensive team building. This team building, with its focus on the team itself, shifts to a focus on the organization during the mission formulation phase of the process, then externally to a focus on the competitive environment during the performance audit phase. If the team members understand these shifting foci early in the process—as the consultant guides them through the early phases—they will not be as likely to feel lost when the shifts occur.

EDUCATING THE PLANNING TEAM AND THE ORGANIZATION

From the very beginning of the Applied Strategic Planning process, efforts are made to achieve meaningful involvement of a significant number of people in the organization. Although these efforts are made to improve the quality of the product, their most important impact is to build a broad constituency who can personally feel an investment in and ownership of the resulting strategic plan.

Involvement and Commitment

The value of developing a broad and deep interest in and commitment to the strategic plan is immeasurable when it comes to implementing the plan. The potency of achieving this commitment is so high that, at every step of the process, we examine the question of who *could* be involved, either as making an input to or in developing implementation considerations related to that particular phase of the process. The emphasis here is on identifying potential opportunities for involvement, not on restricting them. Also, this involvement should not be treated as an obligation—something that people should do—but as an opportunity. Tasks that one "should" do are rarely approached with verve and enthusiasm, and these tasks are too important to the success of strategic planning to have them approached with anything short of complete enthusiasm.

Training the Planning Team

Much of the resistance to any change effort comes from misunderstanding or, at least, not understanding. Therefore, it is important to devote significant energy at the end of the planning to plan phase to inform the planning-team members of how they were selected and what is expected of them. To this end we have developed a publication, *Applied Strategic Planning: An Abridged Guide* (Goodstein, Nolan, & Pfeiffer, 1992b), to reinforce an overview presentation of two to four hours. The publication is also intended to serve as a road map, once the formal planning process has begun; and it helps the members of the planning team to identify (a) where they are in the process, (b) where they have been, and (c) where they are going. It should be part of the strategic planning kit used by team members.

We strongly recommend that the above-mentioned *Abridged Guide* also be distributed to key members of the organization who have not been selected for the planning team. We recommend that these individuals be given a separate orientation for the purpose of educating them in the process of Applied Strategic Planning.

Training the Organization

Another significant step is to inform all members of the organization about what is taking place. As noted before, developing commitment is a significant by-product of involvement. One way of achieving a modest level of involvement throughout the organization is through communication about what is going on. *A Brief Introduction to Applied Strategic Planning* (Goodstein, Nolan, & Pfeiffer, 1992a) can be distributed to every member of an organization. It should be accompanied by either (a) a brief orientation from the CEO or (b) a cover letter from the CEO. Either method should stress the CEO's commitment to the process, and it should identify the planning team, its goals, and the projected time frame. "Don't let them guess about what you're up to when you're willing to tell them" is a solid axiom for any CEO.

Planning the Feedback Loop

Keeping all members of the organization well-informed about the progress and direction of the planning team is also essential. The mecha-

The Organization Must Be Informed

nism (meeting or memorandum) and frequency (quarterly or after each planning session) should be established and communicated as part of the orientation meetings or memorandum. This is an essential element of the application considerations (an ongoing process) as well as the implementation phase (the last step in the Applied Strategic Planning process).

INVOLVING THE OTHER STAKEHOLDERS

Typically, there are several other groups who are not formally members of the organization but who feel that they have an investment in the organization. These groups are called *stakeholders,* and the only requirement for being a stakeholder is a sense of involvement—a very fluid criteria. In addition to managers and other employees, the usual stakeholders of organizations include the board of directors, labor unions, local and state governmental bodies, the surrounding community, and, in fact, any constituency that perceives that it will be impacted by a significant change in the organization. Figure 5-3 presents a simple model of a typical organization's stakeholders.

These stakeholders may be influenced in terms of status, resources, relationships, discretion, or activities; and the perceived impact of a change in the organization on different stakeholders rarely will be the same.

It must be determined whether or not any of these key stakeholders are capable of sabotaging the development and implementation of the plan, even if there is sufficient commitment from the CEO. Resistance to the development and implementation of a formal planning process must be identified, evaluated, and, where appropriate, dealt with in a decisive manner. To fail to do so places the entire process at dire risk. There likewise may be key stakeholder groups that can support the strategic planning process and its outcomes, especially if they learn that it is in their best interest to do so. Careful attention to these groups can be of real benefit to the planning process.

The reactions of stakeholders to perceived impact can be sudden and disruptive if not thought through in advance. For example, one strategic planning team decided to change the shift hours in its manufacturing plants. In one community, there was an overwhelming negative reaction. The morning-shift change would coincide with the beginning of the school day, creating serious traffic problems for the community. The strength of the negative reaction to this seemingly trivial change almost sidetracked the entire implementation effort.

The lesson to be learned here is a relatively straightforward one. It is critical to identify the organization's stakeholders and to include them, or at least regularly inform them, of the organization's strategic planning activities and to permit them to provide feedback whenever possible. If it is not possible to involve a stakeholder group directly in the process, their responses should at least be anticipated so that plans can be made accordingly.

Board of Directors

The organization's board of directors, however, is a special class of stakeholder and requires different treatment. The board is one of those key stakeholder groups that actually can force the organization to abandon the strategic planning process and thus needs to be involved in a way very different from that of other stakeholder groups.

One option is to have a member of the board involved in the entire process, either as a participant or as an observer. Another is to have the board members involved in a parallel process, that is, developing a strategic plan for themselves and their role in the organization. This approach can work well for public organizations, wherein the city council or a board of education—for example— can operate on a level different from that of the city department or school systems they supervise.

Nevertheless, whatever process the organization selects to involve its board, it cannot be neglected or simply told about what is going on after the fact.

Figure 5-3. A Model of a Typical Organization's Stakeholder Relationships

The Final Product

A related issue is the nature of the final strategic plan. A central question that needs to be answered as part of planning to plan is the target audience of the final planning document—for whom it is being written. Our general contention is that the process of Applied Strategic Planning is far more important than its final product, the plan. Nevertheless, a plan must emerge at the end of the process, and understanding its audience is critical to its crafting.

In general, there are two possible audiences for a strategic plan—internal and external. A plan written for internal use within the organization is far more narrow, technical, and detailed. A plan written for external use—for shareholders, government agencies, or the community—is broader, more general, less technical, and less detailed. While either can be a useful product, one document rarely serves both audiences. We believe that there must be a document for internal use, because the primary purpose of planning is internal organizational clarity and to assure the creation of the ideal future. It may be appropriate to draft two plans, one for each audience, but they will be rather different. What needs to be understood is why and for whom the plan is being written and how it will be used. These decisions should be made as part of the initial planning to plan phase.

CONTRACTING FOR STRATEGIC PLANNING

In strategic planning, as in all major consultation processes, clarity about the nature of the consultation process is important. This is especially true in strategic planning, because the topic on the table is the future of the organization and the players are from the very core of the organization. In contrast to some consultations, in Applied Strategic Planning our expectations as consultants are reasonably clear, expectations we feel must be fulfilled if the process is to be successful. Among these expectations are the following:

1. The top of the organization will visibly and dramatically model commitment to the process;
2. The organization will hold line managers responsible for implementing the plan; and
3. The organization will identify and reward those managers who enable the plan to be implemented and will effectively deal with those who do not.

These are essential requirements for a successful implementation and must be part of any psychological contract for Applied Strategic Planning.

Contracting for the Initial Phase

The authors prefer to contract the planning to plan phase separately from the remainder of the Applied Strategic Planning process. Given the description earlier in this chapter about the unquestionable need for organizational readiness and CEO commitment, it is possible to complete the planning to plan phase only to discover that, at least for the present, it is inappropriate to move on to the successive phases. At this point the consulting strategy should be to specifically detail what needs to be accomplished by whom before the process continues. The planning consultant then exits the system while the remediation takes place. It is, of course, possible to involve the consultant in the getting-ready/building-commitment phase. The pros and cons of this alternative are addressed later in this chapter in the section on "Identification of Other Training and Data-Collection Needs."

Another way in which this matter can be approached is to contract for four to six days initially, essentially for the team-building part of Applied Strategic Planning. Since any issues that stand in the way of strategic planning will need to be addressed and since they can be better addressed by a fully functioning team, such team building is time well spent by the organization. These days are ordinarily spent in interviews of key managers (two days), an executive briefing on the model (one day), and in a two- to three-day off-site meeting dealing with planning to plan, the values scan, and a first pass at formulating a mission statement.

Setting Realistic Time Expectations

Another key issue that requires contracting is how long the planning process will take. The answer, almost inevitably, is "longer than anticipated." Although the size of the organization and the complexity of products and/or services offered have some impact on the time needed to complete the planning cycle, the three most significant factors that influence the time needed to do the necessary work are the following:

1. Self-awareness,
2. Interpersonal conflict-management skills, and
3. The degree to which the key stakeholders have a harmonious view of the organization's future.

The time horizon for the planning process will also impact the time involved. Although there are no clear-cut rules for determining the horizon for planning, it should be short enough for the planning team to see the results of their effort and long enough for the plan to be truly strategic, that is, to change the scope and nature of the work performed by the organization, if appropriate, or to refocus on the existing mission and goals if this is not the case.

Another factor in determining the time needed to complete the planning process is the availability of data required for the performance audit. Organizations that lack skill in the management of interpersonal

Time Commitment Is Vital

data take more time and more of the consultant's energy to gather and consider the data than do interpersonally skilled groups of managers.

Realistically, an organization should expect to spend between ten and twenty full days of meetings to complete the Applied Strategic Planning cycle. Assuming no significant change in the planning team (nor in key stakeholders) and performance within the targeted ranges, successive iterations can shorten the planning time.

In an ideal model, the first full process can be completed in six months. In such circumstances, the planning team would meet fairly regularly, perhaps every six weeks, for two or three days at a time. Ideally, the team would work effectively toward values consensus, develop a mission statement that is rapidly and enthusiastically endorsed by the organization, and then create a strategic business model expeditiously. The resulting action plans would then be developed, tested, integrated, and implemented promptly. However, it is more likely that significant stumbling blocks—which must be addressed and resolved before the team can move on—will arise at various points in the sequence.

For example, in the six weeks between planning-team meetings, various members of the organization may be researching, compiling, and cataloging data that are necessary for the team to consider in the next stage of the process. If such data are readily available, the planning team may be able to meet sooner than scheduled. If, however, gathering and processing the required data severely burden the resources of the organization, the planning team may decide to postpone its next meeting for a week or two.

Strategic planning has direct impact on budgeting considerations in the organization. In fact, the strategic plan should be at the core of the organization's budget process for the following year, and it is essential that the plan be completed prior to the start of the new budgeting cycle.

As the strategic planning process is repeated on some regular basis, the gathering and processing of information will become easier, and the relationship between the planning process and budgeting considerations will become more obvious, more automatic, and more harmonious. Membership on the Applied Strategic Planning team is not permanent, and the planning team needs to be reconstituted each year. In particular, people who detract from the process should be replaced by people who have the potential to contribute to the process. Different participants may be required to reflect new directions that the organization is taking. Over time it is helpful to have differing points of view represented at the planning table. It is critical that the planning team not become a closed society. However, the CEO and key senior managers must be involved every year.

Location

Another significant issue is where the strategic planning sessions should be conducted. To be effective, the site used must be away from the interruptions of the daily work routine. We have successfully used hotel/motel meeting rooms, retreat-type conference facilities, condominium and private clubhouses, vacation homes, and personal residences. The key is to assist the planning-team members in isolating themselves from daily work routines that can inhibit the kind of envisioning and confrontation that is essential to the strategic planning process.

We have also been successful in using the regular conference room in the organization's own facility for weekend sessions. Depending on the organizational culture, some of the planning may be done on weekends. However, too much formal weekend work will detract from the day-to-day functioning of the operation. This also can build resentment among team members and send the incorrect message that strategic planning is not "real work."

Cost of Doing Formal Planning

The two major sunk costs associated with Applied Strategic Planning are (1) the time foregone to the organization in the meeting time of the planning team and (2) the additional time foregone for the planning team and others in out-of-meeting activities to generate the data for planning-meeting consumption. These costs should be estimated for the organization by the consultant after the planning team is selected.

If an organization makes extensive use of an outside consultant, which we recommend because it adds objectivity and enhances the productivity of the planning team, the consultant should set some realistic expectations with the client regarding the overall costs, including the costs for his or her services, the costs of meeting-room rental, and so on. A final estimate of both the out-of-pocket and sunk costs should be provided to the CEO prior to the initiation of the planning process in order to provide a clear basis for contracting.

An effort should be made to weigh this cost against the expense of not planning or against the potential payoffs that should be derived from the process. Adopting such an investment mind-set is far more beneficial than a mere examination of the costs. If the organization cannot perceive clear-cut benefits from planning, then the planning process should be abandoned.

Identification of Other Training and Data-Collection Needs

The Applied Strategic Planning process will identify needs for the type of activities used in organization development (e.g., climate survey/feedback, departmental team building, conflict resolution on an interpersonal and departmental level, customer-service programs, market research, sales training, and market studies). There is a potential for the planning consultants to do this work as they go along. We believe that it is a trap and should be avoided. Despite the apparent need for such additional work, it has a high potential to take both the consultant's and the CEO's eyes off the salient issues, that is, getting through the strategic planning cycle reasonably close to the target time and expense allocations.

Where possible, these emergent needs should be incorporated into the HRD plan and be dealt with as yet another competitor for the limited resources of money, time, and energy in the integrating action plans phase. If the need cannot be deferred until the end of the strategic planning cycle, then the Applied Strategic Planning consultant should assist the system in finding another consultant to do the OD work. This somewhat purist point of view will enable the strategic planning consultant to keep a focus on the macrotarget.

APPLICATION CONSIDERATIONS

Each phase of the Applied Strategic Planning process has some immediate application considerations; that is, some things need to be done to implement what has been accomplished during that aspect of planning. Marketing the strategic planning process internally is the most important implementation step of the planning to plan phase.

To maximize the likelihood of success for strategic planning, it is critical that the people who will be important to the implementation of the plan feel a sense of involvement in its creation. This sense of involvement results in an enhanced sense of ownership of the plan, which in turn results in much more spirited efforts to implement the plan successfully—a key ingredient for its overall success. People will work much harder to implement something that they see as "our" plan than they will for "management's" plan.

Opportunities to involve others in the organization exist throughout the process, but that involvement must start as soon as the process itself starts, with the planning to plan phase. Involvement alone, however, will not achieve the level of psychological ownership that is being sought. Special efforts at marketing the process and its benefits must be made.

When Applied Strategic Planning is initiated, it is helpful to make an effort to emphasize the payoffs of the process to those who are important to its implementation. This can be done through a combination of meetings, training sessions, and written information to employees, board members, and stakeholders important for the plan's success. It is important that the CEO be seen as clearly initiating and supporting this communication process.

At every step of the Applied Strategic Planning process, people need to be informed and involved. It is also important for them to understand that the communication—about completing a values instrument, responding to a mission statement, and so on—is part of the strategic planning process. It is unwise to assume that they ordinarily will make that connection. All too often, they do not.

Each time a product (e.g., a values or mission statement) is brought back to the organization, it must be identified as a product of the planning process and a result of the joint efforts of the planning team and others—each of whom should be specifically identified. A brief internal marketing plan should be created to identify the planning process, the involvement of various people and groups in the process, and the potential benefits of the process. As with any marketing plan, different groups (labor unions, board of directors, employees, etc.) would be approached according to their unique interests and needs.

During the planning to plan phase, planning-team members need to understand that the most important test of implementation is the degree to which organizational members, especially managers, use the strategic plan in their everyday management decisions. A strategic plan is being implemented if the initial response of a manager—when confronted by a problem—is to consider whether an answer is found in the organization's strategic plan. Although guidelines for every decision will not be provided in the planning process, consideration of the plan as a first step is the best evidence of the plan's implementation. This concept needs to be widely disseminated throughout the organization's management as part of marketing the strategic planning process.

In conclusion, it is crucially important in planning to plan to establish the proper climate for successful strategic planning by instituting appropriate norms and contracts and by avoiding an inappropriate rush for action that all too often typifies unsuccessful planning efforts. The time involved in planning to plan is time well spent and, if properly done, will go a long way to assuring the success of the planning process. Figure 5-4 provides a convenient checklist for the consultant and the planning team to use to make certain that the steps necessary for a successful planning to plan phase have been taken.

____ Identification of planning-team membvers and their roles.

____ Clearance of contract, individual commitment, planning schedule, locations.

____ Stakeholder's considerations clearly identified and involvement defined.

____ Awareness of competitive environment and preferred planning horizon.

____ Awareness of the Applied Strategic Planning model and process.

____ Consideration of factors that support successful strategic planning.

____ Determination of organizational interventions to enhance the planning effort.

Figure 5-4. Checklist of Necessary Outputs in Planning to Plan

SUMMARY

Planning to plan is the in-depth consideration of how the planning will be conducted. It includes determining readiness, developing commitment, identifying planning-team members, educating the organization, determining key stakeholders, and contracting for the strategic planning. Each phase of Applied Strategic Planning has application considerations, and planning to plan is no exception. Marketing the strategic planning process internally is the most important application consideration in this phase.

REFERENCES

Goodstein, L.D., Nolan, T.M., & Pfeiffer, J.W. (1992a). *A brief introduction to applied strategic planning* (rev. ed.). San Diego, CA: Pfeiffer & Company. (In press.)

Goodstein, L.D., Nolan, T.M., & Pfeiffer, J.W. (1992b). *Applied strategic planning: An abridged guide* (rev. ed.). San Diego, CA: Pfeiffer & Company. (In press.)

Lewin, K. (1975). *Field theory in social science.* Westport, CT: Greenwood.

Pfeiffer, J.W., & Jones, J.E. (1978). OD readiness. In J.W. Pfeiffer & J.E. Jones (Eds.) *The 1978 annual handbook for group facilitators.* San Diego, CA: University Associates.

Steiner, G.A. (1979). *Strategic planning: What every manager should know.* New York: Free Press.

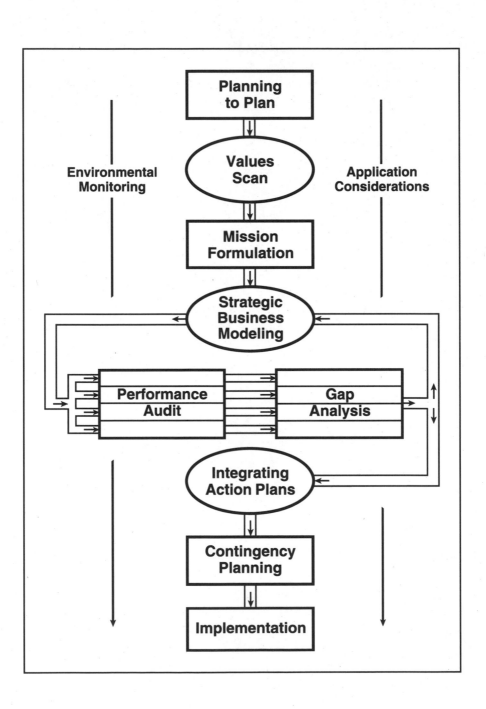

Chapter Six

Environmental Monitoring and Application Considerations

Info, info everywhere, but no one stops to think.

H. Krantzberg
1990
"Peer Review, Refereeing,
Fraud, and Other Essays."
American Scientist, 78, 265-266.

The Applied Strategic Planning model consists of nine sequential steps (or phases) plus two continuous steps—environmental monitoring and application considerations. These two continuous steps are necessary because each of the nine sequential steps involves both environmental monitoring and some immediate application or action steps.

Environmental monitoring is generally necessary to provide data to the organization in the daily work and is especially necessary for the planning team at every sequential step. There is a need to know what is occurring both within the organization and in the external environment. Each of the sequential phases requires the organization to take some action steps; the planning team must at least provide feedback to the organization about what decisions have been made. Although the implementation of the final plan requires a tidy conclusion to the planning process, there is much to be done in the interim. This chapter is concerned with these two continuous phases of strategic planning, with the bulk of attention directed toward environmental monitoring, as it is a relatively generic process. Application considerations, on the other hand, require specific processes, depending on the sequential phase of the overall planning.

ENVIRONMENTAL MONITORING

All organizations have a vital need to track what is occurring, or about to occur, in their environments. While change has been the only constant in our world, the rate of change is accelerating; and organizations that do not anticipate and attempt to manage these rapidly increasing changes face precarious futures. Only by monitoring an organization's environments can the organization track and understand these changes. As Murphy (1989) concluded from his review of the literature on such monitoring, it is poorly and inconsistently done in most organizations, and—even when it is done well—the information gleaned from this environmental monitoring is not used in developing alternative futures.

Strategic planning requires that an organization take time out to seriously examine how it monitors the environments that directly impact its future and how it processes the information obtained. Because the Applied Strategic Planning model assumes that environmental monitoring is an ongoing, continual process in organizations, there is no single point in the planning sequence at which environmental monitoring begins or ends. Thus, the model shows environmental monitoring as a continuous aspect of the planning process. The data produced in the organization's ongoing monitoring process should continually provide information to the planning team and to the entire organization about what is happening and what is likely to happen that might affect the organization's current operations, its planning process, and its future.

The Process and Scope of Environmental Monitoring

Two essential aspects of environmental monitoring need to be confronted in the planning process. The first concerns the types of information to be obtained and the ways this information—facts, hypotheses, intuitions, guesses, and the like—should be used. The second aspect concerns the effectiveness of the organization's system for gathering, storing, processing, integrating, and disseminating environmental intelligence. In most cases, an organization's data are fragmented and incomplete, and its monitoring system—especially its competitor analysis—is woefully inadequate. One of the side benefits of the Applied Strategic Planning model is that it helps the organization confront and evaluate its environmental monitoring system and, where necessary, develop a more effective system.

The particular kinds and forms of information that are needed by a given organization will, of course, depend on the organization and the nature of its environments. This information should identify emerging opportunities and threats in the organization's external environment. It should further identify the organization's strengths and weaknesses for meeting these opportunities and threats. Additionally, the environmental monitoring process should surface a variety of important factors, both internal and external to the organization, that have been overlooked to date but that need to be considered as part of the strategic planning process. Examples of these might include cyclical economic trends, the development of new but yet untested technologies, the emergence of new and untested competitors, and the gradual disappearance of a set of critical job skills in the labor force. The public sector is equally affected by such trends (e.g., total quality management, customer service, and cost-benefit analyses).

One of our clients provides a pointed example of the usefulness of this approach. As part of its environmental monitoring, a number of modest facts, rumors, and shrewd guesses were put together and allowed the planning team to conclude that a new Taiwanese group was buying and remodeling an outmoded factory and would be able to directly compete with our client in approximately eighteen months. Although all these data were available to the organization prior to strategic planning, they had not been collated, processed, and integrated into a meaningful conclusion. Once this was done, appropriate plans

The Environment Must Be Monitored

could be drawn up to combat the heretofore unseen competition in a timely and much more effective manner. Until these data and their implications were integrated into the consciousness of the planning team, no action plans could have been formulated or executed.

In general, the following four environments should be scanned on a regular basis (also see Figure 6-1):

1. The macro environment,
2. The industry environment,
3. The competitive environment, and
4. The internal organizational environment.

During the planning process information about each of these environments must be available to conduct the values scan, to draft the mission statement, to formulate the strategic business model, to identify the competition, and so on.

The Macro Environment

During the past decade few, if any, organizations have not been affected by the introduction of the microcomputer, the rising prices of petroleum, the changes in foreign-currency exchange and interest rates, the rise of consumerism, the changing attitudes of employees toward

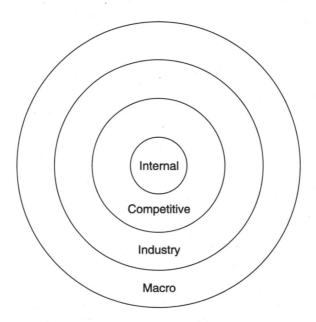

Figure 6-1. Environments to be Monitored

work, the taxpayer rebellion, and a host of other broad, societal-based trends. These changes in the macro environment—in the economy, in technological developments, in the body politic, and in the society—clearly affect most or all organizations, but in different ways and to differing degrees.

A number of social observers have spelled out some of these changes. One of these, Naisbitt (1982), identified the following emerging trends that will transform our lives—especially our organizational lives:

1. The change from an industrial society to an informational society;
2. The development of a high-tech/high-touch requirement;
3. A shift from a national to a world economy;
4. A movement from short-term to long-term thinking, managing, and planning;
5. A movement from centralization to decentralization;
6. The re-emergence of self-help to replace institutional help;
7. A change from representative democracy to participatory democracy;
8. A shift from hierarchical forms of management to networking;
9. In the United States the development of the South as a center of energy and organizational life; and
10. A shift to searching for multiple options rather than an either/or solution.

More recently, Naisbitt and Aburdene (1990) have identified ten overarching trends that build on and extend Naisbitt's original list. These trends, according to the authors, will provide important bridges from the present into the twenty-first century and include:

1. The booming global economy of the 1990s;
2. A renaissance of the arts;
3. The emergence of free-market socialism;
4. Global lifestyles and cultural nationalism;
5. The privatization of the welfare state;
6. The rise of the Pacific Rim;
7. The decade of women in leadership;
8. The age of biology;
9. The religious revival of the new millennium; and
10. The triumph of the individual.

In a similar vein, Cetron and Davies (1991) have identified fifty trends that are "shaping our world." While their list is too extensive to reproduce here, it is divided into twelve major categories: (1) population; (2) food; (3) energy; (4) environment; (5) science and technology; (6) communications; (7) labor; (8) industry; (9) education and training; (10) world economy; (11) welfare; and (12) international alignments.

While one may certainly argue about the accuracy of any of these sets of predictions, they help to focus our attention on these important areas and provide a frame of reference for considering how these trends and developments may affect the future of our organization. Such considerations could provide a worthwhile structure to the organization's strategic planning efforts to add definition to how the future might impact the organization.

Organizations that monitor such broad societal changes and integrate the potential impact of such changes into their planning process obviously have a competitive edge over other organizations. The economic, technological, political, and social aspects of the macro environment should be considered by the planning team as part of the process. Each of these is examined below.

Economic Aspects. Among the economic factors to be considered are the current phase of the business cycle, changes in interest rates, and the general business climate. The business cycle and the organization's response to that cycle are of special importance to the strategic planning process.

Figures 6-2 and 6-3 demonstrate the typical relationship between business cycles and an organization's expansion modes. When an organization is new, it will most probably be in a survival mode and be relatively unconcerned with such cycles. As the organization matures, however, such cycles should become an important aspect of its planning processes.

As the mature organization sees the business cycle rising, it will probably start thinking of expanding; but all too often organizations wait until the business cycle peaks before they start the expansion. While the cycle is still high, when buying is expensive, and when good labor is scarce, the typical organization goes into the expansion mode. As it sees the benefits of expansion, it can easily be trapped into thinking if a little expansion is good, then a lot of expansion is even better. So it continues to expand, even though the business cycle has started to decline.

In fact, an organization typically will not start contracting until the business cycle is at the very bottom or close to the bottom. Then it discovers that it has money tied up in machinery, equipment, or other property that is lying idle. Also, too many employees are on the payroll. Because the organization went into expansion at the wrong time and/or

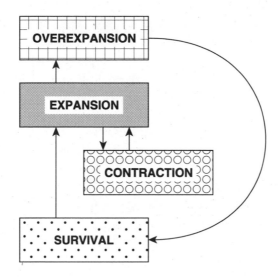

Figure 6-2. Expansion Modes

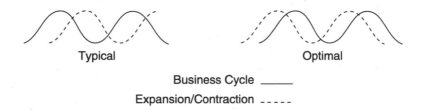

Typical   Optimal

Business Cycle _____
Expansion/Contraction - - - - -

Figure 6-3. Business Cycles

stayed in it too long, it reached overexpansion and soon finds itself back in the survival mode.

An important goal in strategic planning is to keep within the expansion/contraction mode and to avoid the overexpansion and survival modes. Let us consider how an organization can do this. If a company begins to expand just as the business cycle begins to rise, it can buy at lower prices than it can later in the cycle and will have a good selection of human resources. Then just as the cycle starts to fall, the company should simultaneously start the contraction process. It should stay in the contraction mode until the business cycle begins to increase again. Thus, it would continually be moving from expansion to contraction to expansion but avoiding the overexpansion and survival modes. Without understanding the impact of this proper timing in strategic planning, an organization might continue the expansion-contraction-expansion-contraction out of phase with the business cycle.

An example of how a company can be on top one day and down the next was seen in a *New York Times* article (Downtime, 1985). It told how a manufacturer of computer chips celebrated Christmas "with typical Silicon Valley flamboyance—a $700,000 employee Christmas party," which featured a rock group and a fifty-piece orchestra. Six months later the company was "making its employees work longer hours for no extra pay" and planned to close its factories for two weeks to cope with "plunging earnings and possible losses." It introduced an austerity program called STAUNCH: "Stress Those Actions Urgently Needed to Check Hemorrhaging."

Technological Aspects. The influence of changes in the technological aspects of the macro environment is equally pervasive and important. Among the clear technological trends that might be considered are the increasingly widespread use of the microcomputer, the development of robotics, the use of composites as substitutes for basic metals, and electronic information transmission (e.g., electronic banking). Although the degree to which any specific organization will be impacted by such technology will vary, rarely will any organization be unaffected.

An example of this impact was seen in a financial-service organization to which the authors were consultants. The entire secretarial force had been centralized in a secretarial pool, and each manager was given a computer terminal to replace the missing secretary. Those managers were required to draft their correspondence on their terminals and receive finished copies from the pool. Although the cost savings were substantial—because the number of secretaries was reduced—the loss of the personal relationship between the remaining secretaries and their former supervisors was disconcerting to both groups. Several years after this change, considerable residual bitterness remained on the part of both the secretaries and their former bosses about this matter, with the natural negative impact on morale and productivity.

Political Aspects. A number of political trends have also affected broad segments of our society. The most important of these in the United States are changes in governmental regulation, with a simultaneous increase in governmental concern about the physical environment; the ever-changing taxation policies as they affect organizational policies, such as investment or research and development; the expansion of equal-opportunity requirements to include more categories (e.g., the handicapped, the aged, and gays and lesbians); the development of special-interest-group politics; and the ever-changing role of government. In the United States, there is a decrease in Federal-government involvement and power in many policy areas, particularly in some areas of environmental protection, and an increase in state- and local-government involvement and power.

Issues of trade promotion on one hand and protectionism on the other, as evidenced by international product quotas and tariffs, have significant impact on the future of the globalization of markets. An interesting response to this problem has been the virtual globalization of some products that are designed in one country, have their parts manufactured in several countries, assembled in yet another country or group of countries, and marketed and sold world-wide. Still another critical development is the elimination of tariff barriers in Europe in 1992 with the full realization of the European Common Market. Although the impact of these political aspects has affected and will continue to affect organizations differentially, some of the impact has been widely experienced and, over time, these impacts will be more substantial. Such political changes need to be carefully monitored by organizations.

Environmental monitoring is especially important in globalization. Consumer preferences about product and service features vary from culture to culture, and carefully monitoring these differences is necessary as organizations begin to cross national boundaries. Although this function is often seen as belonging to a market-research group, it really needs to permeate the awareness of the entire organization. However, more than awareness is necessary; the organization needs to react promptly to the data gathered. Such prompt action can pay rich and unexpected dividends.

Stanley Works, the U.S.-based manufacturer of hand tools, sent a small group of key managers to tour the Far East to see competitors in their own environment, test the market, and generally acquaint themselves with this new and different environment. In this process, the group discovered a double-toothed handsaw that had been used widely in Asia for a generation—a saw that cut both on the upstroke and the downstroke—but one that was unknown in the West. Stanley successfully produced and marketed these saws in the United States and also exported them widely abroad. The point of this story is that environmental monitoring need not be a highly complex process, but what is seen needs to be acted on promptly if it is to have an impact on the organization's future.

Social Aspects. Social aspects are those broad changes in the society that occur over time and that directly affect the way organizations operate or should operate. These changes include changing demographics, especially the aging and the increasing diversity of the work force, consumerism, and the increasing concern with protecting the environment and with the quality and costs of health care and education.

An example of one such social trend was presented in a table in the *New York Times* (Greying, 1983). It gives an analysis based on U.S. Census Bureau projections of the "greying" of the U.S. population over the next hundred years and predicts that by the year 2080, 23.5 percent of the U.S. population will be 65 or older. The impact of these changes on health care, retirement, housing, and so on are already widespread. This phenomenon of an aging population, of course, is but one of many such social trends.

Another example is the increasing diversity of the U.S. work force. In many areas and in some industries the majority of the work force is Hispanic. As a result, the Marriott Corporation, a hotel chain, has decided that all first-level supervisors must be bilingual in both English and Spanish within a fixed period of time. Language classes are made available, at company expense and at the work site, to help achieve this goal. However, this organization is an exception in its clear-cut response to this social challenge. These social changes can strongly impact all organizations and need to be included in their environmental monitoring processes.

The Need for Current Data. To be helpful, information on these trends in the macro environment must be current. There are numerous

Current Data Are Needed

sources of up-to-date information on these changes. For example, the Naisbitt Group publishes a yearly forecast (*The Year Ahead: 10 New Trends that Will Shape the Way You Live, Work, and Make Money*) and a monthly newsletter; the World Futures Society holds an annual conference and provides a variety of publications on future trends; the Club of 1000 publishes forecasts on a variety of trends of concern to business organizations; many banks publish monthly or quarterly newsletters that focus on local or regional financial trends; business schools of many universities provide published summaries of their research findings on local business trends; and, of course, the national business magazines, such as *Fortune, Forbes,* and *Business Week,* provide information on the macro environment, especially on how it may impact businesses generally.

Another important source of current data are the several on-line computer data bases. For example, ABI/Inform—a service of UMI/Data Courier, headquartered in Louisville, KY (800-626-2823)—provides over 500,000 abstracts and full texts from over 1,200 business and management journals from around the world, classified in a variety of ways to facilitate searching specific topics of interest. Over 1,200 new articles are added weekly, making the available information highly current. One way in which such data can be tracked is to develop a list of topics of importance to the organization's future and then assign one key manager the responsibility of tracking such a data base.

Several commercial organizations specialize in tracking social trends. For example, for over twenty years Yankelovich Clancy Shulman of Westport, Connecticut, has tracked a number of specific social issues for its clients, including environmentalism, children and youth, minorities, especially Hispanics, and demographics in general. While such research services tend to be rather expensive, they are quite comprehensive in their coverage and are less costly than developing such information on one's own.

A careful analysis of all these macro environmental trends needs to be included in the strategic planning process. Despite the inherent difficulty in quantifying the latter two factors—political and social—their importance to organizational success makes it mandatory to include them in any comprehensive environmental scan.

The Industry Environment

Among the factors to be considered as part of the industry environment are changes in the structure of the industry; in how the industry is financed; in the degree of governmental presence in the industry; in the engineering, processes, and typical products used in the industry; and in the typical marketing strategies of the industry.

The adoption of faster cycle time (FCT) (Blackburn, 1990) by an industry is an example of such a trend. This ongoing ability to identify, satisfy, and be paid for meeting customer requirements *faster* than anyone else changes the parameters of competition in that industry. Faster cycle time, in turn, requires total quality management, as FCT involves the assumption that all products are produced to meet customer requirements. As trends like this begin to impact an industry, the way business is done changes. The organization that detects and positively responds to these changes has a competitive edge.

The industry environment is best monitored through reading the various technical and trade journals in that industry. One of our regular surprises as we begin to work in an industry unfamiliar to us is the plethora of journals, magazines, and newsletters that are part of that industry's information-disseminating network, all new to us. One aspect of developing a comprehensive monitoring process involves reviewing the available industry literature and making certain that it all is being covered and that the information gleaned from this coverage is being systematically fed into the organization for review and analysis.

The Competitive Environment

Monitoring the competitive environment includes consideration of changes in competitor profiles, in market-segmentation patterns, in commitment to research and development, and so on. The initial questions are concerned with who the competition is and how it competes. The traditional way to answer to these questions is by looking at other organizations that provide the same products or services, but this approach is incomplete. Another way is to consider those products that customers might perceive as reasonable alternatives for meeting their needs or wants. For example, a manufacturer of potato chips has not only other manufacturers of potato chips as competition (the initial answer to our hypothetical question), but also the manufacturers of all other snack foods—pretzels, pizzas, nuts—that a potential customer might consider in making a choice. This second approach requires the organization to cast a net in answering the critically important question of who the competition is. Competitor analysis is so important that Chapter 10 deals with it again, in conjunction with the performance audit.

The Internal Environment

Among the factors to be considered as part of the internal organizational environment are changes in the structure of the company, in its culture, in its climate, in its productivity, and in its distinctive strengths and weaknesses. In addition, the internal environment includes the many structures and systems that typically are used for day-to-day planning and control within the organization, such as inventory control, distribution, and quality control.

The areas of concern are how well these systems are functioning and whether they are improving or deteriorating. Since the members of the strategic planning team are part of this internal environment, they may be nearsighted in observing it. Therefore, an external consultant can be especially helpful at this point in the strategic planning process. An external consultant has the obligation to make certain that the evaluation of the internal environment that is developed in the planning process is fair and that it pays equal attention to the strengths and the weaknesses of the internal environment.

Although it is crucial to monitor employee satisfaction regularly as one measure of the internal environment, it is equally important to develop clear means of tracking how customers—the life blood of any organization, including those in the public sector—perceive that internal environment. How well the internal environment operates directly impacts customer satisfaction, and it is imperative that this data be regularly tracked. For example, poor internal communications between organizational segments—such as shipping and billing or marketing and quality control—will cause customers problems that can adversely affect the future of the organization. These can be tracked by simple methods, such as including a customer-satisfaction form with every order and systematically tracking responses that are received, appointing a customer-satisfaction representative to deal with complaints and then tracking exactly what problems are surfaced, or regularly calling customers and asking what went well or poorly in their last dealings with the organization.

An Approach to Monitoring

Since there is no end to the changes regularly occurring in these four environmental arenas, there is always a question of how this monitoring process should be conducted. Effective environmental monitoring requires that careful attention be paid to those issues that have high potential impact on the future success of the organization. A simple way to approach the task of establishing a useful environmental monitoring process is for the planning team to review each of the four areas systematically and to develop comprehensive lists of possible changes that might impact the organization. Each of these potentials should be rated for importance and then for probability. Changes that would have high impact and that are reasonably probable need careful monitoring. While the other areas should not be neglected, they can receive less focused attention.

In summary, each of these four aspects of the environment needs thoughtful attention during the strategic planning process. Although the degree to which an organization needs to consider each factor will vary, every organization should identify how each of these four aspects might impact its future plans and to what degree the plans could be impacted. Sorting out how changes in any one of these environments may impact the organization over time and carefully tracking the most important of these constitute the essence of sound environmental monitoring. Although environmental monitoring will identify a variety of internal and external factors, these four broad areas make a useful starting point for understanding and managing the process of environmental surveillance. However, the other areas identified should be programed into the environmental monitoring process and considered during strategic planning.

The most important single decision related to environmental monitoring is *which* of the important aspects of the environment should be regularly monitored. One of the positive consequences of strategic planning is the determination of how well the organization is monitoring its environments and how that process can and should be improved.

Environmental Monitoring and Driving Forces

Although Chapter 8 discusses driving forces in conjunction with mission formulation, they have an impact on environmental monitoring. Organizations vary enormously in how they concentrate their monitoring, apparently as a function of the dominant driving forces that differentiate the various organizations. For example, Procter & Gamble—with marketing as its primary driving force—devotes most of its monitoring energy to the competitive arena, while Walmart—with distribution as its primary driving force—devotes most of its monitoring energy to its internal environment (inventories, transportation, and the like). The control-room panel of Walmart's headquarters in Bensonville, Arkansas, probably resembles NASA's launch control center more than it does a typical retailing-chain network; it is devoted to tracking the status of Walmart's distribution system.

Two lessons can be learned from this observation of driving forces. The first is that this single-mindedness may prevent an organization from adequately monitoring those areas that are outside its usual focus of attention. To the degree that this is true, some redirection of energy may be required to complete the strategic planning process successfully. The second lesson—a mirror image of the first—is that the organization's environmental monitoring reveals its dominant driving force, which is also useful information for the planning process.

Organizing Environmental Data

Most organizations are exposed to tremendous amounts of environmental information. They have multiple subscriptions to trade journals, association newsletters, and business and financial publications and frequently send representatives to trade shows and conventions. Despite all this information, the data are often incompletely surveyed, organized, analyzed, and stored and, as a result, are unavailable for either management decisions or strategic planning. In other words, the surveillance of the environment is, in most cases, undirected, haphazard, and nonfunctional.

To create some order in this typically chaotic state, Aaker (1983) recommended that organizations utilize a strategic information scanning system (SISS). The SISS is a simple, formal, five-step system for identifying organizational information needs, assigning members of the organization to specific monitoring tasks to obtain that information, and feeding the information into the strategic planning and management processes. The five steps are as follows:

1. Identify the organization's information needs, especially for the next round of strategic planning;
2. Generate a list of information sources that provide core inputs (e.g., trade shows, publications, technical meetings, and customers);
3. Identify those who will participate in the environmental monitoring process (they do not have to be members of the planning team);
4. Assign monitoring tasks to several members of the organization; and
5. Store and disseminate the information.

The SISS should be as simple and as manageable as possible. All the important areas (such as identifying actual or potential changes in strategy by competitors) should be covered, but the surveillance tasks should be kept simple and direct. Information needs can be rated on

Data Must Be Organized

their importance to and impact on the organization. For example, if a serious threat is likely to occur immediately, then information in this area is much more important than data about unlikely threats in the distant future. An extensive list of information sources should be developed (e.g., through brainstorming), and then the sources that are routinely and regularly accessible should be determined. Those that have been ignored or overlooked should also be identified. This procedure will help an organization to rationally develop a core set of information sources. People from various parts of the organization should be tapped as a source of information from vendors, customers, advertisers, etc. Many people outside the planning team have easy access to valuable information and will be happy to report their findings.

Figure 6-4 illustrates how the SISS could be conducted and monitored. Various information sources are shown along the horizontal axis, and several information needs are displayed along the vertical axis. The names represent specific people who are assigned to monitor each of the sources in order to meet the information needs. When several people are assigned to the same source, each person monitors that source for a particular information need based on his or her background and interest. For example, a prime technical journal might be monitored by one person for marketing information, by another for new applications, and by still another for competitor information.

The information can be stored in any convenient form, from a simple set of manila folders to a complex computer-data-based system. However, the storage method should be congruent with the work styles

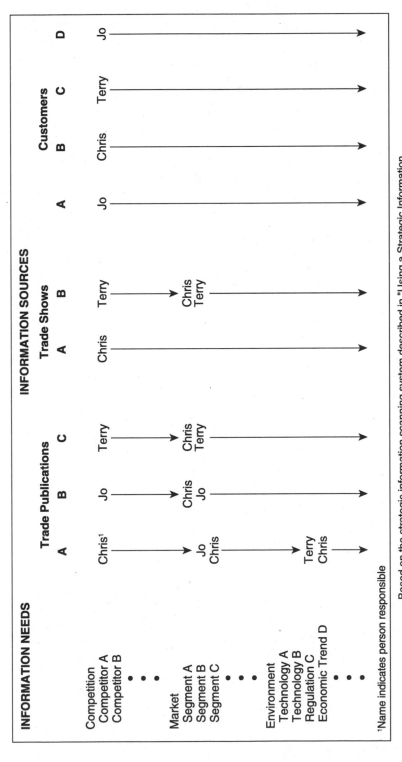

Based on the strategic information scanning system described in "Using a Strategic Information Scanning System" by D.A. Aaker, 1983. In *California Management Review, 25*, pp. 80-81.

Figure 6-4. Information Needs and Sources

and traditional means of information storage and retrieval in the organization. Larger, more complex organizations may wish to develop strategic-information systems, rather than mere environmental monitoring processes. Finkelstein (1989) provides a highly sophisticated, computer-based approach to developing these systems and argues that a new professional subspeciality, information engineering, be used to manage such systems.

Nevertheless, regardless of who manages the data produced by environmental monitoring, time and care must be devoted to the development of the storage system so that it can adequately serve the needs of the planning process. One of the clear responsibilities of the strategic planning team is to make certain that both a comprehensive environmental monitoring process and an easily accessible storage system be operational early in the planning process.

Effective Environmental Surveillance

Organizations that carefully and continually monitor their critical environments obtain a competitive advantage from that process. Pitney Bowes, the ubiquitous manufacturer of postage meters, offers an outstanding example of how this happens. Over the years, that company has developed and maintained a symbiotic relationship with the U.S. Postal Service. Pitney, on one hand, needs to know how mail service is going to be changing; the Postal Service, on the other, needs to protect its revenues, and postal meters are seen by the Service as providing opportunities for fraud by unscrupulous users of the meters. Thus the Service must be constantly working on developing systems to prevent that fraud, while Pitney must be constantly working to upgrade the equipment to meet the needs of the market.

To maintain the lines of communication, Pitney maintains a full-time director of postal relations in Washington, D.C., and his office is across the street from U.S. Postal Service headquarters. The director's role is to obtain all the information possible about the future plans of the Service; Pitney wants no surprises from the makers of the rules and regulations that control its business. This communication system works so well that senior postal officials have been known to call Pitney's Washington office for information about what is happening in their own organization.

These close relationships regularly pay off for Pitney. The Postal Service had been developing a system for "manifesting" the postage on bulk mail, a system that prepares, tracks, and documents the volume of bulk mail sent out by mass mailers. What is surprising about this is that

Pitney Bowes had a pilot model of that system available *before* the Postal Service released its official specifications. The competitive edge that such close monitoring provides is clearly apparent. What are necessary are both excellent intelligence about potential changes *and* the ability and willingness to act on the information. Without both of these, the data are essentially useless, except as an academic exercise.

Highly focused newsletters to help track potentially important developments in specific organizations are commercially available. Offered at significant annual subscription fees, such newsletters are devoted to a single organization, such as IBM or General Electric, and provide one way of monitoring that organization to potential vendors, competitors, and others whose futures can be impacted by such Goliaths.

Continual Process

Various aspects of environmental monitoring are discussed as appropriate in other chapters. However, during the planning to plan phase, the planning team should gain a thorough understanding of what the process entails and how it should operate in the organization. The environmental monitoring process should be continual, so that the appropriate information about what is happening or about to happen in the various environments is always available. Applied Strategic Planning provides an opportune time for a major use of these data. Learning not only to collect relevant information, but to organize, interpret, and use this information is critical to strategic success. For this reason, each key manager—and perhaps even groups of employees—should be given permanent assignments of vital areas to be monitored. They also must be given a clear and simple way in which to channel useful information back to the organization's leadership. It is important that this monitoring, interpreting, and application of data become a constant way of life in an organization. We cannot overemphasize the importance of developing with the organization the willingness and ability to act on environmental intelligence promptly and with enthusiasm.

APPLICATION CONSIDERATIONS

One of the most important ways in which the Applied Strategic Planning model differs from other models is in its preoccupation with broad-scale involvement in the process. The following three rules should be followed in designing such involvement:

1. Broad-scale involvement should begin as soon as possible;

There Should Be Involvement to the Greatest Extent

2. There should be involvement to the greatest extent possible and practical; and

3. There should be as much participation as feasible in decision making about the plan.

Obviously, not every member of the organization can or should sit at the planning table, but every member of the organization needs to be involved in one way or another as soon as possible. Also, the way in which the accomplishments of the planning team will be applied or implemented must be considered as soon as possible.

Even though the *implementation* phase is the final step of the Applied Strategic Planning model, application or implementation must continually take place throughout the strategic planning process. As Chapter 5 ("Planning to Plan") noted, every stage of Applied Strategic Planning contains application aspects. For example, if the values scan identifies incongruous values in segments of the organization, these need to be addressed as soon as they are identified, not held until the final implementation phase. As new clarity is achieved regarding organizational values, this should be shared broadly in the organization. This clarity will help current efforts of the organization and will keep the organization's members informed and excited about the planning process.

The mission statement needs to be distributed to all the relevant stakeholders for comments and suggestions before it is accepted, and no further planning should be done until there is consensus on the mission statement. Each step of the Applied Strategic Planning process

Strategic Planning Must Be Implemented

has its own application considerations, and each of these considerations should be addressed during that phase, not postponed until final implementation of the plan. This book devotes one chapter to each phase of Applied Strategic Planning, and each of these chapters addresses application considerations for the corresponding phase. Overall, we are seeking to build involvement in the process. The outputs from each step help establish and sustain this involvement. These outputs are tangible demonstrations of the accomplishments of that phase of the planning process and allow for input to the next phase.

The final implementation phase involves the initiation of the various action plans designed at the unit and functional levels and their integration at the top of the organization. This may, for example, involve new construction, initiation of management development or technical training, increased research and development, or marketing of new products or services. All parts of the organization need to have a clear feeling that there is activity at all levels of the organization that will bring about the successful completion of the organization's mission.

As the strategic plan is "rolled out," the ways in which people have been involved in the planning process should be reviewed. Given the duration of the planning cycle and the press of current operations, it would be easy for people to forget their involvement and their commitment. This should not be allowed to happen.

In addition to the nine sequential steps of the Applied Strategic Planning process, the two continual steps—environmental monitoring and application considerations—have been identified and described.

These are important processes and need to be considered as integral parts of strategic planning. The integrity of Applied Strategic Planning rests on their effectiveness; without them, strategic planning becomes a closed event that is disconnected from organizational and environmental realities. The planning process must receive the visibility it deserves within the organization. If this does not occur, the psychological ownership of both the process and its resultant plan is reduced for organizational members who are not members of the planning team and the likelihood of quality plan implementation is dramatically reduced.

SUMMARY

In addition to the sequential phases of Applied Strategic Planning, there are two continuous steps: environmental monitoring and application considerations. Information gathered while monitoring the environment should help the organization to identify strengths and weaknesses within its internal environment and also the emerging opportunities and threats from the external environment. Four environments should be monitored on a regular basis: the macro environment, the industry environment, the competitive environment, and the internal environment. However, data gathering is a mere exercise unless action follows data analysis. An organization's environmental monitoring is a function of driving forces and may reveal the organization's foremost driving force. Each phase of the Applied Strategic Planning process has its own application considerations, and these should be addressed during that phase, not postponed until the final implementation phase.

REFERENCES

Aaker, D.A. (1983). Using a strategic information scanning system. *California Management Review, 25,* 80-81.

Blackburn, J.D. (1990). *Time-based competition: The next battle ground in American manufacturing.* Homewood, IL: Dow Jones-Irwin.

Cetron, M.J., & Davies, O. (1991, September-October). 50 trends shaping the world. *The Futurist,* pp. 10-21.

Downtime in technological industries. (1985, March 24). *New York Times,* Sec. 12, p. 10.

Finkelstein, C. (1989). *An introduction to information engineering: From strategic planning to information systems.* Sydney; Addison-Wesley.

The greying of the U.S. population. (1983, August 12). *New York Times.*

Murphy, J.J. (1989). *Identifying strategic issues. Long-Range Planning, 22*(2), 101-105. Reprinted in J.W. Pfeiffer (Ed.). (1991). *Strategic planning: Selected readings.* San Diego, CA: Pfeiffer & Company.

Naisbitt, J. (1982). *Megatrends: Ten new directions transforming our lives.* New York: Warner Books.

Naisbitt, J., & Aburdene, P. (1990). *Megatrends 2000: Ten new directions for the 1990's.* New York: William Morrow.

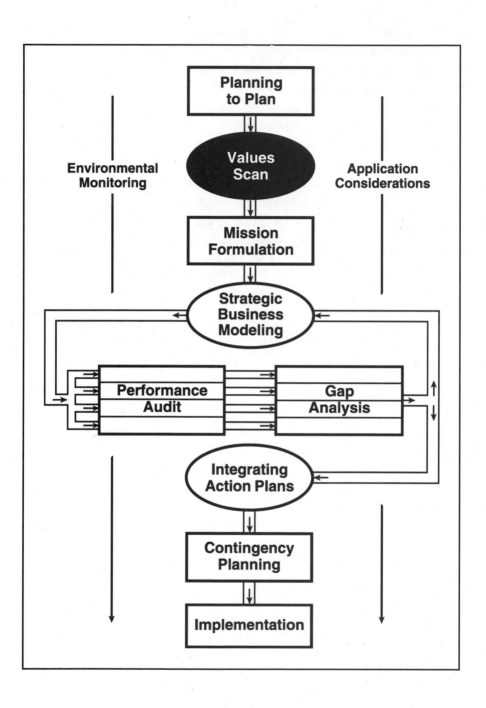

Chapter Seven

Values Scan

Life has a value only when it has something valuable as its object.

Georg Wilhelm Friedrich Hegel
Philosophy of History, 1832

All business decisions are based on values. Indeed, all organizational decisions are value-based. Schwartz and Davis (1984) put it a slightly different way. They argue that the choices senior managers make reflect their view of reality—the values, beliefs, and norms that served them well during their own rise to power.

These strong statements are frequently contested by managers, especially those from traditional business organizations. They argue that business decisions are typically based on "bottom-line" considerations, that is, on how profitability will be affected by the decision. While we might point out that the choice of the bottom line as the criterion for making a business decision is itself a value, we usually choose another line of argument. We ask how the decision is made to choose between the taking of profit out of the company—for dividends to shareholders or bonuses to managers—and investment in growth, or at least how these two alternatives are weighted in the decision-making process. Another alternative is to ask how the trade-off between short-term and long-term profits are made. Since these are such typical issues that top management must resolve on a fairly regular basis, we soon see the light of understanding in the manager's eye.

One of our clients faces such a decision on a regular basis. Part of a large corporation, it is a manufacturing plant that produces computer peripherals, and it is expected to meet its quarterly production goals—which are measured by units shipped out the door. At the same time, the organization expects very high quality standards to be met. For these particular peripherals, quality can best be ascertained by a hundred-hour *burn-in* period, in which the units are continuously run for one hundred hours to check for defects; over 90 percent of all defects emerge during that period. For a variety of reasons, the plant invariably is unable to meet its shipping quota—unless it cheats on the burn-in time. The choice that the plant management regularly must make is between meeting its shipping quota or its quality standards, yet another example of the role of values in organizational life. Most organizations are not clear about their values, and this lack of clarity causes problems to emerge regularly—problems that could best be resolved by surfacing and resolving the underlying values dilemmas. Without such values clarification early in the planning process, it is difficult or impossible to develop a usable strategic plan.

One unique aspect of the Applied Strategic Planning model is its emphasis on the values scan. Many others who write about and practice strategic planning suggest that the underlying values of the organization need to be considered in the planning process and that understanding the organizational culture is essential to a successful planning activity. Nevertheless, they provide little advice and few suggestions about how to tackle this critically important aspect of the work. This chapter is intended to remedy this problem.

VALUES CONGRUENCE

Before we begin our discussion of the values scanning process, let us re-emphasize the necessity for congruence between the organization's values and its strategic plan. Strategic plans that do not take values into account will be in trouble and may even fail. For example, consider the acquisition of the Fireman's Fund Insurance Company by American Express. Although a variety of financial and marketplace considerations were important, we wish to focus on the differences in the values of these two organizations and how these unexamined differences led to problems in implementing the acquisition. At the time of the acquisition, the Fireman's Fund was an old-line, San Francisco based company that prided itself on its long tradition of service, its commitment to policy holders, and its record of paying off all claims from the turn-of-the-century San Francisco earthquake and fire. American Express, on the other hand, was a comprehensive financial-service organization with a hard-nosed profit orientation. Fireman's Fund was committed to strong humanistic values in dealing with its employees and had one of the most comprehensive HRD programs available, whereas American Express was much more traditional in employee relations and had little in the way of HRD programs.

The clash of these two cultures was inevitable, and the CEO of American Express found it necessary to devote much time to a hands-on management of the Fireman's Fund, a move that required him to spend the bulk of his time in the Fireman's Fund headquarters. It is clear from the array of newspaper and magazine reports, as well as reports from personal informants, that—although the acquisition of the Fireman's Fund made sense in terms of marketing strategy—the failure to check out the differences in values between the two organizations and to make appropriate plans to manage them is an important reason for the difficulties that were encountered.

After several years of such effort, it was announced in the summer of 1985 that American Express was divesting itself of the Fireman's Fund because it was "incompatible with its investment strategy." The incumbent president of American Express announced his resignation "to seek career opportunities elsewhere." The moral of this tale is self-evident

ASSUMPTIONS

The basic assumptions organizations use in their decision-making processes must also be considered prior to the formal initiation of the values scan. In the discussion of organization culture, Chapter 3 pointed out that organizational values rest on the assumptions that the organization makes about the world and how it operates. Every organization has tacit assumptions about the way the world works that have profound consequences on how members of that organization perceive and interact with suppliers, customers, competitors, employees, labor unions, governments, and others. Without exposing these tacit assumptions, or what Ulrich and Wiersma (1989) term *mind-sets*, an organization is unlikely to understand fully the behavior of its members, much less to be able to modify that behavior.

One of the elements of the strategic planning process is to help managers understand the role of these mind-sets, to raise their awareness of those that operate in their organizations, and to question their utility. One task that precedes the actual values scan is helping the organization recognize some of its assumptions about how things work and test how true they are in fact and how much consensus there is about these assumptions. Such a discussion provides a solid starting point for the values scan and considerably enriches that process.

The following are some common, but *false,* assumptions (Zimmerman, 1985, pp. 13-14)[1] found in organizations. They are offered as a starting point for a discussion of assumptions and their role in the life of the organization.

1. The top managers share a common understanding of the organization's strategy.
2. If something is longer range, it is strategic; and if it is shorter range, it is operational. *(Strategy is, in fact, measured in terms of impact on direction.)*
3. If business units' strategies are clear, the organization's strategy is clear.
4. We have a long-range plan, so we know where we are going. *(This is an operational trap.)*
5. Our top team has the experience and ability to think strategically.

One function of the strategic planning consultant is to make certain that these assumptions and others of importance are surfaced and tested by the management team. It ordinarily requires some courage on the part of the consultant to confront these somewhat touchy issues and on the part of the planning team as it moves through uncharted waters, questioning basic assumptions and beliefs. This often turns out to be good training for the planning team for the systematized aspects of the values scan.

ELEMENTS OF VALUES SCAN

The values scan in Applied Strategic Planning involves an in-depth examination of following five elements:

1. The personal values of the planning team;
2. The values of the organization as a whole;
3. The organization's operating philosophy;
4. The organization's culture; and
5. The organization's stakeholders.

---

[1] Adapted from "The Frontiers of Strategic Thinking: An Interview with John W. Zimmerman." *Kepner-Tregoe Journal 14*(4), 13-16. Used with permission. Kepner-Tregoe is an international organization development firm specializing in strategic and operational decision making. World headquarters are located in Princeton, New Jersey.

Basic Assumptions Should Be Challenged

The examination of each of these elements is built on examination of the prior element; and each examination can be both threatening to members of the planning team and, as a consequence, time consuming. These elements are often the ones that require the highest degree of facilitator competence.

In this context, we are using Rokeach's (1973) definition that "a *value* is an enduring belief that a specific mode of conduct or end-state of existence is personally or socially preferable to an opposite or converse mode of conduct or end-state of existence. A *value system* is an enduring organization of beliefs concerning preferable modes of conduct or end-states of existence along a continuum of relative importance." That is, our values lead us to regard some goals or ends as more legitimate or correct and other goals as illegitimate or wrong. Our values also lead us to regard certain ways of reaching those goals or means as proper and appropriate and others ways as improper or inappropriate. Since these values are deeply ingrained in our belief system, they are relatively unchangeable.

This "enduring organization of beliefs" determines what both individuals and organizations consider to be appropriate and inappropriate behavior. Such belief systems or values determine norms (i.e., the standards for action) in organizations. For example, the norm of following the chain of command in an organization is based on the value system that the older and more senior members of the organization have both the experience and expertise to make appropriate decisions and, even more importantly, that experience and expertise are the most important factors to consider in making decisions. It is based further on the belief that a formal organization of decision making is critically important. Thus, organizations with such an underlying value system are unlikely to hold innovation and change as important values unless they come from age and experience. It is often much easier for an organization to identify its norms than the underlying values that led to and support the norms. In working with a group, the consultant must examine both the norms and the underlying values.

Personal Values

The first step of the values scan is an examination of the personal values of the members of the planning team. Since values exist on both the individual and organizational levels, as well as within various segments of the organization, there needs to be clarity regarding the level at which the assessment is occurring. The first cut of the values scan should take place on the individual level. It is particularly important for the key decision makers in an organization to be clear about their personal values and to recognize those differences in values that exist among them. If any of these key organizational decision makers are not members of the planning team, then an assessment of their values needs to be part of the values scan.

Consider, for example, an individual for whom risk taking is an important personal value. This person will envision an organizational future that is quite different from the one envisioned by a person who

Include *All* Members of the Team

holds security as a high personal value. Likewise, the goals and dreams of an individual who holds professional reputation as a value and is less interested in power will be different from those of a person whose priorities are the reverse.

These differences have clear implications for the organization's future direction, its structure, decision-making processes, and all other work of the management team. If the differences in values are not identified, clarified, and understood, there can be little agreement about how the organization's desired future would meet the personal expectations of the individual members of the management group.

There are several important reasons for starting the values scan on the personal level. One is that differences in personal values among the members of the planning team will impact the course of strategic planning. As noted earlier, values about critical issues such as risk taking, profitability, and growth are at the heart of the strategic planning process. Unless these differences are surfaced and fully explored with some degree of resolution, they will continually crop up and interfere with the process of planning. While we are not suggesting that deep divisions among the people holding strongly different values are readily resolved, we insist that the surfacing and testing of these differences provide a much more solid basis for planning than would otherwise be the case.

A second reason is that these personal values provide the basis for the values of the organization. The founders of organizations are typically people who have strong values in common. They, in turn, recruit like-minded people to work in that organization—the process of selection—and then the new members are further shaped by those existing organizational values in order to strengthen those values—the process of socialization. Over time, these shared personal values serve to make the organizational values potent in the life of the organization. Thus understanding personal values provides a basis for understanding how certain organizational values evolved.

The most direct and effective technique for surfacing personal values is to ask each member of the planning team to complete a simple values questionnaire. The consultant can then calculate the range and averages of these scores and post them. The group should then be asked to attempt to characterize itself along these dimensions. Ordinarily members will then begin to share their individual scores and discuss the meaning of their scores and the implication of these for their own individual behavior and its impact on the group. Differences among group members quickly surface and become the focus of the conversation.

In conducting the values scan, one of our clients, a large public service agency, identified quality of life as a shared, important personal value. This quickly led to a discussion of work loads, norms about time spent at work, taking work home in the evening, and so on. This discussion led the planning team to examine seriously the assumptions that the organization made about the role of the manager, how work should be accomplished, what a "timely" response was, and so on. The strong agreement of the planning team allowed it to reach a decision about changing some of those norms and the assumptions that they rested on. By the end of the strategic planning cycle, there were notable differences in managerial behavior about the length of the typical work day.

Managing Differences in Personal Values

All too often there are clear differences among members of the strategic planning team that have the potential to interfere with the planning process. Scherer's (1983) model for managing such differences (those that can cause "pinches") suggests a process for people to use in dealing with differences in values. This process involves the following steps:

1. Do not ignore a "pinch." Work on the difference before it becomes a "crunch." A cooling-off period may be necessary, with an agreed-on time to deal with the issue later.
2. The two people with the differences should talk to each other and attempt to resolve the differences themselves.
3. It is O.K. to ask a consultant for suggestions on how to approach the other person or how to define the issue better.
4. If someone approaches you with a values difference, be willing to work on it with that person. You also may wish to seek a consultant's help in clarifying your own point of view.
5. If, after you have tried to work on the issue on your own, there has been no change and the differences in values still exist, seek help from a consultant on next steps.
6. If someone complains to you about the values of another person who is not present, encourage the person who has approached you to discuss the matter directly with that other person. Do not become entangled in such triangular relationships.

Surfacing such values issues in an organization, especially for the first time, often reveals differences between espoused values and actual values, as well as differences in the values of the several segments of the organization and in the values held by members of the planning team. Without some resolution of these differences—at least at the level of agreeing to disagree, developing mutual respect for these differences, and considering how these disagreements can be used to improve the quality of organizational decisions—little effective planning can occur.

One way of working through such differences in values involves the use of an analytic tool, a two-by-two matrix with differences in values along the horizontal axis and the nature of the consequences along the vertical axis (see Figure 7-1).

		VALUES	
		Similar	Different
ORGANIZATIONAL CONSEQUENCES	Productive	1	2
	Nonproductive	3	4

Figure 7-1. One Tool for Working Through Differences in Values

When individuals share similar values and this congruence has productive consequences (Quadrant 1 of Figure 7-1), there is nothing to work through. When there are differences in values and these differences have productive consequences (Quadrant 2), then working through should focus on these positive consequences rather than on these differences. Consider, for example, the positive consequences in a manufacturing facility of having the production manager pushing for output while the quality manager insists on quality. The creative tension of that dialogue should enhance both productivity and quality, providing that these differences are not taken personally and the conflict is effectively managed.

However, similar values can have nonproductive consequences (Quadrant 3). Strong agreement about such basic values as avoiding risk or smothering conflict can have clear-cut negative consequences for organizational vitality. One of our client organization insists that it makes all of its policy decisions on the basis of consensus. Nevertheless, managers in that system never really feel empowered to speak their mind; they know that the CEO abhors conflict. Discussion about policy matters are stilted and the options are never really explored. Under these circumstances it is easy to reach "consensus," but to an outsider it appears much more like collusion, especially around issues that involve some degree of risk. It would be far more productive for an organization to have some managers pushing to take certain risks while others argue for caution. Such differences in risk management should lead to better risk assessment and improved decision making.

When there are sharp differences in values that have nonproductive organizational consequences (Quadrant 4) and those differences cannot be resolved in any other fashion, changing the players involved may be the only solution for the organization. Continual conflict over values, especially when it is covert and destructive, saps organizational vitality and must be stopped. It is the organizational consequences of values differences that need to be understood, because such differences can be productive, provided the conflict is managed.

Because very few groups have the skills to continue to confront such emotionally loaded and difficult-to-resolve issues as values differences and values clarification, attempts by the planning group to resolve these matters frequently deteriorate into personal arguments and power struggles; or the group may retreat into unrelated and more readily resolved areas. The frequency and severity of such problems prompt us to insist on an external facilitator for most groups. The facilitator must be able to recognize and surface legitimate differences among group members, provide a safe environment to test these differences, ensure that all points of view are expressed, and promote enough resolution of the differences to allow the group to move on.

The Abilene Paradox. One consequence of the failure to allow differences to surface is a situation that has been termed the "Abilene paradox" (Harvey, 1988). The term comes from a story of a family who drove a nonair-conditioned car to Abilene for dinner on a hot summer night. Although nobody wanted to go, each person—thinking all the others wanted to make the trip—was unwilling to express disagreement. Organizations that put a high value on managing agreement, rather than surfacing and legitimizing disagreement, may often find themselves on a trip to Abilene. One of the important purposes of Applied Strategic Planning is to make certain that organizations do not dine in Abilene, except by clear-cut choice.

Our view of organizations as social systems leads us to give heavy emphasis to the values scan as an early and critical phase of strategic planning. Many organizations have given little attention to the values underlying the behavior of their members, particularly their leaders, or to the organizational values that have driven organizational decisions. An excellent example is an organization's values about conflict management—how conflict should be handled between the organization and its competitors, between and among organizational units, or between individual members of the organization. These values are always present and are important determinants of behavior; yet rarely are they consciously established; and even more rarely are they discussed in an open fashion, using a cost-benefit analysis to determine whether the retention of these specific values is warranted.

When there is clarity on the personal values of the members of the planning team and an agreement about how the differences in values can be managed, the strategic planning process can move ahead. This stage of Applied Strategic Planning is very much a values-clarification process, and the actual strategic plan for an organization represents the operational implementation of the shared values-based vision of the management team.

Organizational Values

Once the individual values of the management planning team have been worked through, the desired values of the organization as a whole must be considered. That is, given the personal values of the members of the planning team, what values do they want to have this organization espouse and use in its decision making? While the analysis of the planning group's personal values focused on the question of what they wished to stand for as individuals, the question to be asked here is what they want their organization to stand for. Typically at this point, the team raises issues such as profit versus growth, being a good corporate citizen, and being seen as a value-added organization or a good place to work. In other words, the task of the planning group during the organizational aspect of the values scan is to articulate the things that the organization will value as it implements its strategic plan. The organizational values can be determined by using instruments similar to those employed in the personal-values assessment.

Values lie at the heart of almost all organizational decisions. When managers say that the XYZ department can always be counted on to fulfill its promises or that the ABC organization would never sell unsafe products because it is a highly ethical firm, they are explaining those organizations' behaviors in terms of their value bases. In this part of the values scan the important issue to work through is what values the planning team want to have the organization operate on in the future. It then may be useful to determine if there are differences in desired values among the major segments of the organization.

Application Considerations

If the values scan identifies desired values in one segment of the organization that are incongruous with those in another segment, this difference needs to be addressed immediately. Some degree of values articulation and some resolution of strong values differences are mandatory for a successful strategic planning process. The envisioning of an organization's future state is a values-based activity. How an organization considers ordinary marketplace decisions (such as those regarding market share, dealing with the competition, innovation in products and services, and customer or client service) is a natural outgrowth of the fundamental values that the organization holds—values that need to be examined, or re-examined, as part of the strategic planning process. When a planning team arrives at a resolution about the values of the organization, this information needs to be disseminated to the rest of the organization.

Operating Philosophy

An organization's values typically are organized and codified into a philosophy of operations, which explains how the organization approaches its work, how its internal affairs are managed, and how it relates to its external environment, including its customers or clients. This type of formal statement integrates the organization's values into the way it does business.

Some organizations have explicit, formal statements of philosophy, such as "Hoechst Celanese Values" (Figure 7-2), the "Five Principles of Mars" (Figure 7-3), and the "Johnson & Johnson Credo" (Figure 7-4). These statements have evolved over the years and are these organizations'

Some Organizations Have Explicit Philosophies

VALUES

Performance

- Preferred supplier, dedicated to understanding and meeting customer expectations
- Commitment to safety, employee health and protection of the environment
- Responsible corporate citizen
- Earnings to support long-term growth
- Consistently superior to competition
- Commitment to continual improvement

People

- Respect for individuals and appreciation for contributions each can make
- Diversity accepted and valued
- Concern and fair treatment for individuals in managing business change
- Equal opportunity for each employee to achieve his or her potential
- Employee pride and enthusiasm
- Informed employees through open communication

Process

- Openness and trust in all relationships
- Innovation, creativity and risk taking encouraged
- Teamwork throughout the organization
- Participative goal setting, measurement and feedback
- Decision making at the lowest practical level
- Actions consistent with clearly understood mission and long-term goals
- Recognition for quality achievements
- Resources committed to ongoing training and development

Figure 7-2. Hoechst Celanese Statement of Values

attempts to clarify and explicate the values by which they attempt to run the businesses.

All these organizations (Hoechst Celanese, a major chemical manufacturer; Mars, the candy manufacturer that is probably the world's largest privately held corporation; and Johnson & Johnson, a major health-care products manufacturer) regularly update their explicit philosophy statements, have regular seminars with employees to ensure dissemination of these values, and actually hold managers accountable for operating in accord with these philosophies. In Hoechst Celanese business meetings, it is common to hear a manager ask the question, "Is what we are proposing congruent with our values?" Such public statements provide managers with clear-cut guidelines about decision making.

As a further example, given the first sentence of the Johnson & Johnson Credo, that "our first responsibility is to the doctors, nurses, and patients, to mothers and all others who use our products," we should not have been surprised when the managers of McNeil Consumer Products Company, a wholly owned subsidiary of Johnson & Johnson, decided to recall all of the retail stock of Tylenol (31 million bottles) when several people died after taking capsules that had been tampered with. Although it was clear that the tampering had taken place after the product reached the retail level (and it was ultimately determined that only seventy-five capsules in eight bottles had been tampered with), commitment to the end users required this action. Persons knowledgeable about the event state unequivocally that the only issue confronting management was *when* the recall could take place, not *if* a recall was in order. This is a clear example of how a values-driven organization made a decision by applying those explicit values.

---

1. **Quality**
   The consumer is our boss, quality is our work, and value for money is our goal.

2. **Responsibility**
   As individuals, we demand total responsibility from ourselves; as associates, we support the responsibilities of others.

3. **Mutuality**
   A mutual benefit is a shared benefit; a shared benefit will endure.

4. **Efficiency**
   We use resources to the fullest, waste nothing, and do only what we can do best.

5. **Freedom**
   We need freedom to shape our future; we need profit to remain free.

Figure 7-3. The Five Principles of Mars

The Tylenol decision is not just a single, well-known instance. Equally impressive but less well-known is the decision by Johnson & Johnson to stop its marketing campaign for using its Baby Oil as an aid for sun tanning. This decision was made when employees pointed out

Our Credo

We believe our first responsibility is to the doctors, nurses and patients,
to mothers and all others who use our products and services.
In meeting their needs everything we do must be of high quality.
We must constantly strive to reduce our costs
in order to maintain reasonable prices.
Customers' orders must be serviced promptly and accurately.
Our suppliers and distributors must have an opportunity
to make a fair profit.

We are responsible to our employees,
the men and women who work with us throughout the world.
Everyone must be considered as an individual.
We must respect their dignity and recognize their merit.
They must have a sense of security in their jobs.
Compensation must be fair and adequate,
and working conditions clean, orderly and safe.
Employees must feel free to make suggestions and complaints.
There must be equal opportunity for employment, development
and advancement for those qualified.
We must provide competent management,
and their actions must be just and ethical.

We are responsible to the communities in which we live and work
and to the world community as well.
We must be good citizens — support good works and charities
and bear our fair share of taxes.
We must encourage civic improvements and better health and education.
We must maintain in good order
the property we are privileged to use,
protecting the environment and natural resources.

Our final responsibility is to our stockholders.
Business must make a sound profit.
We must experiment with new ideas.
Research must be carried on, innovative programs developed
and mistakes paid for.
New equipment must be purchased, new facilities provided
and new products launched.
Reserves must be created to provide for adverse times.
When we operate according to these principles,
the stockholders should realize a fair return.

Johnson & Johnson

Figure 7-4. The Johnson & Johnson Credo

that such tanning was a health hazard, and promoting an aid to a health-risk activity was incongruent with their Credo.

Regarding the "mutuality" statement in the Five Principles of Mars, a story is told about a Mars buyer who was able to secure cacao beans from a distressed broker at a figure well below the market price. He returned to his company with the self-assurance that he would be lauded for the money he had saved Mars. Much to his surprise, he was disciplined, and the contract was rewritten at a fairer price to the broker. He was told that his company valued its suppliers too much to take advantage of them during a depressed period; and furthermore, Mars could someday be the distressed party and would want reciprocal treatment.

Values-driven organizations, such as Hoechst Celanese, Mars, and Johnson & Johnson, spend a great deal of time and energy in disseminating and tracking the impact of their philosophies on all organizational behavior. In such values-driven organizations all members of the organization are expected to know and understand the operating philosophy and to use it in their day-to-day work. Furthermore, serious sanctions are invoked against any member who violates the philosophy. In these organizations there is usually a great deal of folklore about the philosophy and many stories are told—both about the people who were rewarded for acting according to the philosophy and about people who were punished for not acting in accordance with it.

Even those organizations that do not have explicit, written philosophies of operations have implicit philosophies. Members of this type of organization can readily answer questions about its philosophy of operations in action: how work is done, how conflict is managed, how much customer service is provided, how soon bills are paid, and so on.

Another aspect of an organization's philosophy of operations that is worth surfacing in this process is how marginal employees are managed. By "marginal employees" we mean those employees whose performance is never poor enough to warrant discharge but never good enough to make them solid performers. Typically, this is the 20 percent of the work force who occupy 80 percent of management's time. The philosophy of operations about such employees is usually implicit and rarely addressed directly by management. Surfacing this issue is frequently highly cathartic for a planning team and frequently results in an organization's addressing the issue directly—often for the first time.

An organization's philosophy of operations often includes a series of assumptions about the way things work and the way in which decisions are made. Such assumptions in the profit-making sector include "No profit can be made doing business with the government" or "Allowing a labor union to organize our hourly production people would destroy this company." In the not-for-profit sector, typical assumptions are "If we do not spend all of this year's budget, it will be cut next time," and "You have to go along to get along." Some general assumptions are that the organization's growth is assured by an expanding and more affluent population or that there never will be a satisfactory substitute for the organization's major product or service.

Unless such assumptions are examined in terms of their current validity and relevance—regardless of whether or not they ever were true or relevant—the organization will continue to assume that they are true and operate accordingly. Thus, an important part of the strategic planning process is to identify the assumptions that the organization makes about its environment, its markets, its operations, and how things do or should work and to examine their validity.

One important part of the strategic planning process is to create an explicit philosophy of operations, because this philosophy becomes the vehicle for disseminating the organization's values both internally and externally. Also, the strategic plan needs to be built on the organization's philosophy of operations, or that philosophy needs to be changed to conform to the strategic plan.

There is no simple and direct way for an organization to produce an explicit philosophy of operations if it does not have one. It is often useful for the strategic planning team to attempt to develop one as part of its work, using examples such as those from Johnson & Johnson or Mars. It is useful for the strategic planning consultant to keep a record of the various organizational assumptions that were encountered during earlier work with the organization and, at appropriate times in the planning process, to raise them as issues for the planning group to examine for truth or falsehood and for agreement or disagreement. Organizations typically make untested assumptions about their competition, their marketplace, compensation schedules for both exempt and nonexempt workers, the role of the government, the problems of unionization, and so on. Although raising such issues for a reasoned analysis is a difficult, anxiety-arousing task for a consultant, it is an important part of the strategic planning process.

Organizational Culture

As Chapter 3 noted, an organization's assumptions about the way the world works, its members' individual values, the values of the organization as a whole, and its philosophy of operations all come together to produce the organization's culture. An organization's culture ties the people in the organization together and gives meaning and purpose to their day-to-day work lives.

It is becoming more and more obvious that those organizations that have "strong cultures," that is, organizations that have a clearly stated mission and a clear system of informal rules that spell out how organizational members should regularly behave and that enable members to feel good about their jobs and their employers, are consistently high-performing systems (Denison, 1990; Levering, Moskowitz, & Katz, 1984). As Levering, Moskowitz, and Katz point out in their analysis of the one hundred best American companies to work for, these are companies whose cultures provide a working life that is really worth living and one to which the employees can look forward on a regular basis. Denison demonstrated, as we summarized in Chapter 3, that the more profitable organizations are those whose cultures are mission driven and regularly involve their employees in the work of the organization, both aspects of organizational culture.

Some Organizations Have Strong Cultures

In identifying and understanding the origins of an organization's culture, we need to investigate three elements, in addition to the desired organization values, that are the heart of the culture: the organization's heroes, its rites and rituals, and its cultural network.

Heroes

An organization's heroes are those people who personify the organization's values and about whom stories are told. These are the organizational members who serve as clear role models for others and epitomize the uniqueness of the organization.

It is no surprise that founders of organizations are frequently in this role. J.W. Marriott, Sr., the now-deceased chairman of the board of the Marriott Hotel Corporation, was a hero in his organization for his faithful reading of customer comment cards in order to make real the Marriott slogan, "We do it right." Forrest Mars, former CEO of Mars, is legendary for his preoccupation with the quality of product and his extravagant temper when he found that his expectations about quality were violated for any reason. An organization with a strong culture always has a hero or two whose exploits help clarify and personalize organizational values. Learning about an organization's heroes is an integral part of learning about its culture.

Rites and Rituals

An organization's rites and rituals are the ceremonies and other programed routines that help define an organization's expectations (and the underlying values) for employees. An organization that regularly rewards career employees for longevity with recognition dinners and five-year pins that are proudly worn is rather different from one that pays no attention to length of service and lavishly rewards its top salespeople and other top performers; and these are both different from organizations that have rites and rituals for both. Such symbolic acts tell us much about the organization and need to be carefully observed. In one high-growth organization that was experiencing a 20-percent compounded growth in staff, resulting in a doubling every four years, new employees would "accidentally" wash their ID badges in the washing machine with their clothing in order to avoid being seen as a "new hire." High-performing organizations have a variety of rites and rituals as part of their strong culture, and these need to be identified as part of the strategic planning process.

Cultural Network

A strong culture requires a cultural network of informal communications to tend and spread the culture—storytellers who keep the culture alive by telling tales about the organization's heroes (and villains), priests who worry about any intrusion of foreign values into the organizational culture, whisperers who transmit cultural information into otherwise inaccessible places, and so on. These people are the important actors in maintaining and extending the organizational culture and are invaluable informants to the strategic planning process. They also play a critical role in facilitating the acceptance of the strategic planning process and the assimilation of the strategic plan into the ongoing working life of the organization.

Behavioral evidence about the organization's culture is everywhere—in the organization's physical structures and sites, in how it greets or guards itself from outsiders, in its "war stories" told about the good (or bad) old days, in those regarded as the organization's heroes and villains, in the rites and rituals of the organization, and so on. All this must be decoded—a rather difficult job, because it involves drawing inferences about the underlying meaning and significance of behavior, a frequently controversial task. It thus often becomes one of the tasks that needs to be initiated and managed by the strategic planning consultant.

An organization's culture provides the social context in and through which the organization performs its work. It guides the organization's members in decision making, how time and energy are invested, which facts are examined with care and which are summarily rejected, which options are looked upon favorably from the start, which types of people are selected to work for and in the organization, and practically everything else that is done in the organization.

Clearly the culture of an organization will either facilitate or hinder both the strategic planning process itself and the implementation of whatever plan that process produces. A formal assessment of the organization's current culture and its potential impact on the implementation of the strategic plan is ordinarily performed as part of the performance audit and gap analysis phases of the Applied Strategic Planning process. However, a discussion of the organization's culture—especially the roots of that culture in the assumptions, values, and beliefs of the management team—often begins during the values scan. It can be a useful and important part of that phase, providing a link to the performance audit and gap analysis phases of the planning process. An analysis of the organization's culture is also useful in surfacing issues that may interfere with the strategic planning process itself, and it may enable the planning team to manage those potential blockages better.

The Stakeholder Analysis

The final step of the values scan is the stakeholder analysis. By "stakeholders," we mean those individuals, groups, and organizations who will be impacted by or who are likely to be interested in the organization's strategic plan and the planning process. Included are all who believe, rightly or wrongly, that they have a stake in the organization's future and not merely those whom the planning team believes have a reasonable or legitimate right to such a stake. Each of these stakeholders needs to be identified and a determination must be made of how they are likely to respond to the plan, the planning process, and the implementation of the plan.

In this analysis it is necessary to take into account the presumed values of the various stakeholder groups and their respective resources, status, freedom of action, relationships, and activities that may be impacted by shifts or changes in the organization's strategic direction. Given the diversity of stakeholder interests, however, it will never be possible to satisfy all of them. Rather, these stakeholder interests should be assessed and considered in terms of the consequences of either meeting or not meeting them. Such an assessment would reduce the surprises that might overwise impact both the strategic planning process and its implementation.

Exchange Processes

In his discussion of stakeholder analysis, Ackoff (1981) points out that business organizations engage in six direct exchange processes with stakeholders:

1. An exchange of money for work with employees, including managers;
2. An exchange of money for goods and services with suppliers;
3. An exchange of goods and services for money with customers;
4. An exchange of money paid later for money received now with investors and lenders;
5. An exchange of money paid now for money received later with debtors; and
6. An exchange of money for goods, services, and regulation with government (police and fire protection, antitrust regulation, pollution control, tariffs, water, sewage, etc.).

Ackoff's conceptualization is presented graphically in Figure 7-5. Ackoff goes on to insist that the appropriate objective of a business organization is not to serve any one of its stakeholder groups to the exclusion of any other, but rather to serve all the stakeholders by increasing their ability to pursue their own objectives more efficiently and effectively. In other words, Ackoff argues that the overriding purpose of an organization ought to be to serve the interests of all its stakeholders,

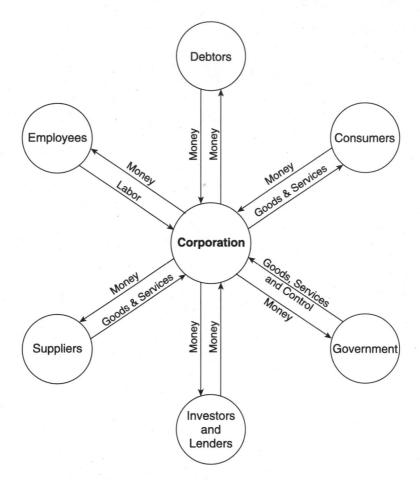

From R. Ackoff, *Creating the Corporate Future,* p. 31. Copyright 1981 by John Wiley
& Sons. New York: John Wiley. Used with permission.

Figure 7-5. A Stakeholder View of the Organization

not just its investors (the group whose interests are typically emphasized
by an organization).

The purpose of presenting Ackoff's position is to raise two important issues affecting the strategic planning process: (1) who the
organization's stakeholders are and (2) how the organization intends to
address the values of those stakeholders. Identification of the stakeholders and their values permits the planning team to consider the impact of
various future states on each of them. The stakeholder analysis enables
the planning team to identify the various constituencies that need to be
considered in the planning process.

Identifying Stakeholders

A straightforward way to approach stakeholder analysis is to have the members of the planning team, first independently and then as a group, identify the various stakeholders. They should work to understand the values of the stakeholders. This can be done by examining the overt behaviors of these stakeholders over time and "backing out" the underlying values these behaviors represent. Then it is necessary to attempt to understand the nature of the current exchange process with each of these stakeholders. The construction of a diagram similar to Figure 7-5 is a useful way to record these data.

This analysis should provide the planning team with a template for understanding and meeting the different expectations of the several stakeholder groups during the course of the planning process. For example, in considering its relationships with its suppliers as stakeholders, one planning team concluded that its suppliers wanted an ongoing partnership—characterized by open communication, mutual respect, and appreciation for what the partners could provide for each other. This led to a fundamental change in the organization's relationship with its suppliers; in the new relationship, the organization diligently tried to deal with its suppliers in the same fashion that it hoped its customers would deal with it.

Similarly, one organization—in dealing with its employees—came to the understanding that they strongly valued a high quality of working life, including the opportunity for professional and personal development. Attending to these employee values would enable the organization to be a strongly preferred employer, able to both attract and retain its human resources. Pitney Bowes, whose outstanding environmental monitoring processes were discussed in Chapter 6, holds an annual job-holder meeting, in addition to its traditional shareholder meetings. The purpose of these two meetings is more or less identical: to allow a group of significant stakeholders to learn about the company's progress and plans and to share questions and concerns. These job-holder meetings are one of several reasons that Pitney Bowes is included in the Levering, Moskowitz, and Katz (1984) list of the one hundred best companies to work for in America. Of more general significance, however, is that without such attention to the several groups of stakeholders whose lives and futures are intimately tied into the future of the organization and its plans, any strategic planning process is incomplete.

The values scan is the critical second step of the Applied Strategic Planning process. It forces the strategic planning team to analyze and understand the underpinnings of the organization and how it operates—the assumptions upon which it operates, the personal values of the planning team, the desired values of the organization as a whole, the organization's philosophy of operations, its culture, and its stakeholders. An understanding of these elements and their interrelations is essential to a successful strategic plan, one that truly will provide future direction for the organization. Figure 7-6 provides a convenient checklist to verify that all the necessary outputs of the values scan have been obtained.

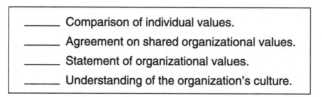

Figure 7-6. Checklist for Values Scan

SUMMARY

All business decisions are based on values. The values scan phase of Applied Strategic Planning involves an in-depth examination of personal values, organizational values, the operating philosophy, the organization's culture, and the stakeholders. The strategic plan must be congruent with the organization's values; if not, either the values or the plan must change.

REFERENCES

Ackoff, R. (1981). *Creating the corporate future.* New York: John Wiley.

Denison, D. R. (1990). *Corporate culture and organizational effectiveness.* New York: John Wiley.

Harvey, J. (1988). *The Abilene paradox and other meditations on management.* San Diego, CA: Pfeiffer & Co.

Levering, R., Moskowitz, M., & Katz, M. (1984). *The one hundred best companies to work for in America.* Reading, MA: Addison Wesley.

Rokeach, M. (1973). *The nature of human values.* New York: Free Press.

Scherer, J. (1983). *The pinch package: For renewing relationships at home and work.* San Diego: University Associates.

Schwartz, H. & Davis, S. M. (1984). Matching corporate culture and business strategy. *Organizational Dynamics, 4*(4), 30-48.

Ulrich, D., & Wiersma, M. F. (1989). Gaining strategic and organizational capability in a turbulent business environment. *Academy of Management Executive, 3*(2), 115-122.

Zimmerman, J. (1985). The frontiers of strategic thinking: An interview with John W. Zimmerman. *Kepner-Tregoe Journal, 14*(4), 13-16.

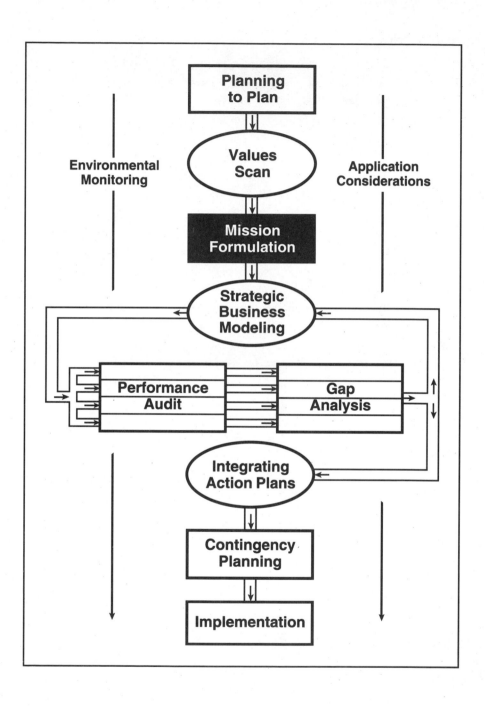

Chapter Eight

Mission Formulation

So may a thousand actions, once afoot,
End in one purpose, and be well borne
Without defeat.

W. Shakespeare
Henry V, I.ii. 211-13

O ne of the most important and, often, one of the most difficult aspects of the strategic planning process is the development of a mission statement, that is, a brief, clear statement of the reasons for an organization's existence, the purpose(s) or function(s) it desires to fulfill, its primary customer base, and the primary methods through which it intends to fulfill this purpose. The mission statement provides the context for the formulation of specific lines of business in which the organization will engage and the strategies by which the organization will operate; it sets the arena in which the organization will compete; and it determines how resources will be allocated by the organization and what the general pattern of growth and direction will be for the future. The primary purpose for having such a mission statement is to bring clarity of focus to members of the organization, to give them an understanding of how what they do is tied into a greater purpose. Thus the focus of the mission should be internal to the organization, not external for other stakeholders.

FORMULATING THE MISSION STATEMENT

The development of a mission statement follows the completion of the values scan. The mission statement must be congruent with the desired organizational values that the planning team developed during the values scan. A mission statement that is not congruent with the organization's desired core values and its desired philosophy of operations will not perform the expected task, that of providing a guiding star by which to steer the organization. Even worse, any attempt to develop a mission statement without congruence with desired organizational values will likely meet with considerable resistance, especially if the planning team has done its job in disseminating these desired values throughout the organization and secured the necessary buy-in.

A mission statement addresses the organization's fundamental *raison d'etre* (reason for being) and specifies the functional role that the organization is going to play in its environment. A mission statement should clearly indicate the scope and direction of the organization's activities and, to the extent that is feasible, should provide a template for decision making by people at all levels in that organization. An effective mission statement will prevent people in the organization from developing and proposing many plans and projects that will not be accepted by top management, because they will be able to see that such plans or projects are not within the scope of the mission statement.

In formulating its mission statement, an organization must answer four primary questions (see Figure 8-1):

1. *What* function(s) does the organization perform?
2. For *whom* does the organization perform this function?

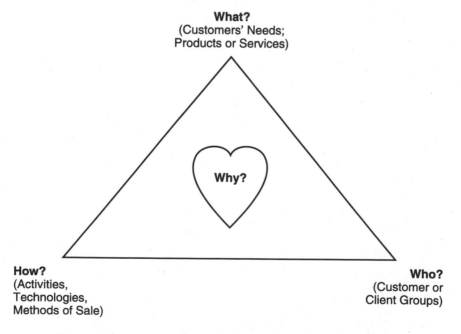

Figure 8-1. Four Basic Elements of the Organizational Mission

3. *How* does the organization go about filling this function?
4. *Why* does this organization exist?

What

The first question, that of "what," involves defining the needs that the organization is attempting to fill. Chapter 1 pointed out that it is critically important to avoid "marketing myopia" (Levitt, 1960) in answering the "what" question. It is also important not to accept superficial analyses of what business the organization is in.

The classic story of Avis nicely illustrates this point. For years Avis thought that it was in the car-rental business. If one is in the car-rental business, then a rental car—once its life as a rental vehicle is over—is a waste product with only salvage value. When Robert Townsend became president of Avis, he began an in-depth analysis of the organization's mission and determined that Avis was really the world's second largest producer of used cars and that should be its mission! Given this clarity, the entire operation of the Avis rental-car business changed: Rental-car maintenance became more important, rental vehicles were not kept in service as long as was previously the case, and an entirely new sense of excitement began to permeate the organization. Avis was the first rental-car organization to push the retail sale of its cars with the development of its own retail used-car lots and the development of the "Avis yearling" marketing campaign. The important point in this story is the profound impact that this clarification of direction has had on the day-to-day operations of Avis, from the higher quality of the cars Avis initially purchases, to its maintenance program, to how long it continues to rent the cars before reselling them, and even to how often Avis washes its cars.

"Marketing myopia" causes an organization to define the "what" in terms of goods or services provided rather than in terms of needs to be served. As Chapter 1 mentioned, Levitt points out that the failure of the railroads to see themselves as being in the transportation business was the critical reason for their rapid decline.

Thinking about *what* needs the organization is attempting to fill for customers or clients should make the organization more sensitive to a clear initial identification of those needs and a continual monitoring of those needs. As those needs change, need-conscious organizations are more likely to develop new goods and services to meet the emerging needs of their customers and clients and are less likely to experience obsolescence and decline. For example, an organization that sees itself in the business of assisting people in cleaning garments is much more likely to view a new ultrasonic cleaning process as an opportunity and part of its ongoing mission than is an organization that sees its mission as manufacturing detergents.

Nevertheless, simply defining the "what" in terms of needs is no guarantee of success. It can lead to success—as it did when the oil companies redefined themselves as being in the energy business rather than the oil business and acquired coal mines. On the other hand, when the business is defined too broadly, it can lead to failure—as it did when those same oil companies defined themselves in the "natural resources" business. Examples of these failures include Gulf's acquisition of the Bunker Hill Mining and Smelting operations. Such a broad definition allows the organization to consider a broader range of options; but each of these options needs to be carefully evaluated, and tough decisions will still need to be made. A mission statement is no substitute for good management and intelligent decision making.

Successful organizations try to identify value-satisfying goods and services that meet the needs of the public and include these considerations in their mission formulations. A major issue in mission formulation typically is achieving consensus on how broadly or narrowly to answer the "what" question. The fact that values regarding risk taking, conflict avoidance, and growth versus profit quickly surface during mission formulation is one of the important reasons for completing the values scan prior to formulating the mission statement. Gup (1979) provides a useful analysis of how to distinguish between narrow and broad lines of business and offers advantages of each approach.

The failure of United Airlines' attempt to broaden its mission from being an airline to being in the travel business with its acquisition of Hertz Car Rental Company and the Westin Hotel chain is often offered as an example of the risks inherent in developing a broader mission statement. Rather, we see this example as a failure to take into account stakeholder interests in the mission formulation. The CEO of United Airlines at that time simply announced his plan without adequately involving either the board of directors or the several powerful unions in the process. Their outcries of outrage not only scuttled the plan, but also led to replacing the CEO.

The positive impact of a properly broad mission statement is seen in that of Pitney Bowes, which no longer sees itself as just in the postage-meter business but rather in the mail-automation business. This broader mission has enabled Pitney to develop machines that take letters from a computer disk, print them on organizational letterheads, collate them with other relevant materials, properly fold the material, insert the collated and folded materials in an envelope on which it also

Defining the Business Is Important

has printed the recipient's full name and address, seal the envelope, apply the proper postage, and sort the envelopes by postal code. Such one-stop mailing automation has enabled Pitney to retain its place as the industry leader.

On the other hand, organizations that have defined themselves narrowly can be highly successful in fulfilling that narrowly defined mission. For example, the Wrigley Company is clearly and solely in the chewing-gum business and has no apparent interest in broadening that mission. The most consistently successful company in that business, it has not reconceptualized itself as a snack-food organization or anything else. Its two prior diversifications, as owner of a major-league baseball team—the Chicago Cubs—and as owners of the Cubs' playing field, Wrigley Field, convinced it that being the largest and most successful chewing-gum manufacturer was a sufficiency.

In the not-for-profit sector, answering the question of *what* function the organization serves is a critical one. For example, once a large metropolitan library became clear that its function was the dissemination of information, and not merely distributing books, options for new services became apparent, as did new community support. Regardless of what venue an organization operates in, it must be clear on what functions or purposes it intends to meet.

Who

The second aspect of mission formulation is identifying the "who," that is, which market or segment of the market the organization is attempting to serve. No organization, regardless of size, is large enough to meet the needs of all possible customers or clients. Few, if any, organizations are large enough to attempt to serve everybody; and, in any event, everybody does not have the same needs. Mission formulation requires a clear identification of what portion or segment of the total potential customer base the organization has as its primary market. The process of sorting out an organization's actual and potential target is called *market segmentation.*

There are many ways in which a market can be segmented: by geography, age, wealth, ethnicity, and a variety of other factors. The needs of Sun Belt consumers are different from those of Frost Belt consumers. Federal Express serves customers who are willing to spend more than the price of ordinary postage to ensure next-day delivery of packages. Kosher foods have devout consumers, as do soul foods. An organization can segment its market by single or multiple factors; for example, products can be developed for middle-class housewives throughout the United States, or middle-class housewives only in the Northeast, and so on. Clarity about its market segment enables the organization to be more sensitive to the needs of that segment and to focus its resources on its prime target.

There clearly are different needs and different resources in various market segments. Organizations may elect to serve only one small segment of the market; consider, for example, the difference between a small boutique and a large department store. Large organizations may also develop subunits to focus on various market segments; these are actually smaller businesses within the overall business. For example, General Motors has been enormously successful through the past forty years with distinct lines of automobiles: Chevrolet, Pontiac, Oldsmobile, Buick, and Cadillac—each designed and priced for auto buyers at a particular socioeconomic level and marketed accordingly. This strategy is now obsolete according to management guru Peter Drucker (1991). He argues that the wants and needs of American automobile purchasers are best expressed in different "life styles," that is, self-selected values and expectations that are expressed in their choices of autos. A life-style market place is not clean-cut and definitive, rather it is fuzzy and fluid. The Japanese automakers have been aware of this change in the marketplace and their short design and production cycle has enabled the Japanese to produce a range of options that is far more responsive to this changing marketplace than those of their American competitors, and thus they take market share away from Detroit. While the negative consequences of this loss should be obvious, there is little sign that any of the Big Three American automakers are likely to change their traditional approach to the marketplace.

Understanding the marketplace is also important for the not-for-profit sector, especially organizations that are publicly funded. Clarity about the two kinds of the critical clients—those who control the funding sources and those who are the recipients of the organization's service—and meeting the needs and expectations of both sets of clients are important ingredients of success in this arena. When the needs of the recipients are at odds with the needs of the funding source, managing the organization can be difficult.

How

The third question addressed by the mission statement should be concerned with how the organization will attempt to achieve its goals, for example, what technologies will be used by the organization in meeting the needs identified in its market. The "how" may involve a marketing strategy, such as becoming the low-cost producer, providing innovative products, or providing the most reliable products; it may involve a distribution strategy, such as providing no-appointment dental or medical services in shopping malls, adding regional warehouses, or offering electronic shopping through computers; it may involve direct-mail marketing, door-to-door selling, or telemarketing; or it may involve any of a variety of processes through which the organization can develop, produce, market, and deliver products and/or services to a defined group of consumers or clients.

The "how" question also needs to be addressed by organizations in the not-for-profit sector. For example, the mission statement of the Center for Creative Leadership states, "We accomplish our mission through research, training, and publications—with emphasis on the widespread, innovative application of the behavioral sciences to the challenges facing the leaders of today and tomorrow." The "how" question must be addressed as in integral part of mission formulation.

Even when the "what" and "who" questions are readily answered in the planning process, answering the "how" question can raise unexpected problems. For example, in a large, private foundation devoted to alleviating the pain and suffering caused by a particular disease, during strategic planning a sharp disagreement surfaced between those who wished to devote all the foundation's resources to supporting the basic

The Third Question Is "How?"

research necessary to find and eliminate the cause of the disease and those who wished also to put a goodly portion of these funds into providing support, including nursing and medical care, to those people who had already contracted the disease. This fundamental difference has long been an important factor affecting the foundation's operations, but the differences were resolved only after they had been clearly articulated at the strategic planning table.

Another important aspect of *how* involves considering acquisitions and mergers. If, for example, growth or movement into new lines of business becomes a significant part of the strategic plan, then such growth or movement can often be most readily obtained through acquisition or merger and should be included as part of the how portion of the mission statement. Deciding which specific paths the organization will follow on its road to the ideal future is critically important.

Why

The question of *why* an organization performs the functions that it does—the existential question—frequently is an important one for both profit-oriented and not-for-profit organizations. Many organizations feel that they need to include some simple statement of their *raison d'etre* as part of their mission statements. It can appear as the "heart" in the diagram of the triangular relationship of the what, who, and how questions (see Figure 8-1). For example, the mission statement of Warner-Lambert, the U.S.-based pharmaceutical manufacturer starts off its creed with the following mission, "To achieve leadership in advancing the health and well being of people throughout the world..." while the Johnsonville Sausage Company, of Sheboygan Falls, Wisconsin, includes the following: "We, here at Johnsonville, have a moral responsibility to become the best sausage company ever established..." Sun Oil includes the following in its mission statement: "We must be responsive to the broader concerns of the public including the general desire for improvements in the quality of life, equal opportunity for all, and the constructive use of natural resources." Dow Chemical's statement includes, "To share the world's obligation for the protection of the environment." These examples show a broad concern extending beyond what many would think is the proper content of a mission statement.

In the not-for-profit sector, the Center for Creative Leadership in Greensboro, North Carolina, states, "Our mission is to encourage and develop creative leadership and effective management for the good of society overall." The New York State Board of Equalization and Assessment "seeks to improve the administration and understanding of the real property tax to achieve equity for the tax payers of New York State." The County of Los Angeles Public Library mission statement includes the following: "We are committed to supporting lifelong learning and knowledge through self-education." An Ann Arbor research and knowledge-dissemination organization begins its mission statement with the following: "The renewal and continued vitality of manufacturing is essential for improving the quality of American society. The Industrial Technology Institute exists to catalyze that renewal and vitality by accelerating the development of manufacturing technology and by creating methods and tools to foster their widespread use."

Such statements are often a natural outgrowth of the organizational-level values scan, and the Applied Strategic Planning model promotes the inclusion of such a statement. The "why" statement enables the organization to place what it does in a societal context and provide a more meaningful focus for its activities. As we learn more about the psychology of work and the importance of employee commitment and satisfaction, the role of why statements becomes ever more important.

Pre-Existing Mission Statements

Consultants often encounter organizations with pre-existing mission statements, which were outcomes of previous organizational processes. The question that typically arises is how to handle these pre-existing mission statements. At the risk of appearing glib, we answer simply "with care."

Regardless of the quality or potential usefulness of a pre-existing mission statement, organizations take great pride in having such statements. The single most useful approach to take is to simply acknowledge the existence of such statements, suggest that they be set aside for the time being, and attempt to craft a new mission statement, one that represents the new desired future that the organization will work toward. Later the pre-existing mission statement can be re-examined to determine what, if anything, should be added to the newly developed statement.

Slogans

Organizations sometimes summarize their mission statements into brief slogans. For example, the British Airways slogan, "The World's Favourite Airline," draws attention to its service-based, growth strategy and helps tie its marketing program into its mission statement. The Rouse Company, a builder of such large community projects as the design and construction of Columbia, Maryland—a totally planned community— and the reconstruction of Baltimore's Inner Harbor, has effectively used the slogan, "Creating the best environment for people," in much the same fashion.

While such a brief, highly emotional slogan can be developed on the basis of a mission statement and usefully used both internally and externally, it poses a danger if the slogan is not anchored in the realities of the values of the organization and its mission statement. Such a slogan also runs the risk of becoming superseded by the realities of the marketplace. For example, AT&T's former slogan of "Universal Service" seems quite inappropriate following deregulation of the telecommunications industry, as does Sears, Roebuck's slogan of "Quality at a good price." While mission statements can and should be modified with the changing environment, a world-wide advertising slogan that catches on is rather more difficult to change. In order for the mission to achieve its desired impact, the necessary change should be made, regardless of the effort required.

DRIVING FORCES

Another important factor that must be considered as part of mission formulation is the identification and prioritization of the organization's driving forces. Organizations, on the basis of their successful experience operating in the marketplace, develop mind-sets for approaching strategic questions. These forces that drive an organization are a reflection of what the managers of that organization see as that organization's competitive advantage (South, 1981). These mind-sets, or driving forces, help both determine and integrate the strategic choices of managers in these organizations. Tregoe, Zimmermann, Smith, & Tobia (1989) identify the following eight basic categories of driving forces:

1. *Products Offered.* The organization is committed primarily to a product or service—such as retail banking, chemical manufacturing, or automotive manufacturing—and limits its strategy to increasing the quantity and quality of that product or service. The unique product characteristics provide these organizations with their competitive advantage. Dow Chemical and General Motors are both good examples of organizations that are driven by products offered.

2. *Market Served.* Market-served organizations recognize that their strongest competitive edge is their continuing relationship with the customers and markets they serve. Such organizations therefore continually survey their customers to discover unfilled needs for goods and services. Once these are identified, these organizations develop products or services to fill those needs. Procter & Gamble and Fisher-Price are examples of such companies.

3. *Technology.* Organizations that are technology driven continually try to develop products and services that are based on their technology. Bringing "cutting-edge" products to the marketplace is seen as their competitive advantage and thus is given a high priority. Among such organizations are the Minnesota Mining and Manufacturing Company (3M) and the Digital Equipment Company.

4. *Low-Cost Production Capability.* Low-cost capability organizations strive to produce goods or services at a cost lower than their competitors' costs. They concentrate on developing advanced process technology and cost control in order to beat their competition and thus provide their competitive advantage. Wal-Mart and International Paper Company are examples of such organizations.

5. *Operations Capability.* An organization with an operations capability seeks maximum use of that capacity. Such organizations have a primary commitment to keeping their existing production

capacity utilized; for example, to have hospital beds filled or to keep the continuous-process plant from shutting down. Operating at capacity provides these organizations with their competitive advantage. American Airlines, Alcoa, and CSX are examples of such organizations—as are the hospitals operated by the Department of Veterans Affairs.

6. *Method of Distribution/Sale.* The methods of distribution and sale—such as an elaborate network of warehouses and vehicles for delivery, door-to-door selling, direct mail, or premiums and bonus programs—direct the strategy of these organizations. These distribution and sales channels provide these organizations with their competitive advantage. The Southland Company (7-11 Stores), Mary Kay, and Lands End are examples.

7. *Natural Resources.* Certain organizations are strategically driven by their ownership of natural resources, such as coal, timber, petroleum, land, or metals. They must convert these natural resources to products usable by their customers. The competitive advantage of such organizations is in the quality, quantity, location, and form of these natural resources. Weyerhauser and Shell Oil, who own large amounts of their resources, are examples of such organizations.

8. *Profit/Return.* Some organizations set their highest priority on profit margins or return on investment and make strategic decisions in order to achieve these goals. Such a driving force is quite different from the usual concern that all businesses have with making a profit. Meeting predetermined profit or return on investment goals is the *sole* criterion of business success in profit- or return-driven companies. General Electric and IT&T are examples of such organizations.

This list of eight driving forces is useful, but it may be incomplete. While many organizations may understand themselves better by using this analytic tool, there are many that cannot. An entrepreneurially driven firm may have as its driving force the interests of the entrepreneur at its helm—which may not be included in the above eight categories. These categories also do not adequately capture the driving force of growth. Growth—almost a religion in some organizations—drives decisions in ways that often do not overlap with the above eight categories. Finally, not-for-profit and governmental organizations will find it difficult to apply these categories to themselves.

All eight of these driving forces need to be considered in formulating an organization's mission. Tregoe, Zimmerman, Smith, and Tobia believe that an organization must clarify which of the eight factors is its primary driving force; when decisions require choosing from these eight forces, the decision makers in the organization must clearly and mutually understand which one is the primary force. For example, it is impossible for an organization to be both the low-cost producer *and* the technology leader. Further, decisions may need to be made on whether resources should be allocated to research and development or to the development of a sales force to achieve growth or whether they should be retained as profits. If there is clarity on the organization's driving force, these decisions can more easily be made.

In contrast to the position of Tregoe et al., we have found it more useful for the strategic planning team to prioritize these eight driving forces in terms of their perceived importance, rather than identifying only the sole, primary force. The importance of gaining consensus on these priorities should be apparent. Most major strategic decisions that organizations make involve the allocation of resources according to a set of priorities. If there are inadequate resources or if the choices are incompatible, the rank of the eight strategic areas can determine how resources will be allocated or which direction will be chosen. A consensual rank order, with the most important driving force in first place, enables the planning team to make otherwise difficult decisions rather easily. However, it may be important to include in the mission statement the driving force that has been identified as the most important.

DISTINCTIVE COMPETENCY

The final ingredient of the mission statement requires the identification of the distinctive competency or competencies of the organization: What quality or attribute of the organization sets it aside from its competitors? How is it, or how will it be, different from the rest of the pack? Its distinctiveness may be a function of its market niche; for example, it may be the only educational institution to provide management education after work and on weekends in its geographical market. Its distinctiveness may be a function of the products or services offered or a function of being a low-cost producer or providing superior service. Peters (1984) suggests that there are only three truly distinctive sets of such skills: (1) a focus on total customer satisfaction; (2) a focus on continual innovation; and (3) a focus on all-out commitment. He argues that these three sets of skills are the only effective source of long-term, sustainable advantage.

Defining the distinctiveness of an organization is no easy matter, even for the planning team. Glib generalizations such as "We are a communications company," or "We serve the leisure-time industry" are simply not distinctive competencies. Contrast those generalities to the clarity of Marriott's CEO, J. Willard Marriott, Jr., who sees Marriott's distinctive competencies as three fold: (1) running hospitality and food-service operations; (2) building hotels and other lodgings; and (3) packaging these properties for sale to investors. This clarity helped Marriott make the decision to sell its cruise-ship business, its theme parks, and its travel agencies.

Robert (1991) terms these competencies an organization's "strategic heartbeat," which it can leverage to develop strategic advantage. He identifies the fusing of glass and metal as the key competency of Phillips, the Dutch electronics giant. The Daimler-Benz heartbeat has been the "best engineered car in the world," while Wal-Mart sees having the most cost-efficient warehouse system as its competitive advantage and 3-M uses it knowledge of the applications of polymer chemistry to produce over 60,000 products. Merck's distinctive competence in integrating immunology, biochemistry, and molecular biology enabled it to create its array of trail-blazing drugs during the past decade. Identifying its distinctive competencies is a process by which the organization can focus its energies and resources to move in a particular direction; it also helps provide a rallying point for both managers and rank-and-file employees.

The Mission Statement Should Be Brief

There is a growing awareness of the importance of identifying and using an organization's distinctive competencies as one base of the strategic planning process. Indeed, some strategists have begun to argue that the traditional focus—correctly defining what business an organization is in—is not the proper question to focus on. Rather these strategists insist that the proper focus is: "What are we really good at and how can we build on those special skills?" C. K. Prahalad has become a spokesperson for this point of view (see Hamel & Prahalad, 1989; Prahalad & Hamel, 1990). Using such examples as Kodak's identification of "imaging" as its core competency to justify its acquisition of a five-billion-dollar pharmaceutical company because the processes involved in producing that company's drugs were the same as those involved in imaging. Similarly, when AT&T established its own credit-card company, many wondered how this could be justified. Once we understand that AT&T's existing billing infrastructure was seen as a core competence, what appeared to be an unrelated business turned out to be an application of that competence to providing a new service. The U.S. Treasury's Financial Management Service (FMS) has a distinctive competence—it moves over two trillion dollars in 750 million transactions annually with a 99.9964-percent accuracy rate. The FMS is building on this distinctive competence, launching two new businesses to train others how to competently manage complex financial systems.

This focus on distinctive competence is critically important. However, we reject the notion that the focus should be taken from the external marketplace and placed solely on the internal examination of distinctive competence. Long-term success will come from a clear identification of the true distinctive competence and a careful and creative search of the marketplace to determine best-fit situations where this competence is marketable.

Once the questions of what, who, how, and why are answered and the organization's driving force and distinctive competencies are identified, these elements can be integrated into the organization's mission statement. The mission statement should be brief, typically a hundred words or less, and clearly identify the organization's basic business. The mission statement, which should be well-known to all members of the organization and understood by them, answers the questions of what the organization does, for whom, how, and why; and it identifies the organization's major strategic driving force. By answering these questions for both internal and external use, the organization can chart its course of action and provide a guide for making routine day-by-day decisions. Figures 8-2 and 8-3 are two examples of a reasonably effective mission statement.

The Alpha Corporation is a low-cost manufacturer and marketer of consumable food-service items for home and industrial use. We intend to maintain our position as a market leader by meeting customer needs and providing a high level of service and quality while maintaining a level of earnings sufficiently high to satisfy our investors.

Figure 8-2. An Example of a Mission Statement

The Beta Company's principal goal is to develop, manufacture, and market man-made fibers and related products for industrial and textile markets in an innovative manner so as to ensure long-term profitability. Our intent is to utilize worldwide and internally developed technology to enhance our leadership position in the quality of goods and services for our customers.

Figure 8-3. Another Example of a Mission Statement

In contrast, consider the following example:

> The Gamma Corporation is a marketing-centered, professional service company that concentrates its efforts on providing services to satisfy the wants and needs of residential and commercial consumers at a value to the consumer superior to the competition.

It is not immediately apparent from its mission statement that the Gamma Corporation is an actual organization that is currently in the business of lawn and carpet care. Its mission statement is so broad that virtually any set of goods and services that met any residential or commercial consumer needs could be included. Such a mission statement is hardly likely to influence day-to-day management decisions, and the distinctive competence of the organization is simply not clear.

Another example of an oblique mission statement is the following:

> The fundamental purpose of the _____ Corporation is to provide products and services of such quality that our customers will receive superior value, our employees and business partners will share in our success, and our stockholders will receive a sustained, superior return on their investment.

While one might conclude that this is an omnibus mission statement—"one size fits all"—it is actually a corporate mission statement that was formulated and adopted by General Motors. As the Cheshire cat noted at the beginning of Chapter 1, if you don't know where you're going, any path will do. Perhaps the mission statement helps to explain why General Motors has been floundering for the past several decades.

Mission statements such as these—although bland enough not to offend anyone—offer no vision nor provide any focus or direction to the organization as a whole or to any of its component parts, nor to any of its members.

APPLICATION CONSIDERATIONS

When the planning team completes the first attempt at mission formulation with a working model of the mission statement, that draft mission statement must be broadly circulated in the organization for comment and reaction. It is especially important to involve all the relevant stakeholder groups in that distribution. Although the draft is preliminary and will later be modified and refined, it is offered as an honest effort to define the organization and its mission. The planning team should recognize that some opposition to the draft mission statement is almost inevitable. No mission statement can completely accommodate all stakeholders, and any effort to placate all of them will vitiate the purpose of the statement. What is important is maintaining involvement and excitement about the process on the part of most members of the organization.

If the planning team is large, a subgroup of the team may need to edit the draft mission statement prior to its circulation to the rest of the organization. Sometimes it is necessary for the subgroup to try to boil the draft down and then bring it back to the team for discussion and approval before it can be circulated. Most planning groups are overly optimistic about the amount of time that it takes to develop a succinct mission statement that covers all the points discussed above, and often there is a need for a subgroup to wordsmith the statement between sessions. It is imperative that some form of the mission statement be distributed as part of the continuing involvement process. It is less important for an absolutely finished product to be distributed than for a reasonable product to be made available promptly.

MISSION FORMULATION
IN ORGANIZATIONAL SEGMENTS

Once an overall mission statement has been developed for an organization, mission statements that are more specific and concrete should be developed for significant units or segments of the organization. Those parts of the organization that are large enough and autonomous enough to function relatively independently (i.e., the strategic business units and the functional parts of the organization) will ordinarily profit by developing their own unit mission statements. Thus in a large organization, units with highly differentiated functions—such as the marketing group or the service department—need their own mission statements, as would each operating company, separate plant, regional office, clinic, school, and so on, of the organization.

Unit mission statements should be more focused and more limited than that of the total organization, but they must be derived from the organizational mission statement. The value of such unit mission statements is that they bring the focus and energy of the mission down to the level where rank-and-file members of the organization can see how that mission statement affects them and their daily work.

**Unit Mission Statements Should Be Derived
from the Organization's Statement**

The first step in developing a unit mission statement is to ask the planning staff of the unit to carefully review the overall mission statement of the organization and consider how the functioning of that unit fits into the organizational mission. In large organizations it may also be necessary to do a unit values audit before writing a unit mission statement. This is especially true if there are different values, beliefs, and philosophies of operations among the various organizational segments or between the top levels of organizational management and other levels of management.

Once a consensus on values and philosophy of operations is achieved in the unit, the unit planning staff (or the management of the unit) should develop the unit's mission statement, observing the same requirements that governed the preparation of the organizational mission statement. The unit mission statement should identify what the unit does, for whom, and how it does what it does, as well as identify its driving force and distinctive competence.

When the unit planning staff agrees on the unit mission statement, it should be forwarded to the organization's top-level strategic planning team and/or top management for endorsement and approval. Each unit mission statement should be based on and reflect the organizational mission statement, and it is the responsibility of senior management to make certain that this is the case. A similar review and sign-off process from other organizational segments (e.g., sign-offs between marketing and sales or manufacturing and quality control) may also be important. Such an exchange and dialog over unit mission statements can go a long way in clarifying the roles and expectations of the various segments of an organization.

In implementing these unit mission statements, it is imperative that prompt steps be taken to inform and involve all the personnel of that unit in the unit's mission statement. This can be accomplished through dissemination of the mission statement by memorandum and/or in a meeting of all personnel in the unit. The following is an example of an actual unit mission statement (Kanter & Buck, 1985):

> The Defense Systems Employee Relations Department provides leadership for progressive human resource planning, policy design, systems, and services which are aimed at fostering productivity, innovation, and a climate of success in the work place. We contribute to business strategy development while being mindful of the self-esteem and well-being of employees and the division's responsibility to the greater community.

Kanter and Buck (1985) also provide an in-depth analysis of the development of this particular unit mission statement, its function as part of an overall unit change strategy, and the way this unit mission statement is intended to fit into the overall Honeywell corporate mission. The positive effect of using an external consultant to facilitate the mission formulation process in this case is particularly noteworthy.

TEN CRITERIA FOR EVALUATING MISSION STATEMENTS

It is useful at this juncture to review and codify the criteria by which a mission statement can be evaluated. Our criteria include the following ten considerations:

1. The mission statement is clear and understandable to all personnel, including rank-and-file employees.
2. The mission statement is brief enough for most people to keep it in mind. This typically means one hundred words or less, which is possible.
3. The mission statement clearly specifies what business the organization is in. This includes a clear statement about:
   a. "What" customer or client needs the organization is attempting to fill, not what products or services are offered;
   b. "Who" the organization's primary customers or clients are;
   c. "How" the organization plans to go about its business, that is, what its primary technologies are; and
   d. "Why" the organization exists, that is, the overriding purpose that the organization is trying to serve and its transcendental goals.
4. The mission statement should identify the forces that drive the organization's strategic vision.
5. The mission statement should reflect the distinctive competence of the organization.
6. The mission statement should be broad enough to allow flexibility in implementation but not broad enough to permit a lack of focus.
7. The mission statement should serve as a template and be the means by which managers and others in the organization can make decisions.
8. The mission statement must reflect the values, beliefs, and philosophy of operations of the organization.
9. The mission statement should be achievable. It should be realistic enough for organization members to buy into it.
10. The wording of the mission statement should help it serve as an energy source and rallying point for the organization.

All ten criteria must be met for the mission statement to fully accomplish all that such statements can accomplish. They are offered here as a template against which the strategic planning team can evaluate the product of its labors. Although it is difficult to develop a mission statement that can fully meet all ten of these criteria, we firmly believe that to the degree that they are met, the mission statement will have the intended impact on organizational clarity and vitality.

MISSION FORMULATION
AS A PROCESS

While there clearly is a product that emerges from the mission formulation phase of Applied Strategic Planning (i.e., the mission statement itself), it is critical to keep in mind that formulating a mission for an organization is a process. A competent mission formulation is an organization's best attempt to determine its desired future—what products or services it desires to provide, for whom these products or services are intended, and how these products and services will be produced and distributed, all based on the organization's distinctive competencies. Nevertheless, the future is a constant moving target and therefore the organization's mission statement needs to be revisited on a regular basis and modified when appropriate. As the environment in which the organization operates changes and as the distinctive competencies of the organization change, the mission statement may have to be changed to reflect how the organization desires to reposition itself to account for these changes.

Where an organization finds itself in its own life cycle will also impact both the process of mission formulation and its content. Mature organizations can become ossified in their identity and the current mission easily defined. What is often necessary in such cases is a planning process that can help them break out of their traditional pattern and define a future-based mission. On the other hand, young, vigorously growing organizations may need a planning process that sets some boundaries and provides badly needed discipline. As organizations change and develop, they need new, more appropriate mission statements that address their current dilemmas and opportunities. The mission formulation process is a reiterative one.

A dramatic example of a changing mission is provided by the Horn & Hardart Company (H&H), an old-line food service company best known for its Automat cafeterias. Food was displayed behind small glass doors that the customers could open by putting the right coins in the slots next to the doors. The Automats were primarily in blue-collar, urban neighborhoods; and when many of the customers left for the suburbs and operating costs soared, H&H found itself hemorrhaging money. Because H&H either owned or had highly favorable leases on the land on which these restaurants stood, they replaced the Automats with an ever-changing variety of fast-food franchises, none of which solved their problems. To help offset their losses, H&H bought Hanover House, a high-quality, low-cost, direct-mail marketing firm that it largely neglected for two decades except to apply its profits to its corporate profit-and-loss statements.

In 1988, a new chairman was brought in to run H&H. He initiated a strategic planning process that turned H&H into a mail-order company, based on its new-found distinctive competencies. Divesting itself of its restaurant operations over time has bred a new sense of energy and direction at H&H. It is too early to determine how H&H will fare in the long run; nevertheless, it clearly has a new sense of direction. While this shift in the H&H mission was fairly radical, most organizations will find that some revisions in their mission become imperative over time. H&H, in fact, represents the rare case of an organization that became aware of and utilized a completely new competency, one that had been unrecognized since the acquisition of Hanover House. Very few organizations, in fact, have such opportunities. A more ordinary example, one representing typical opportunities, is found in Pitney Bowes as it broadened its mission statement from being in the postage-meter business to being in the mail-automation business. There are innumerable other examples of changing mission statements in every segment of the organizational world. Despite the focus of the mission formulation phase on producing a mission statement for distribution, it is the process that counts, a process that continues over time.

THE IMPACT OF CORPORATE MISSION STATEMENTS

There is general agreement among both practitioners and researchers that mission statements are a critical step in the strategic planning process, and the available research summarized by Pearce and David (1987) suggests that organizations that engage in strategic planning outperform those that do not. Until recently, however, there has been no real evidence on the degree to which the content of such mission statements differentially impacts organizational performance. The research of Pearce and David provides some interesting tentative data on this question. They identified the following eight key components of a mission statement.

1. Target customers and markets.
2. Principal products and services.
3. Geographic domain.
4. Core technologies.
5. Commitment to survival, growth, and profitability.
6. Key elements of corporate philosophy.
7. Corporate self-concept.
8. Desired public image.

By mail, they requested corporate mission statements from each of the *Fortune* 500 companies. Only 218 (44 percent) of the companies replied and only sixty-one (28 percent) sent a mission statement usable for their purposes. Another fifty-eight (27 percent) sent documents that were not mission statements in the sense of this discussion. An additional eighty-eight (40 percent) replied that they did not have a corporate mission statement, and eleven (5 percent) said that it was confidential. The sixty-one available statements were then rated for the presence or absence of each of the above eight components and for their financial performance, that is, whether the corporation's performance was above or below average.

The corporate mission statements of the high-performing organizations significantly differed from the low-performing ones on three of the eight components—more of the high performers included elements of corporate philosophy, corporate self-image, and desired public image. While the results must be regarded as tentative in view of the small size of the sample and the unknown biases that were involved, it is nevertheless provocative that none of the more traditional business issues—markets, products, and the like—differentiated the high and low performers, but the more humanistic issues did. Perhaps, as Tom Peters is fond of remarking about American business, "Soft issues really determine the hard issues." Our own experience strongly supports Peters' view. For example, when Battelle Northwest Labs added the phrase "world class" to its mission statement, it dramatically changed its approach to the marketplace, the kinds of people hired, and so on.

FINAL COMMENTS

The process of preparing the mission statement, the hard work of formulating the mission of the organization, is the critical step. It is an extremely difficult and time-consuming task, one in which the choice of a single word may arouse intense controversy. After all, there is a difference between stating that the organization will be "the leading producer" or simply "one of the leading producers" of a product line. The resulting behaviors stemming from these two different driving forces can be quite different. The development of a consensus on such issues is what mission formulation is all about, and it is a long, tough process. Despite our insistence on the brevity of the mission statement, or perhaps because of it, the process of writing and editing the mission statement and achieving the consensus necessary for its adoption cannot be accomplished in a single session. It is a process that usually extends over several sessions and seems to require some time out between sessions. However, developing a truly functional mission statement is well worth the time and effort, because the organization then has an enormously useful management tool with long-term positive consequences that brings focus and energy to the organization and its members. Without the completion of this phase of the process, no further steps should be taken. Figure 8-4 provides a useful checklist to help make certain that all the necessary steps involved in mission formulation have been taken.

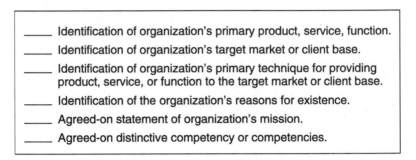

Figure 8-4. Checklist of Necessary Outputs in Mission Formulation

SUMMARY

One of the most important, and perhaps difficult, aspects of strategic planning is formulating the mission statement, which follows the values scan. In developing a mission statement, the planning team must answer the following questions: What functions does the organization perform? For whom does it perform them? How does it perform them? Why does the organization exist? The organization's driving forces and distinctive competencies must also be considered. A draft mission statement must be circulated to relevant stakeholders, and the planning team must reach consensus on the wording of the statement. The mission statement should make most of the members of an organization feel involved and excited. Unit mission statements, which should always be based on the organizational statement, are frequently helpful.

REFERENCES

Drucker, P.F. (1991, June 18). The Big Three miss Japan's crucial lesson. *The Wall Street Journal*, p. A-17.

Gup, B.E. (1979). Begin strategic planning by asking three questions. *Managerial Planning, 35,* 28-31. Reprinted in J.W. Pfeiffer (Ed.). (1991). *Strategic planning: Selected readings* (rev. ed.). San Diego, CA: Pfeiffer & Company.

Hamel, G., & Prahalad, C.K. (1989, May-June). Strategic intent. *Harvard Business Review,* pp. 63-76. Reprinted in J.W. Pfeiffer (Ed.). (1991). *Strategic planning: Selected readings* (rev. ed.). San Diego, CA: Pfeiffer & Company.

Kanter, R.M., & Buck, J.D. (1985). Reorganizing part of Honeywell: From strategy to structure. *Organizational Dynamics, 13*(3), 4-25.

Levitt, T. (1960, July-August). Marketing myopia. *Harvard Business Review,* pp. 45-56. Reprinted in *Harvard Business Review,* September-October, 1975, pp. 228, 33-34, 38-39, 44, 173-174, 176-181. Also reprinted in J.W. Pfeiffer (Ed.). (1991). *Strategic planning: Selected readings* (rev. ed.). San Diego, CA: Pfeiffer & Company.

Peters, T.J. (1984). Strategy follows structure: Developing distinctive skills. *California Management Review, 26*(3), 111-125. Reprinted in J.W. Pfeiffer (Ed.). (1991). *Strategic planning: Selected readings* (rev. ed.). San Diego, CA: Pfeiffer & Company.

Pearce, J.A., & David, F. (1987). Corporate mission statements: The bottom line. *Academy of Management Executive, 1,* 109-116. Reprinted in J.W. Pfeiffer (Ed.). (1991). *Strategic planning: Selected readings* (rev. ed.). San Diego, CA: Pfeiffer & Company.

Prahalad, C.K., & Hamel, G. (1990, May-June). The core competencies of the corporation. *Hatvard Business Review,* pp. 79-91.

Robert, M.M. (1990, Spring). Managing your competitor's strategy. *Journal of Business Strategy,* pp. 24-28.

South, S. E. (1981, Spring). Competitive advantage: The cornerstone of strategic thinking. *Journal of Business Strategy,* pp. 15-25. Reprinted in J.W. Pfeiffer (Ed.). (1991). *Strategic planning: Selected readings.* (rev. ed.). San Diego, CA: Pfeiffer & Company.

Tregoe, B.B., Zimmerman, J.W., Smith, R.A., & Tobia, P.M. (1990). *Vision in action.* New York: Simon & Schuster.

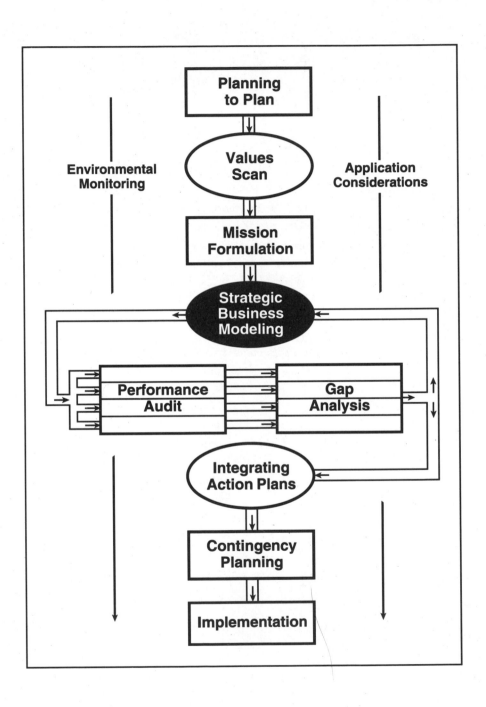

Chapter Nine

Strategic Business Modeling

The best way to have a good idea is to have a LOT of ideas.

Linus Pauling
1958

Strategic business modeling is the process by which the organization more specifically defines success in the context of the business(es) it wants to be in, how that success will be measured, what will be done to achieve it, and what kind of organizational culture is necessary to achieve this success, while remaining consistent with the newly established mission statement. Strategic business modeling involves the organization's initial attempt to spell out in detail the paths by which the organization's mission is to be accomplished and how progress toward achieving that mission will be tracked. Briefly, strategic business modeling produces a concrete and quantified version of the organization's desired future.

In the strategic business modeling phase of Applied Strategic Planning, the planning team is asked to conceptualize a series of specific future scenarios and then to decide which of these futures they wish to achieve. Strategic business modeling is the last opportunity for the planning team to either develop or reshape its vision of an ideal future before getting down to the nuts and bolts of figuring out how to reach that future.

During strategic business modeling, the team will determine the steps necessary for achieving the alternative scenarios, who will be responsible for those steps, and when those steps can be accomplished. The strategic business models that are developed should stem from and be in concert with the overall mission created in the previous phase of the planning process. This phase of applied strategic planning should identify the potential and actual components that can enable the organization to fulfill its mission within its values and philosophy of operations.

There are blocks in almost every organization to taking this strategic view of the future. All too often there is pressure to produce ever-increasing annual profits regardless of the long-term negative conse-quence of this short-range orientation. These pressures need to be ad-dressed directly in terms of short- and long-term trade-offs, the underlying rationale for these trade-offs, and how these trade-offs can be better controlled. Banks and Wheelwright (1979) provide a useful analysis of how this was done in six different companies and offer some concrete advice for managers to use in their management of this issue.

Applied Strategic Planning is distinctly different from long-range planning, and the strategic business modeling phase is the point at which these differences are most clear. Long-range planning is merely an exten-sion of what an organization is currently doing. In a long-range plan an international airline might plan on selling more tickets to new destina-tions through its existing distribution network. A hospital may plan to open a suburban branch. But both of these plans involve only slight variations in or expansion of the product or service offered in existing markets. Such typical long-range planning often is myopic and unduly constraining.

When an organization focuses too heavily on its current products and services and the area of the market that it currently occupies, it runs the risk of overlooking other possible products, services, and mar-kets. Thus, for example, the airline might decide to enter the small-package delivery business, while the hospital might consider preventative health programs. Applied Strategic Planning, with its emphasis on stepping back and envisioning the ideal future of the organ-ization, enables the organization to confirm current directions that are part of a viable future and to explore creative, new directions that would not emerge naturally from the present day's work. When Sony intro-duced the videocassette recorder and the Walkman, it had no informa-tion about the potential market for these products other than these were creative, new products that should meet consumer's needs (Rob-ert, 1990). Strategic business modeling allows the organization's cre-ativity to be applied to the specifics of the envisioned future. The more time spent on strategic business modeling, the more empowering the planning process will be for the organization and the clearer the neces-sary actions will become. As one of our clients noted, "This is where the planning process begins to focus on concrete targets."

STRATEGIC PROFILE

Before we examine the process of strategic business modeling in detail, a number of key factors need to be considered. These factors make up the organization's *strategic profile*—its mind-set or general orientation to strategy formulation. That is, its approach to innovation, its orientation to risk, its capacity for proactive futuring, and its competitive stance are collectively referred to as the organization's strategic profile. Since many of these analyses can profit from technical expertise, especially the futuring and approaches to competition, strategic business modeling is *the* place where technical experts, such as futurists, marketing specialists, and the like, can be brought in to consult with the planning team—but as *experts,* not process consultants. A strong need remains for high-level facilitation by the process consultant who has consistently been engaged in this process.

Innovation

A vision of the future organization should drive the strategic business modeling process, which involves putting flesh on the bare bones of the organization's dream of its ideal future. Without such a vision to drive the process, there is a serious danger that the modeling process will produce just a linear extension of what the organization already is, not what it can be. It is worthwhile, therefore, to begin the process of strategic business modeling with a detailed review of the vision of the future state. Scully (1987), Apple Computer's CEO, described its planning process as projecting Apple at least five years into the future by creating a visual image of what the world economy, the computer industry, and the organization would look like then. Once there was agreement about that future, then the planning group moved back into the present, envisioning what needed to be done to attain that future. This is exactly what we mean by strategic business modeling.

By engaging in strategic business modeling before the performance audit, the planning team will enhance its ability to be *creative* and *innovative* before it must become analytical and critical. We distinguish between the two: creativity involves the generation of new ideas, whereas innovation involves the actual application of those ideas in the real world. In other words, innovation is applied creativity. While strategic business modeling should have a heavy emphasis on focused creativity, this is a useless activity unless some innovations stem from this creativity. Time should be provided for generating free-flowing ideas that are rich in diversity and that stretch normal limits. The best ideas typically surface during the latter part of a brainstorming session, so sufficient time should be allowed for the full development of ideas.

Strategic business modeling allows another opportunity for the planning team to develop a vision, albeit a more focused and targeted vision than was the case earlier. Success in this process is most likely to be found when the planning team restricts itself to areas within the competence of the organization. Multiple possibilities should be explored, but it is neither realistic nor productive to attempt to explore all possibilities. For example, it is much more productive for a manufacturer of steel fasteners to generate ideas that relate to at least the general areas of manufacturing and the production of comparable products than to generate ideas that emphasize retailing or delivery of services—areas in which the organization has little experience or competence. In a process as time-constrained as Applied Strategic Planning, such unfocused creativity would be a costly luxury.

The question here is what lines of business and what possible new activities the organization should engage in. The strategic planning process of a cash-strapped, elementary-school district in the southwestern United States provides a clear example of this process. Both the board of education and the district administrators understood that their principal line of business was providing quality education from kindergarten through the sixth grade but were quite lost as to what else the district might do, especially given its serious financial situation. During a brainstorm session, they began to develop options—day care before the formal school day began, day care after the formal school day was over, adult English-as-a-second-language instruction (the district had a majority Hispanic population), a foster grandparent program, and many others. Not only were most of these programs adopted, but they also turned into modest but important sources of funds for the district. Without the creativity unleashed in this phase of Applied Strategic Planning, none of these would have happened.

The innovative new ideas developed during the strategic business modeling phase will be tested in the gap analysis phase. It is possible, therefore, that many of these ideas will never become part of the strategic plan. Hence, the planning team should be cautioned not to communicate these ideas broadly in the organization as a definite plan. Any mention of them should carry the label of "tentative plans." Here is one place in the planning process where too much openness can backfire.

Orientation Toward Risk

All organizational actions, like all personal actions, involve some degree of risk. As part of strategic business modeling, the planning team is asked to determine the degree of risk that the organization generally prefers and can support. A better understanding of that degree of risk sets an important context for the strategic business modeling phase, one that will underlie many of the decisions that the group will make during the course of planning.

All Actions Involve Some Degree of Risk

Orientation toward risk results from a mixture of forces. The marketplace may dictate high or low amounts of risk for current inhabitants and potential entrants. High-risk markets tend to be those dominated by two or more leaders that are likely to engage in severe competition with one another. The high costs of exiting a market (such as car-rental, magazine-publishing, and airline businesses) also present high risks. If an organization owns facilities that it cannot readily sell, subscriptions or contracts that it must honor, or facilities on which other parts of its organization depend, exiting from that business is more costly than it would be if these encumbrances did not exist. Therefore, when an organization is contemplating entering a market with these kinds of risks, the decision makers must determine the amount of risk, the payoff for success, and whether the organization could withstand failure in the market. See Chapter 10 for a discussion of entrance and exit barriers.

Markets dominated by two or more leaders that are engaged in—or that are likely to engage in—severe competition tend to be high-risk areas for all involved. For the leaders, such competition is likely to cut heavily into profitability; price cutting, expensive advertising, and a struggle to maintain or expand carefully guarded market shares increase the risk of failure. For those not in leadership positions in their markets, the future can be equally treacherous. Not only are economies of scale working against organizations with small portions of their markets, but these differences in market portions are magnified by the fierce competition of the market leaders.

A good example is the soft-drink market, which has long been dominated by Coca-Cola and Pepsi-Cola. This marketplace sees extensive advertising by the two leaders and constant price cutting by those with smaller market shares. Other entries into this market—even Seven-Up, operating with marketing expertise and dollars from its parent, Phillip Morris—tend to capture only small or unprofitable amounts of the market share or fail entirely. As the leaders compete with each other, the others are left even farther behind with their smaller advertising budgets and more expensive costs of operation.

Orientation toward risk is further defined by forces internal to the organization. Internal cash or other reserves facilitate risk taking, as does a strong, diversified organizational market mix. Management must decide its own orientation toward risk. It should ask whether the interests of stakeholders are better served through a more risky (and often potentially more profitable) approach to the marketplace or through a more conservative approach. Another important question is whether the decision makers desire to take a risk position, an issue of organizational culture. Determining the appropriate level of risk taking is discussed later in this chapter.

The planning group needs to assess carefully the risks inherent in a desired marketplace, as well as how those risks are likely to change and how comfortable the organization will be in accepting those risks. Also an assessment must be made of the resources available to support the organization in a risky situation. The desires of the key players—and the interests of those they represent—must be honestly evaluated. Collectively, the personal risk-taking orientation of the planning group becomes the organization's risk-taking posture.

A useful model for jointly assessing approaches to risk taking and creativity is found in Byrd's (1986) *C&RT: The Creatrix Inventory*. Figure 9-1 provides an overview of the model, which allows respondents to plot their scores from the inventory on two dimensions—risk taking and creativity. According to Byrd, those high on both dimensions are *Innovators*, those high on creativity and low in risk taking are *Dreamers*, those high on risk taking and low in creativity are *Challeng-*

ers, and those low on both are *Reproducers,* with a variety of other descriptors for middle-range scores. The instrument is useful to help the planning team understand differences among its members and to produce a composite profile of the group.

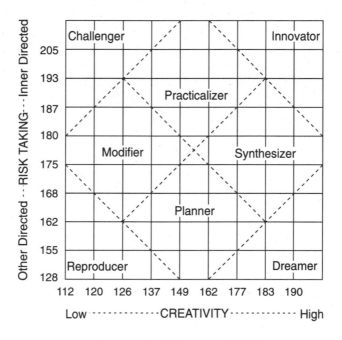

Figure 9-1. The Creatrix Model

Capacity for Proactive Futuring

Strategic business modeling should be done within the context of "proactive futuring" (Ackoff, 1981). Although no one can fully predict the future, significant aspects of the future can be anticipated, a desired end state can be conceptualized, and the organization can work proactively to make this desired future occur. In proactive futuring, the organization takes responsibility for its own future. Rather than guessing what the future will bring, through proactive futuring an organization can balance the skills of anticipating the future and managing itself to attain the desirable goals. Proactive futuring focuses responsibility for the future on leaders and other members of the organization rather than on unseen external forces.

Proactive futuring enables an organization to create a future that might otherwise not have existed. Marketing-driven companies are the most frequently successful organizations in accomplishing such proac-

Proactive Futuring Comes in Many Guises

tive futuring. They determine potential customer needs and develop new products or services to meet those needs. The success of Procter & Gamble in creating the disposable-diaper business by their invention is a good example. Prior to the introduction of Pampers, this type of business did not exist. Procter & Gamble created a different future by its actions. More recently, the wide-spread marketing and use of FAX machines have dramatically changed the nature of organizational communications and further enriched the Japanese electronics industry. Apple Computers created the multibillion dollar personal-computer (PC) industry. As John Scully, Apple's CEO, points out in his discussion of Apple's planning process, "We don't limit idea creation to the practical in the beginning—it can only hinder the possibilities. Wild dreams are transformed into pragmatics later in the process" (Scully, 1987, p. 295).

Competitive Stance

An important aspect of strategic business modeling is defining the organization's competitive stance or its general approach to its competition in the markets in which it has decided to compete. Porter's (1980) work in the area of competitive strategy has become the standard in the field. He describes three generic strategies: differentiation, cost leadership, and focus.

- Differentiation—creating something that is perceived in the marketplace as being unique.

- Cost leadership—achieving overall cost leadership in an industry through a set of functional policies aimed at this basic objective.

- Focus—focusing on a particular buyer group, segment of the product line, or geographic market.

Competition by differentiation requires the development of a unique product or service in the marketplace. The 3-M Corporation successfully competes in the marketplace with its continual stream of new products (witness the success of its Post-it^{TM} products). Others, of course, come along with "me-too" products later; therefore, competing by differentiation requires an organization to produce a constant stream of new products. Competition on a cost basis is the attempt to consistently offer products or services to customers at costs that are lower than those of the competition. Both the K-Mart and Wal-Mart chains have used cost competition as their primary strategy, which helps account for their fierce competitiveness. The focus strategy is practiced by carving out a distinct piece of the marketplace—a niche that is readily defensible—and carefully serving that market segment better than the competition does. Focus strategy was exemplified by IBM when it moved into the PC market with its reputation of quality and service. More recently, as PCs have become more and more a commodity, IBM found it harder and harder to maintain its niche position.

A strategy of differentiation would require a commitment to marketing, a high degree of creativity, strong research and development skills, and a positive product or service image. Control would be less evident. There would be a drive to encourage product or service innovation that would foster the goal of differentiating the organization from the competition.

To achieve a competitive advantage within Porter's framework, an organization must make a series of congruent decisions. To achieve a cost advantage, an organization would typically institute tight cost controls, aggressively pursue innovative ways to deliver services or manufacture products at low cost, pursue low-cost distribution systems, and achieve ongoing economies of scale. Tight control, in general, would be typical. To implement a strategy of focus, careful selection of an appropriate market segment is critical. Having made this selection, the organization would need to develop the appropriate mix of cost and differentiation tactics to achieve leadership. GM's long-term strategy has been one of focus, and GM has been highly successful in that

One Competitive Stance Focuses on a Select Segment

strategy. However, with its market segmentation no longer in place, the organization no longer prospers.

Porter strongly advises that it is dangerous to select and concentrate on more than one of these strategies at the same time. An attempt to be both a cost leader and a differentiated competitor often leaves an organization caught in the middle. Porter gives numerous examples of financial losses or failures that were due to this type of combined strategy. In fact, succeeding with one competitive strategy often obviates another strategy. For example, the controls necessary to become an overall cost leader would most likely eliminate the creativity needed in a differentiation strategy. On the other hand, the expense of marketing and maintaining a well-differentiated product or service often means that the company cannot deliver it to the marketplace in a low-cost manner, negating any hope of cost leadership. Also the selection of one segment of a market means nonselection of other segments. This aspect of focus strategy will often dictate the related moves regarding cost or differentiation.

Organizations in the public and not-for-profit sector have been unaccustomed to thinking about competitors and rarely have included such analyses as part of their strategic planning process. However, those days are over. There are few such organizations that do not have either actual or potential competitors. For example, since the beginning of civil aviation in the United States, air-traffic controllers have been trained at the Federal Aviation Administration's Academy. Those who had been trained during their military careers were sent to the Academy for a refresher course. In 1991 a college-based consortium in the Midwest began training air-traffic controllers, providing a genuine competitor for the first time. Many other similar competitors can be found in other previously public-service functions—waste disposal, fire protection, mail handling, primary and secondary education, and so on. The reasons for the development of such competition are complex, but one universal factor is the belief that others can provide both better and less expensive services than those offered by the current system. Any public or not-for-profit organization that does not include the approach-to-competitors element as part of its strategic business modeling is, in fact, choosing a head-in-the-sand strategy—at its own peril.

In strategic business modeling, an organization must determine how to position itself in reference to competition. As leaders in an organization conceptualize a future, the choice of a competitive strategy is a key aspect of the process. Once the decision is made, this choice further helps to focus the creative process and to identify steps for achieving the desired end state. If, for example, an organization determines that it wants to be a market leader in the greeting-card business (the desired end state), it must determine whether to position itself as a cost leader in greeting cards, differentiate its product line—for instance, by using a particular comic-strip character on all its cards—or focus on a select segment—such as young adults—of the greeting-card market (approach to competition). It must also determine its capability and willingness to risk organizational resources in achieving the desired leadership in the greeting-card industry (orientation to risk).

THE ELEMENTS OF
STRATEGIC BUSINESS MODELING

Strategic business modeling involves establishing clearly quantified objectives of the organization. The outcomes of the strategic business modeling process consist of four major elements:

1. Identifying the major lines of business (LOBs) or strategic activities that the organization will develop to fulfill its mission.
2. Establishing the critical success indicators (CSIs) that will enable the organization to track its progress in each LOB that it intends to pursue.

3. Identifying the strategic thrusts by which the organization will achieve its vision of the ideal future state. Strategic thrusts are organizational initiatives that are neither LOBs nor the CSIs to assess those LOBs; however, strategic thrusts typically can impact LOBs and usually are themselves trackable by CSIs. Examples of strategic thrusts include the development of a total quality management (TQM) process (Sashkin & Kiser, 1991), the creation of a fully functioning human resources department, and installation of a point-of-sale inventory system.
4. Determining the culture necessary to support the achievement of those LOBs, CSIs, and strategic thrusts.

Each of these four elements must be determined and independently worked through during the next two phases of Applied Strategic Planning (i.e., the performance audit and gap analysis phases) and, if necessary, looped back and revised before the planning team moves on to the next element.

Lines of Business

The challenge of strategic business modeling to conceptualize alternative futures is also helpful as a check on prior decisions. Raising questions about what LOBs the organization wants to be in—rather than assuming that the current LOBs should be the future LOBs—will enable the planning team to question and discuss the organization's presence in current markets. Although an LOB may also be a strategic business unit (SBU), one criterion for an SBU is that it has a free-standing accounting system. This may or may not be the case for an LOB. While there can be no absolute criteria for how to differentiate LOBs, it is useful to consider as different LOBs those activities that produce either significantly different products or services or that are directed at significantly different markets.

Every organization, except for the most simple, offers its customers more than one product or service. General Motors offers its five major automotive lines, as well as GM Trucks, and a variety of other products and services, including GMAC (its financing company), Hughes Aerospace, and EDS (its recently acquired data-processing capability). The neighborhood pharmacy offers a variety of nonpharmaceutical products, including a fast-food counter (or at least ours used to). The Social Security Administration (an example from the public sector) offers retirement programs, disability benefits, and health insurance for the aged.

The difficulties in deciding what are LOBs is nicely illustrated by a comparison of the Coca-Cola and Pepsi-Cola corporations. In their rather different patterns of development, Coke has remained completely focused on being a global soft-drink marketing company while Pepsi broadened its mission to become "the best consumer products company in the world" and acquired Frito-Lay, whose snack foods complement Pepsi's soft drinks, and three major restaurant chains—Pizza Hut, Taco Bell, and Kentucky Fried Chicken, all of which serve Pepsi exclusively. The LOB analysis of these two companies would thus be very different, with Coke perhaps conceptualizing its LOBs as its different soft drinks, while Pepsi would have a far more complex LOB analysis to perform. Likewise, each organization has to perform an LOB analysis that fits its unique approach to its mission and the way it conceptualizes its opportunities.

While public and not-for-profit organizations tend not to think of themselves as having LOBs, they in fact do have LOBs. While they might be called functional strategic activities rather than LOBs for their purposes, we prefer to use "LOB" to emphasize the similarities of such organizations with the usual business environment and to further the sense of discipline in the process that such nomenclature connotes. Regardless of what we call it, this diversification of products and services is virtually inevitable as organizations, both private and public, attempt to meet within their own competencies the emerging needs of their customers.

The planning-team members should start by identifying what business they want the organization to be in as they examine their ideal future. Once that has been done, the mission statement needs to be re-examined to determine what additional LOBs can potentially be included in that portfolio of activities in order to achieve the mission. The selection of a new LOB should be based on the existing and nascent distinctive competencies of the organization, the potential contribution of that LOB to the organization's bottom line, and the fit of that LOB into the organization's value system. For example, one would hardly expect Ben & Jerry's Ice Cream Company, with its professed concern for environmental protection, to go into the business of manufacturing nondegradable plastic cups, even though such a new LOB would be a traditionally vertical-integration strategy.

Another important element in bringing a new LOB into an organization's portfolio is the presence of a strong personal advocate for that LOB, someone who genuinely cares about turning that idea into reality and has the personal energy and commitment to follow through. Without such a champion, there is little hope for that LOB, regardless of how much sense it makes for the organization or how many other resources may be invested. New LOBs, like all start-ups, need champions in order to succeed.

LOB Analysis

The LOB analysis involves deciding the mix of products and/or services the organization wishes to offer in the future in order to fulfill its mission. After each such LOB is identified, the relative size of that LOB must be agreed on—in terms of gross revenue, marketing required, profit potential, investment required, and so on. The LOB analyses allow an organization to change its product/service mix—to drop those that the planning team feels are less attractive, have a more limited future, are too far gone in their product-life cycle, or seem incompatible with the new strategic thrust of the organization. For example, as a result of its strategic business modeling, a law firm decided to abandon its maritime-law and patent-law practices, as the firm's new strategic thrust was to focus more on local legal needs that did not require these specialties. In another case a government agency decided on the basis of its planning process to reduce its heavy focus on management-information-system consulting and to begin instead to focus on general-management consultation in order to better fulfill its new mission of providing general-management support. The changing mix of LOBs in these cases arose out of the desired future envisioned by the planning team, not because of poor performance. Similar actions can be taken by an organization as a result of poor performance, but they would occur in the performance audit, not in strategic business modeling.

In a more complex example, Time, Inc., acquired a major producer of paper products—not as a step in vertical integration, but as a countercyclical investment strategy. When Time changed its mission from being a print publisher to being an "information/entertainment company" (through the acquisition of several cable TV businesses as well as HBO and Show Time), its requirements for capital dramatically changed and its LOB analysis led Time to spin off its Forest Products Division to free needed capital for its new LOBs. Lines of business need to be re-examined on a regular basis to make certain that the mix is appropriate to the organization's mission and that they are carrying their weight in accomplishing that mission. It is important to recognize that Applied Strategic Planning is a multi-year process, one that permits the organization to systematically review where it stands and what needs to be done on a strategic level.

The formal portion of the analysis of each of the LOBs, sometimes called the business-case analysis, is not conducted by the total planning group. It is best for a small task force, including some members of the planning group, especially the champion, to conduct this analysis during one of the long breaks between planning-group meetings. The task force needs to develop a detailed business plan for the LOB, including a pro forma, and a realistic analysis of the pros and cons of developing that LOB. Before the planning team adjourns and turns the matter over to the task force, it is important to surface all the concerns that people have about these LOBs. It is extremely useful to appoint a "designated cynic" to each of these task forces—someone who had directly questioned or challenged the notion of that LOB. These designated cynics are extremely useful in sorting out the pitfalls in the plan and finding ways to reduce the risk to the organization. The task force not only saves an enormous amount of time that would be spent in arguing the issues in the planning-group meeting, it regularly produces better plans.

After all of these business-case analyses are completed, the planning group needs to consider all the potential LOBs and make tough, clear decisions about which to embark upon, which should be postponed to a later, specified date, and which must be abandoned. In other words, the aggregate plan needs to be tested against the available resources of the organization, and clear-cut priorities for specific new directions need to be established. This is the core purpose of strategic business modeling.

In considering new LOBs, planning teams sometimes forget the realities of organizational life—that ordinarily things take longer to accomplish than we expect. Typically, organizations have many plans already in motion that precede the initiation of strategic planning and that will be difficult to stop or modify. When sorting out the LOBs, the planning team needs to take these existing plans into account and consider what can and cannot be done within a realistic plan. It is also useful to schedule a "second-chance" meeting, in which all the decisions about LOBs can be revised and a determination made if these decisions are still appropriate in the cold light of a later time. During a second-chance meeting, even previous supporters of a particular LOB are encouraged to poke holes in the idea. This second look enables the team to reject untenable LOBs and augment its problem-solving skills to strengthen those LOBs that it continues to find worthy.

Establishing Critical Success Indicators

As the organization conceptualizes its future, it must identify the specific means of measuring its progress toward that future, setting the critical success indicators (CSIs) for each LOB and then for the organization as a whole (Leidecker & Bruno, 1984). If vision is the *soft* side of strategic business modeling, then CSIs are the *hard* side. A series of pie charts (with each slice representing an LOB) can help the planning team to make that distinction and to analyze the total mix of LOBs by several CSIs, especially potential total revenues and profits, in order to see what potential contributions these LOBs can make to the organization's success, and at what cost.

CSIs are the subgoals or gauges to calibrate the progress toward achieving the organization's mission. The target year(s) for each CSI must be specified if the CSIs are to have any motivating properties for the organization. Critical success indicators are typically a mix of hard financial figures such as sales, margins, and return on investment (ROI) and soft indices of success, such as opinions of customers about service, employee morale, and the attitudes of stakeholders inside and outside the company (see Figures 9-2, 9-3, and 9-4). Figure 9-5 provides a format for developing an LOB by CSI analysis.

Dozens of measures (such as new-product introduction, increased market share, revenue, and profits) can be selected to track progress toward goals. Measures selected during strategic business modeling should be relevant to the organization's mission, to the business the organization will engage in, and to those who are responsible for achieving the defined goals. A limit on the number of measures will facilitate tracking. When all the indicators are selected, they should then be listed in the order of their importance. They will also be used to describe the desired targeted levels of success at the year of the strategic planning cycle (three, four, or five years in the future). Specifying CSIs

Critical Success Indicators	1992 - 1995 Target
1. Profitability	20%
2. Liquidity	No exceptions on payables; $100,000 line of credit; minimum of $15,000 per $1 million in sales or 1 1/2% of revenue.
3. Compensation-to-Revenue Ratio	1984 rate + 10%
4. Size/Growth	>15% but <20%
5. NPD Reserve	No decrease.
6. Employee Satisfaction	At least as good as 1984 audit.
7. Customer Satisfaction	Develop system for monitoring.
8. Inventory Turnover	No worse than for last 3 years.
9. Marketing-Revenue Ratio	Budget on basis of 1989 - 91.
10. Income-Tax Rate	12 1/2% per year (average over 4 years).

Figure 9-2. An Example of Critical Success Indicators - Company A

Critical Success Indicators	Annual Target in Five Years
1. Sales Growth	$100 million
2. Sales per Employee	$100 thousand
3. Pretax Income	5% of sales
4. Cash	Equal to pretax income
5. R & D Expenditures	Not more than 6% of sales
6. General & Administrative Costs	14% of direct labor rate
7. Overhead Rate	200% of direct labor rate
8. Inventory Turnover	3 times a year
9. Manufacturing Parts	Critical parts: manufacture in house; Others: base on cost

Figure 9-3. Another Example of Critical Success Indicators - Company B

Critical Success Indicators	1992 Target
1. Number of Users	30% Overall, 3-County Area
2. Service Expansion	4 New Programs
3. Percentage of Self-Funding	40%
4. Funder Expansion	25% Corporate
5. Volunteer Satisfaction	Match '87 Baseline
6. User Satisfaction	'87 Baseline + 15%
7. Board Profile	Matches Desired Make-up
8. Liquidity	No Exception on Payables; $25,000 Line of Credit
9. Employee Satisfaction	'87 Baseline + 10%

**Figure 9-4. An Example of Critical Success Indicators
from a Not-for-Profit Organization**

by year is critical to the process of making the targets real and trackable. While it is recognized that these numbers are "guestimates," deciding on them makes the process real in a way that nothing else can do.

Prioritizing the CSIs is necessary to assure that the most important indicators will be in focus when decisions are made. If profitability, for example, is a key feature of the mission statement, then it should show up as a high-priority success indicator. Prioritization of success indicators is achieved through consensus of all of the planning-team members so that later support and careful goal setting are ensured.

Lines of Business	Performance Targets		
	Year 1	Year 2	Year 3
1.			
2.			
3.			
Total			

Figure 9-5. A Format for Developing a CSI/LOB Analysis

Figure 9-6 provides common financial ratios that may be applied across most organizations. These ratios are divided into four orientations: liquidity, profitability, activity, and leverage. A number of success indicators that will reflect each of these dimensions should be selected.

Output measures that are not reflected in these financial ratios include industry-specific indicators such as promotion analysis (for direct-mail companies), occupancy rates (for hotels and hospitals), warranty work (for manufacturers), test scores (for educational institutions), and recidivism rates (for correctional facilities). Relevant indicators are best selected after careful study of the business in question. The measures selected should supplement financial ratios in an effort to describe the selected future and to regularly and periodically monitor progress toward this future.

Soft Indicators

The soft indicators (such as the image in the marketplace, customer satisfaction, attitudes of employees, and satisfaction of stakeholders) are also important. Although such measures are frequently hard to gather with a high degree of accuracy, they often represent a major variable in the success or failure of an organization. Any indicator selected, however, must be capable of being tracked.

Time and effort as well as ingenuity are required to develop useful indices in these soft areas, and their development should be tracked. For example, the U.S. Internal Revenue Service (IRS) has the following as part of its strategic plan (1991-1996): "By September 30, 1992, develop a taxpayer burden index that takes into account the time, expense, record keeping, required contacts, professional fees, and other measures of the cost and frustration experienced by taxpayers in fulfilling

RATIO	FORMULA	HOW EXPRESSED
1. Liquidity Ratios		
Current ratio	$\dfrac{\text{Current assets}}{\text{Current liabilities}}$	Decimal
Quick (acid test) ratio	$\dfrac{\text{Current assets} - \text{Inventory}}{\text{Current liabilities}}$	Decimal
2. Profitability Ratios		
Net profit margin	$\dfrac{\text{Net profit before taxes}}{\text{Net sales}}$	Percentage
Gross margin	$\dfrac{\text{Sales} - \text{Cost of sales}}{\text{Net sales}}$	Percentage
Return on investment (ROI)	$\dfrac{\text{Net profit before taxes}}{\text{Total Assets}}$	Percentage
Return on equity (ROE)	$\dfrac{\text{Net profit after taxes}}{\text{Average Equity}}$	Percentage
Earnings per share (EPS)	$\dfrac{\text{Net profit after taxes} - \text{Preferred burdens}}{\text{Average number of common shares}}$	Dollar per share
Productivity of Assets	$\dfrac{\text{Gross Income} - \text{Taxes}}{\text{Equity}}$	Percentage
3. Activity Ratios		
Inventory turnover	$\dfrac{\text{Net Sales}}{\text{Inventory}}$	Decimal
Net working capital turnover	$\dfrac{\text{Net Sales}}{\text{Net working capital}}$	Decimal
Asset turnover	$\dfrac{\text{Sales}}{\text{Total assets}}$	Decimal
Average collection period	$\dfrac{\text{Accounts receivable}}{\text{Sales for year} \div 365}$	Days
Average payable period	$\dfrac{\text{Accounts payable}}{\text{Purchases for year} \div 365}$	Days
Cash turnover	$\dfrac{\text{Cash}}{\text{Net sales for year} \div 365}$	Days
Days of inventory	$\dfrac{\text{Inventory}}{\text{Cost of goods sold} \div 365}$	Days
Price earning ratio	$\dfrac{\text{Market price per share}}{\text{Earnings per share}}$	Ratio
4. Leverage Ratios		
Debt ratio	$\dfrac{\text{Total debt}}{\text{Total assets}}$	Percentage
Times interest earned	$\dfrac{\text{Profit before taxes} + \text{Lease charges}}{\text{Interest charges}}$	Decimal
Coverage of fixed charges	$\dfrac{\text{Profit before taxes} + \text{Interest charges} + \text{Lease charges}}{\text{Interest charges} + \text{Lease obligations}}$	Decimal
Current liabilities to equity	$\dfrac{\text{Current liabilities}}{\text{Equity}}$	Percentage

From Wheelan & Hunger, *Strategic Management & Business Policy,* © 1983, Addison-Wesley, Reading, Massachusetts. Pp. 28-29, Table 2-1. Reprinted with permission.

Figure 9-6. Financial Ratios

their tax burden." This index or soft CSI, in turn, will be used to monitor the decrease in this index over time—a goal devoutly to be hoped for. However, the important point in this example is that there is a CSI for the establishment of a rather different CSI. Without this clarity and the setting of a target date, this later index might never be developed and implemented.

Priorities thus need to be set for establishing these CSIs to make certain that the most important indices will have been established in a timely fashion and will be closely monitored over time. And a tentative timetable for reaching particular levels for each of these indices also must be established. While the performance audit and the gap analysis phases of the planning process will examine the current resources of the organization to meet these new requirements and determine achievability, they need to be spelled out here, at least conceptually.

Strategic Thrusts

Strategic thrusts typically are tasks, processes, or goals that are seen as necessary steps in the achievement of the organization's total strategic plan. Strategic thrusts are best seen as ways of accomplishing the organization's mission. They are neither LOBs, nor CSIs, although these strategic thrusts eventually may have CSIs attached to them. Strategic thrusts may be short-term focused activities or long-term far-reaching ones, ranging from the improvement of the organization's inventory-control system to the development of complex organizational structures such as globalization of the organization's marketplace. In the public sector, strategic thrusts may include quality of service, diversification, or reducing dependence on governmental funding. These are typically regarded as the province of traditional corporate planners and often are all that is meant by "strategic planning." In the Applied Strategic Planning model, however, these strategic thrusts are but one aspect of strategic business modeling.

One such strategic thrust might be the development of partnerships with suppliers. The CEO of Procter & Gamble tells about a production problem with Pampers disposable diapers. The thinness of the rubber leg strips that prevented the Pampers from leaking caused the manufacturing process to creep. This problem was costing the company untold millions until it tried something that was completely contrary to its way of doing business. It invited the supplier of the ultra-thin rubber filaments to visit the plant to help solve the problem. The supplier, after a brief look at the manufacturing problem, proposed what is now known as the "golf-ball" solution: changing the filament to that used in manufacturing high-quality golf balls. This experience led Procter & Gamble to consider dramatically changing its relationship with other suppliers from a distant, uninvolved provider to a true partner, in which shared expertise and a sense of a common destiny link the supplier and buyer into an ongoing relationship. Such a change in how business is done is not a change in LOB but rather a change in organizational strategy, one that can be tracked by CSIs. It is best developed in the context of Applied Strategic Planning.

Strategic thrusts can also be concerned with the integration of processes. Traditionally, vertical integration was considered a sign of a mature, successful organization. This is no longer the case. For example, Compaq (one of the most successful computer producers in the United States) believes its success stems from its strategic decision not to vertically integrate but to buy its technology from anywhere in the world, "to do things in parallel." It created strategic alliances with more than a dozen hardware and software companies, including many of the industry leaders, to provide the expertise and components necessary to produce its work stations. Compaq has thus become a designer, assembler, and marketer of computer work stations, but not a manufacturer of most of their components.

Perhaps the most common organizational strategic thrust, certainly implicitly, is expansion—that is, bigger is better. If the present size of the organization yields a certain level of satisfaction, including profit and income, it is reasoned that any increases in the size of the organization will lead to an increase in that satisfaction. Indeed, once we take the various economies of scale from size into account, the satisfactions should increase at a faster rate than size. Thomsett (1990), however, suggests that this reasoning ignores the risk of falling into an *expansion trap*. He argues that expansion is not automatically a healthy nor a timely process. There are risks involved in expansion, including having to work harder, reductions in quality, the loss of closeness and sense of family among employees, attracting new competitors, and diseconomies as well as economies of scale. Thomsett recommends that organizations be ready for expansion and willing to grow *when* the circumstances are right and prevent expansion when they are not.

We add to Thomsett's list the fact that costs of expansion are typically underestimated. Consider globalization, for example. The costs of establishing a presence around the globe involves considerable expense, even if it is attempted on a modest scale—such as through distributors or agents. The cost of traveling to find distributors or establish offices and creating the necessary legal entities and accounting systems to comply with the myriad regulations is typically seriously underestimated, and much of this needs to be incurred before a single dollar of revenue is realized from this globalization. The learning curve must also be considered, and it is usually less steep than anticipated. Another example of unanticipated costs occurs when the thrust is automation. The cost of software and humanware (training and so forth) is typically four to six times that of the hardware, without even considering the temporary disruption and loss of productivity.

Grand Strategies

Most texts on business strategy identify eight to twelve widely used strategic thrusts that an organization should consider in deciding how to compete in its particular environment. The specific number depends on how the particular author(s) separate or combine the various strategies. Such a list, sometimes called grand strategies, typically include the following:

1. Concentration on existing products or services;
2. Market/product development;
3. Concentration on innovation/technology;
4. Vertical/horizontal integration;
5. Development of joint ventures;
6. Diversification;
7. Retrenchment/turn around, primarily through cost reduction; and
8. Divestment/liquidation—the final solution.

Clearly, the first three of these grand strategies are also organizational driving forces and one can rightly assume that an organization with one of these as its driving force will have adopted that strategy as its method of competing. The other five grand strategies seem more likely to be selected as a function of the planning team's analysis of the requirement of the situation. Chapter 13 ("Gap Analysis") returns to this matter of grand strategies.

A more original analysis of various strategies available to organizations is offered in *Waging Business Warfare* (Rogers, 1987). Seeing business competition in win-lose terms, Rogers argues that a company should follow the same seven strategies that military leaders over the centuries used to defeat their enemies in warfare. These strategies in terms of business warfare are the following:

1. *Leading.* Good leadership is the first requirement of competitive superiority. This leadership needs to imbue the entire organization with a desire to conquer its competition, initiate the neces-

sary action, and be willing to take the appropriate risks. Chrysler's Lee Iacocca and GE's Jack Welch come quickly to mind.

2. *Maintaining your objective; adjusting your plan.* Winning requires focusing on one thing: winning. Once this objective is clearly in mind, the various plans to accomplish this objective—the means to the end—are secondary. GE's objective to be number one in every market it enters, divesting itself of any business that does not have this potential, provides a current example of how this principle is applied.

3. *Concentrating greater strength at the decisive point.* Concentrating on distinctive competencies, on existing successful products and services—as Wrigley, Mars, Exxon, and many others have done—exemplify this principle.

4. *Taking the offensive and maintaining mobility.* Taking a variety of aggressive actions against competitors and not staying on the defensive is the key message of this principle. For example, IBM has regularly tried to keep Apple on the defensive in the PC war, at least prior to its new strategic alliance. Whether or not IBM will continue this strategy, it was a successful grand strategy for that organization for over a decade.

5. *Following the course of least resistance.* This principle encourages finding the competitor's weaknesses and exploiting them. Wal-Mart, in entering the national market, knew that there was high customer dissatisfaction with K-Mart's service. Wal-Mart therefore exploited that weakness by highlighting its superior service to customers.

6. *Achieving security.* When a dormant competitor suddenly shows a burst of activity, the competitor is telegraphing a competitive move. Success depends on anticipating the competitor's plan and hiding one's own response. This strategy requires a high degree of both environmental monitoring and down-board thinking. Procter & Gamble, Frito-Lay, and Wal-Mart excel in this strategy.

7. *Making certain all personnel play their parts.* A small, dedicated army can conquer a much larger, dispirited one, as the United States learned to its dismay in Vietnam. Winning requires rank-and-file commitment. Hoechst Celanese, British Airways, and Eastman Kodak exemplify the utilization of this strategy.

It is critically important that the planning team review the strategies open to the organization and select those that appear to enhance the potential for the success of the strategic plan. Regardless of which strategy—from any of the above or from elsewhere—that a planning-team chooses, it must reach a clear consensus that the chosen strategy is the right one.

The Culture Necessary
to Achieve the Desired Future

Relative to determining the necessary culture two questions are important:

1. What common understanding do members of the organization need to share to create these LOBs, meet their CSIs, and execute these strategies?
2. What kind of organizational culture is necessary to achieve this success?

As Chapter 3 noted, when Colin Marshall became CEO of British Airways, he immediately understood that to become the "World's Favourite Airline," a special kind of organizational culture—one absolutely committed to providing customer satisfaction—was necessary. He regarded the creation of that new culture at BA as his principal task, one that was essential for achieving his vision for the airline.

However, simply articulating the need for a different organizational culture does not provide a sufficient base for producing it. The details of the new culture need to be articulated and CSIs for achieving those specific targets must be specified. For example, another major international airline also determined that a market-sensitive culture was required—one that recognized the critical importance of meeting passenger needs and was willing and able to provide "seamless service." Such service begins with making reservations and continues through arrival at the departure airport, check-in, boarding, in-flight service, debarking, baggage retrieval, and immigration and customs and finally ends with exiting the airport. In order to accomplish this cultural change, the airline set a 20-percent annual increase in customer satisfaction as a CSI. It would be measured by reductions in passenger complaints, data from focus groups and questionnaires, employee reports, and a variety of other sources.

To achieve such a dramatic increase in customer satisfaction, innumerable changes had to be instituted, both within the airline and in a number of related organizations. For example, one of the serious complaints that customers raised was the slowness of the immigration process on arrival at the airline's international hub. The airline set eight minutes as the maximum time a passenger should spend completing immigration and customs procedures. Working with the local government, the airline was able both to increase the number of immigration officers available, which required a substantial annual grant to the government, and to assist in training these officials in customer service. This extraordinary response was duplicated in a number of other ways. The airport authority helped to change the traffic pattern of access roads to the airport, encouraged upgrading the restaurants and snack bars, and so on. Of course, even more changes were initiated within the airline itself. The baggage procedures were revamped by using a bar-code process, installing new equipment, retraining baggage handlers, and so on.

After the culture requirement has been determined, the degree to which such a culture is present or absent in the organization is typically ascertained in the performance audit phase of strategic planning. In both airline cases, however, the need for a culture change and the awareness of the length of time that such a change would take were so apparent that culture-change efforts were initiated immediately, rather than later in the planning process. Ordinarily, however, the performance audit would evaluate the organization's current culture, and the required culture would be compared with the present culture during the gap analysis to see how discrepant the two might be and what could be done to bridge the gap.

One element of the necessary culture that requires careful examination is risk orientation. All organizational decisions involve some degree of risk, and organizations—like people—develop patterns of risk management. These patterns are an integral part of the organization's culture. Start-up organizations are always more willing to take risks than mature, well-established organizations, because they have much less to lose; and people who sign on with a start-up venture are typically risk takers. However, as both the organization and its members mature, there tends to be less and less risk taking as both the organization and the individuals have more to lose. The question of what level of risk taking is necessary in the organization's culture will depend on a variety of factors; for example, the nature of the industry, the competitive marketplace, and the general state of the economy. Here the question is what risk orientation must the organization adopt in order to fulfill its mission in its particular environment at this stage of time.

Application Considerations

Up to this point in our description of the Applied Strategic Planning process, we have urged complete openness, including the organization's rank-and-file. As the planning group moves into strategic business modeling, however, such openness can lead to some undesirable consequences, namely, an erroneous conclusion that some of the items included in the strategic business model—which still require testing in the performance audit and gap analysis phases—are plans set in concrete. Such a false belief can be very disruptive to the organization's operation. Some employees may believe that their jobs will be abolished when certain LOBs are phased out, while others start to bid for jobs in the hypothetical new LOBs. Although those ideas can be part of the strategic business modeling process, only a few of them will even become part of the final strategic plan.

The planning team has the responsibility of deciding how much of this information can be shared. In a mature, sophisticated organization, it may be possible to share most, if not all, of the possibilities. On the other hand, in most organizations it is not prudent to share much of this data. Nevertheless, some information about what has transpired during this phase of strategic planning needs to be fed back to the rest of the organization. The employees can be told simply that a number of new activities are being considered but that they need to be carefully evaluated before final decisions are made. The general approach used in the phase—the development of a variety of new LOBs, the selection of CSIs, the consideration of strategic thrusts, and the cultural requirements—can be explained, but caution should be used in sharing specifics of the potential new shape of the organization.

ROLE OF MISSION, VALUES, AND PHILOSOPHY OF OPERATIONS

While the mission statement spells out the organization's desired future in big, broad strokes, strategic business modeling involves developing specific scenarios for reaching that future. In defining the desired organizational targets immediately after the development of a clear mission statement, the planning team must ascertain that these targets are not only derivative of that mission statement but also that they are in concert with both the values and the philosophy of operations developed earlier. If they are not, the targets must be regarded as suspect and reconsidered.

Mission Statement

As part of strategic business modeling, the planning team eventually must test the congruence between the elements of its strategic business model and the preceding steps in the Applied Strategic Planning model. To be effective, the strategic business model should be congruent with and build on the mission of the organization. To conceptualize a future that is inconsistent with the mission statement is to invite failure. To help maintain consistency, the planning team should post the mission statement prominently during strategic business modeling, and each element should be tested against the mission statement before it becomes part of the plan.

For example, if the planning-team members propose to enter the consumer-electronics industry, this proposal would be tested against the mission statement. If the mission statement did not preclude such a move, this general direction would be further explored. On the other hand, if the mission statement would not permit such a move, the idea would be immediately dropped. Thus, as a concrete example, the change in the Pitney Bowes' mission statement to move into the mail business rather than simply remain in the postage-meter business legitimized its development of the highly successful new equipment for the total automation of mail. On the other hand, quality work during strategic business modeling can result in insights that lead to rethinking and rewriting the mission statement. Although this should be done if necessary, it should be the exception rather than the rule. A strong, clear mission statement ordinarily will not require such modification.

Values and Philosophy of Operations

When there are obvious, important differences between a course of action and the values or the philosophy of operations, one or the other must be changed. For example, a major chemical manufacturer that included operating in an ethical fashion and protecting the environment as elements in its philosophy of operations decided not to acquire a much smaller competitor that was well-known as a serious environmental polluter. Even though this acquisition otherwise fit the growth-through-acquisition mode of expansion that was the nucleus of its mission and produced the right mix of complementary products, the options of continuing to pollute or investing substantial amounts of money in pollution controls made the deal unattractive. Given these alternatives, the ultimate decision was to abandon the deal and look elsewhere.

ENVIRONMENTAL MONITORING

During the strategic business modeling phase, the economic environment should be carefully scanned. Few people are unaware of the impact of the economic changes over recent decades. The initial OPEC oil embargo and the unstable price of petroleum and petroleum products, the recession of the 1980s, unstable interest rates, the fluctuating strength of the U.S. dollar in foreign exchange, and so on, have had both personal and organizational consequences for our entire society and for all organizations. Any organization that became aware of any of these economic trends early and tracked them in its planning process was at a substantial advantage in the marketplace. Organizations need to become aware of macroeconomic trends and to monitor them carefully.

As each LOB is considered, the potential impact of both macroeconomic and microeconomic influences needs to be included in that consideration, especially in the business-case analysis. If, for example, a new LOB is going to require substantial capital investment, then the prospects for raising that capital—through borrowing, equity financing, or leasing—all need to be considered, as do the potential costs of these various options during the period of their use. While the final decisions about moving ahead with these various schemes should be made during the performance audit and gap analysis phases of Applied Strategic Planning, the data needed for the performance audit (as well as the people responsible for gathering the data and the due dates) should be determined during strategic business modeling.

SUMMARY

At the end of the strategic business modeling phase, the planning team should have developed a strategic business model that consists of the following:

1. A strategic profile, including innovation, risk orientation, proactive futuring, and approach to the competition;
2. A set of statements and a graphic representation to identify both the retained and proposed lines of business;
3. A clear, prioritized list of critical success indicators with defined target dates;
4. A list of the strategic thrusts necessary for the organization to achieve its mission, together with CSIs and target dates for initiating these thrusts; and
5. Specification of the necessary culture that the organization must institutionalize if each of the four prior targets are to be reached.

Figure 9-7 provides a checklist for the planning team to use in making sure each of these steps has been taken. All of these pieces should be developed through consensus and should be clearly stated in writing. This information is mandatory for the next two phases, performance audit and gap analysis, of Applied Strategic Planning.

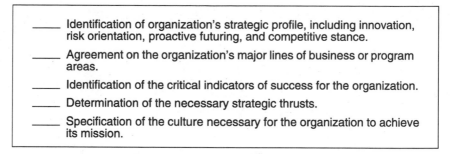

_____ Identification of organization's strategic profile, including innovation, risk orientation, proactive futuring, and competitive stance.

_____ Agreement on the organization's major lines of business or program areas.

_____ Identification of the critical indicators of success for the organization.

_____ Determination of the necessary strategic thrusts.

_____ Specification of the culture necessary for the organization to achieve its mission.

Figure 9-7. Checklist of Necessary Specific Outputs from Strategic Business Modeling

REFERENCES

Ackoff, R. (1981). *Creating the corporate future.* New York: John Wiley.

Banks, R.L., & Wheelwright, S.C. (1979, May-June). Operations vs. strategy: Trading tomorrow for today. *Harvard Business Review,* pp. 112-120. Reprinted in J.W. Pfeiffer (Ed.). (1991). *Strategic planning: Selected readings* (rev. ed.). San Diego, CA: Pfeiffer & Company.

Byrd, R.E. (1986). *C&RT: The Creatrix inventory.* San Diego, CA: Pfeiffer & Company.

Leidecker, J.K. & Bruno, A.V. (1984, February). Identifying and using critical success factors. *Long Range Planning,* pp. 23-32. Reprinted in J.W. Pfeiffer (Ed.). (1991). *Strategic planning: Selected readings* (rev. ed.). San Diego, CA: Pfeiffer & Company.

Porter, M.E. (1980). *Competitive strategy: Techniques for analyzing industries and competitors.* New York: Free Press.

Robert, M.M. (1990, March-April). Managing your competitor's strategy. *Journal of Business Strategy,* pp. 24-28.

Rogers, D. (1987). *Waging business warfare.* New York: Charles Scribner's.

Ross, J.E. & Shetty, Y.K. (1985, February). Making quality a fundamental part of strategy. *Long Range Planning,* pp. 53-58. Reprinted in J.W. Pfeiffer (Ed.). (1991). *Strategic planning: Selected readings* (rev. ed.). San Diego, CA: Pfeiffer & Company.

Sashkin, M. & Kiser, K.J. (1991). *A guide to total quality management.* Seabrook, MD: Ducochon Press.

Scully, J. (1987). *Odyssey: Pepsi to Apple...A journey of adventure, ideas, and the future.* New York: Harper & Row.

Thomsett, M. C. (1990). *The expansion trap: How to make your business grow safely and profitably.* New York: AMACOM.

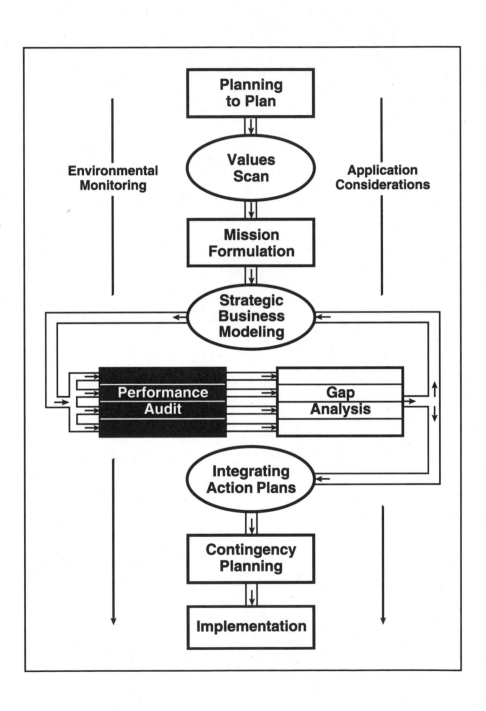

Chapter Ten

Performance Audit

Learn, compare, collect the facts.

Ivan Pavlov
1936

The questions posed by the performance audit are easy to ask but difficult to answer. Having envisioned its future and articulated the strategic profile, the LOBs, the strategies, and the culture necessary to achieve that future, the planning team must evaluate where the organization currently stands on each of these. The gap between the organization's current status and its desired future is the measure of how far it must travel to get where it wants to go. The members of the planning team, like all of us, want such a journey to be both short and sweet. However, before the details of the journey can be planned, the organization's present location must be accurately determined. Coming to a consensual agreement about that location is frequently difficult. Asking for the organization's location is easy; determining its coordinates is much more difficult.

Why is the performance audit so frequently a difficult process? Because it involves taking a hard look at the current status of the organization, the ongoing success of its LOBs (or lack thereof), the validity of its existing tracking systems for critical success indicators (CSIs), and its underlying culture and how it helps and hinders organizational effectiveness. Many of these questions have never been previously addressed with the intensity and thoroughness that must be involved in a strategic planning performance audit, and the prospect of having such a spotlight focused on oneself is often unnerving. In many organizations there is more than a dim awareness that the performance audit will turn over too many rocks, expose too many foibles, and raise issues about too many sacred cows to be comfortable or easy. Yet what is absolutely necessary in the performance audit is honesty and integrity. If defining one's future is one critical element of planning, another is knowing where one is starting from.

It is important for the envisioning of the organization's future through the strategic business modeling process to precede this in-depth analysis of the organization's current performance and capacity. Otherwise, the awareness of the current status can limit the options the planning team considers. Once the strategic business modeling phase is complete, it is time to check those visions against reality. Visions without a reality base are hallucinations. The performance audit is intended to prevent hallucinations.

The performance audit is of critical importance in the Applied Strategic Planning process. The *focused creativity* encouraged in strategic business modeling has likely resulted in some exciting potential goals. The purpose of the performance audit is to establish the bench mark of capability against which these goals can be tested. Failure to do an adequate performance audit could result in a false sense of security—a belief that the organization is more capable of reaching its goals than it really is. This could well mean serious errors in the process of finally establishing strategic goals—and possibly failure to achieve these goals. The purpose of the performance audit is to provide the data for the gap analysis to be conducted—the determination of the degree to which the strategic business model is realistic and workable.

SWOT (STRENGTHS, WEAKNESSES, OPPORTUNITIES, THREATS)

The performance audit is a concerted effort to identify "what is"—where the organization is today. This involves an in-depth, simultaneous study of both the organization's internal *strengths* and *weaknesses* and those significant factors outside the organization that may positively or negatively impact its future, the external *opportunities* and *threats* confronting the organization. A realistic appraisal of where the organization currently stands in these terms is the crux of the performance appraisal phase of Applied Strategic Planning.

The acronym SWOT is typically used to refer to these four internal and external factors. The organization's *strengths* and *weaknesses* are the internal elements, and *opportunities* and *threats* facing the organizations are the external elements. All four factors must be considered in an accurate performance audit. The SWOT analysis is a major way of validating the strategic business model. A SWOT analysis must be completed for each of the actual and potential LOBs the organization has included in its strategic business model and then for the organization as a whole as a final check on the vitality of the total strategic business model. There are other elements that also must be included in the performance analysis. In developing the performance analysis it is useful to consider two broad factors: the internal and the external.

Internal Strengths and Weaknesses

The internal analysis is the process of examining the organization's internal strengths and weaknesses, the first two elements of SWOT. The purpose of this effort is to identify the weaknesses that need to be managed or avoided as the plan is formulated and also the strengths that can be capitalized on in accomplishing the desired future. Many organizations experience some problems in evaluating their internal status. These problems may be due to the inability to identify honestly the weaknesses and to manage the defenses that may surround them, a tendency toward overstating strengths, and/or the general myopia that develops from being too close to a situation.

Few people are excited by focusing on weaknesses, which are often associated with falling short or failure, factors not prized in most organizations. A particular weakness may be associated with a particular person—or may be that person. This factor makes it difficult to identify clearly the weaknesses or to plan the organization's future in light of them. Often a planning team will understate weaknesses or even avoid identifying them, thereby creating a serious flaw in the planning process. The review of strengths can also be problematic if they are understated or overstated by planning-team members who do not have a clear perception of them. It is imperative that the internal performance analysis be competently done, with equal scrutiny to both strengths and weaknesses. The internal performance audit needs to cover at least five key areas:

1. The status of each of the organization's current LOBs and its untapped resources for any LOBs that might be added. This is best determined by reviewing the status of the CSIs for each of the existing LOBs.
2. The status of its tracking systems, that is, the availability of CSIs identified in strategic business modeling.
3. The organization's strategic profile, especially its levels of creativity, its usual levels of risk taking, and its approach to competition.
4. The resources of the system to execute the several strategies that the organization has chosen to achieve its mission, including its structure and its management talent.

5. An analysis of the current organizational culture, including its current way of doing business.

LOBs

The first step in the internal performance audit is to analyze each existing LOB in the context both of the total organization and for each of its separate business units, if such exist. This analysis of existing LOBs should attempt to use the CSIs that were established during strategic business modeling. These attempts will quickly enable the planning team to determine whether or not an adequate tracking system is in place and to plan one if necessary.

One important component of the LOB analysis should be a strategic business unit (SBU) analysis. A strategic business unit is a division, department, or product line that is a business unto itself within the organization; for example, the retail banking operation in a large international bank, the optical department of a large department store, or the group tour division of an airline. The SBU analysis should identify which aspects of the business are losing money, how strengths can be reinforced and weaknesses eliminated, and so on. How the business is organized will determine whether or not an LOB analysis needs to be performed in an SBU. There will be some organizations where SBUs have only one LOB and some where the SBUs have multiple LOBs and thus require additional analyses. For example, if the SBUs are geographic entities and each is involved in a variety of business activities, an LOB analysis will need to be conducted for each of these, but if there is a functional organization of SBUs, that might not be the case.

An interesting example of the importance of such analyses was provided recently by Sears Roebuck, once America's largest retail chain, which has been in the financial doldrums for more than a decade (Caminiti, 1991). Poorly managed with weak cost controls, an out-dated distribution system, and inadequate merchandising know-how, its chain of retail stores constitute one of its SBUs. As part of its strategic planning process, Sears sorted this SBU into seven LOBs: home appliances, home-improvement products, automotive supplies, home furnishings, and men's, women's, and children's apparel. This LOB approach allowed Sears to do something never before possible—determine the profitability of each of these. This analysis, however, required the development of new cost-accounting procedures, which allowed the assignment of real costs against actual sales, rather than using a simple

Some Companies Have Problems Identifying Weaknesses

allocation formula. According to a highly placed Sears executive, "The results were brutally truthful, and we found that a lot of things that we were selling turned out not to be as profitable as we thought." These analyses allowed Sears to take a new strategic direction, focusing its advertising on strengthening the more profitable LOBs, like children's apparel, while attempting to sort out what to do with its less-attractive lines, like men's apparel and home-improvement products. Such actions would not have been possible without the LOB analyses.

To help redirect some of the energy regarding perceptions of strengths and weaknesses, the "Internal Analysis Work Sheet" in Figure 10-1 encourages planning-team members to think about each key component in the organization as having both strengths and weaknesses. Instead of labeling a whole area as strong or weak, members can use this simple format to achieve a more balanced view as well as greater honesty and more detailed information.

The Internal Analysis Work Sheet asks the planning-team members to take two key actions:

1. To review the strengths and weaknesses of an area and identify implications for the strategic planning process.
2. If they identify patterns of weakness or strength, to determine how they want to use these data as the strategic planning progresses.

Internal Analysis Work Sheet

Area Being Analyzed:

_____ Total Organization

_____ Line of Business: _____

_____ Other: _____

Strengths: Weaknesses:

Implications for Strategic Planning Process:

Implication Considerations:

Figure 10-1. Internal Analysis Work Sheet

The Tracking Systems

The internal performance audit, which requires the gathering and studying of a wide variety of performance indicators, is a comprehensive examination of the *recent* performance of the organization in terms of the basic performance indices—cash flow, growth, staffing patterns, quality, technology, operations, service, profit, ROI, cash flow, and so on—that have been identified as critical in the strategic profile. A comprehensive internal performance audit is very time consuming. In relatively simple organizations that maintain strong and numerous outcome measures, it will take the least amount of time to gather the necessary data, but even that level of additional responsibility can be onerous to busy people. Organizations that are more complex will take more time on the performance audit, as will those that must create or gather data not previously tracked. Time will also vary according to the ability of the planning-team members to agree on what the data mean (a discussion prone to "coloring" by individual defensiveness), the ability of key players to give and receive feedback, and the willingness to grapple with unwelcome truths. Figure 10-2 provides a convenient format for the planning team to review the various existing CSIs and their current status.

Instructions: To begin this analysis, list one line of business below and then list its *prioritized* indicators of success, which were identified during your strategic business modeling process. (The numbers in the first column indicate priority.) The "Current State" column is to be completed after this session but before the next.

Line of Business: _____

	Critical Success Indicators	Current State
1.		
2.		
3.		
4.		
5.		

Figure 10-2. Analysis of Lines of Business Work Sheet

Much, but not all, of the data required for the internal performance audit will be available in organizations that have good management information systems, including financial-reporting systems. Furthermore, although data bases may be available (inside or outside the organization), the organization may need to reassign or hire financial staff to research, validate, and analyze the data. Handling and reporting on the data creates a crunch point in many organizations—in terms of time, personnel, expertise. However, it is a critical step that must be completed adequately and on time.

The planning team can also use a variety of tools to survey employees about other issues. The Internal Analysis Work Sheet in Figure 10-1 can be modified to meet specific needs of a particular organization. On the form provided, the planning team is asking those surveyed to focus on the total organization, a specific line of business, or some other component about which information is desired. If an evaluation of strengths and weaknesses in the total organization is desired, employees should be asked to make their comments specific enough to enable planners to identify the particular areas involved. Failure to do so results in suboptimal data utilization, because much of the data may not be interpretable.

Virtually all of this analysis and data gathering will be done outside the planning meetings. While the in-depth discussion of how to interpret the data is best reserved for the planning meetings, the collection and data synthesis are tasks that should be assigned. Although planning-team members may play an active role in this process, it can be delegated to others, especially to staff planners if such exist. Figure 10-3 provides a format that can be used for a checklist to identify what data must be collected, who is responsible, and the dates on which this information is needed. Failure to be specific as assignments are made can lead to frustration, haphazard collection or arrangement of data, lost time, and less solid decision making.

Sufficient time must be allotted to data gathering to allow this considerable amount of work to be accomplished before the next planning meeting. Data must be ready when the planning team meets, and those assigned this critically important task must be held responsible to complete their assignments so that planning meetings will not be postponed nor valuable group time dissipated. The format in Figure 10-2 will enable the planning team to develop an analysis sheet for each LOB and to obtain a quick, clear view of the current state of the LOB—information that will again be used during the gap analysis. The first two columns of such a work sheet can be completed early in the performance audit, and the third column will need to be completed after adequate data have been collected. The format in Figure 10-4 can help the planning team to identify the organization's current position regarding the CSIs selected in strategic business modeling.

Often a general myopia occurs when members of an internal strategic planning team identify strengths and weaknesses. This lack of perspective comes from being too close to the items being discussed.

Data to Be Collected (Be Specific)	Responsible Person	Due Date

Figure 10-3. Data-Gathering Work Sheet

Situations that have been in place for years may be overlooked or underestimated in regard to their positive or negative impact. Entire areas of weakness or strength may be overlooked. This is a point at which an external consultant becomes an invaluable asset to the planning team, pushing them to deal with areas that might otherwise be neglected. What is necessary here is detached objectivity and a willingness to evaluate realistically the internal strengths and weaknesses of the organization, as painful as such an analysis may be.

Strategic Profile

The next step of the performance audit is to evaluate the organization's current strategic profile. At least the following four factors need to be included in the organization's strategic profile:

1. The organization's typical level of creativity;
2. Its prior use of proactive futuring;

Instructions: Fill out a copy of this work sheet for each of the critical success
indicators selected for tracking.

Indicator	Current Level	Time Period Reflected	Comments/ Clarification	Targeted Level

Figure 10-4. Analysis of Critical Success Indicators Work Sheet

    3. Its orientation toward risk; and

    4. Its typical competitive stance.

Where the organization stands on these factors—its strategic profile—
provides a context for understanding how it will go about executing any
strategic plan.

    To what degree has the organization been creative in developing its
LOBs, its products, its markets, and so on? Organizations vary in the
degree to which they welcome and support creativity and innovation.
For example, the 3M Company requires at least one-quarter of the
revenues from each LOB to come from products that are less than five
years old. Critical success indicators at 3M reflect this preoccupation
with innovation, and managers are rewarded accordingly. On the other
hand, each of us can think of at least one organization in which doing
things in the traditional way is the most important element in its way of
doing business. If the strategic business model in such an organization

involves reliance on creativity, it is unlikely to find that long-suppressed creativity. An organization cannot expect a metamorphic change into a 3M overnight.

Proactive futuring involves the organizational mind-set that the future can be shaped by the organization's actions and that it can do better than wait passively for the future to arrive. A strategic business modeling process that involves a dramatic shift in mind-set from passivity to proactivity is more difficult to accomplish than one that merely increases or maintains proactive futuring. The skills in marketing and the comfort level with moving in the face of ambiguity that are necessary for such proactivity take time to develop and that time needs to be factored into the strategic planning process.

Strategic Profiles Must Be Evaluated

Risk orientation is surely the most important factor in the strategic profile. There are certainly elements in the strategic business model that involve risks, perhaps risks that have not even been adequately evaluated. These risks, when considered, may not be acceptable, because that organization may have a habitually lower level of risk taking, a level at which the key members of the organization are comfortable. These habits thus set limits that need to be considered in the planning process.

The organization's competitive stance is also habitual, and the issue is whether the competitive elements of the strategic business model are congruent with that approach. While it is clearly possible for an organization to change its approach to competitors, just as it can change its risk orientation, it is difficult and time consuming to modify these positions. Changing too many of these elements simultaneously is neither possible nor wise, and the strategic profile provides a template for the planning team to hold the strategic business model against to determine its feasibility. There also may be a risk that changing the organization's competitive stance may result in difficulties in exploiting its distinctive competence. For example, if 3M attempted to become a low-cost producer rather than a producer of unique products, that is, moved away from its current differentiation approach, then its distinctive competence would be lost and it would end up with only "me-too" products and seriously erode its customer base.

One could argue that the strategic profile simply represents aspects of the organization's culture. Although that view may not be incorrect, the strategic profile becomes one way of thinking about the organization—about how it has typically approached its environment and how it has achieved whatever success it has attained. Although the organization's culture is involved, the strategic profile provides a necessary opportunity in Applied Strategic Planning to consider the organization on a macro systemic level and is one element of culture that is worth considering separately from the overall cultural analysis.

There is no single agreed-on process for assessing an organization's strategic profile. One approach is for the planning team, with the help of the consultant, to review carefully the organization's recent history, especially how decisions are made and on what basis. Such an analysis is often sufficient to develop a consensual strategic profile. The data collected during the individual interviews that were conducted by the consultant as part of the planning-to-plan process will also help in understanding of the strategic profile. Sharing these impressions about creativity, proactivity, risk taking, and competitive approaches with the planning team helps stimulate and focus discussion about these issues. Also the planning team itself has been a living laboratory for testing these impressions. Providing the planning team with feedback about its own behavior often highlights and illustrates the very issues under discussion.

Resource Analysis

Once the LOB analyses have been completed and the planning team is certain that the necessary tracking system to monitor those LOBs is in place, the team can turn its attention to the resources of the overall system. The desired future of the organization ordinarily involves some new and different activities, some new LOBs, a new approach to marketing, and so on. The question that must be answered first is "What are the current resources of the system?" This includes how competent the current players are, including the management team; where the holes are that will need to be filled and how they can be filled; and what the financial resources for growth are and how can they be augmented.

One of the typical issues uncovered during this aspect of the performance audit is that there are several key actors in the organization whose jobs have grown larger than their capacity to handle those jobs. This is a natural outgrowth of organizational growth. The high-school trained bookkeeper who joined the two entrepreneurs as their first employee and did an outstanding job in that role usually is not the right person to work with venture capitalists on the company's initial public offering. While it may not be necessary to rid the organization of such people, it is necessary both to fill the jobs with people having the necessary competencies and to find other, useful roles for those whose capacities no longer meet the requirements of an expanded role. How the organization deals with such issues needs to be carefully considered, because of its impact on overall organizational morale and productivity.

The LOB analysis may also reveal that certain lines should be de-emphasized, if not eliminated, and this *may* allow some resources to be transferred to other LOBs. Of course, it is imperative to make certain that these people and facilities can perform the tasks necessary in the new LOB or that they can be retrained to perform them. If this is not the case, then the costs of separation must be considered in the resource analysis just as the financial savings from their leaving should be.

Another organizational element to be examined as part the resource analysis is the performance-management system, especially its appraisal and reward elements. Again, a simple question is involved: "What behaviors does the organization's present performance-appraisal system reward and are these behaviors congruent with the organization's mission?" In other words, does the organization's appraisal and reward system help or hinder the achievement of the its mission? In the case of the revitalization of British Airways (Goodstein & Burke, 1991), the CEO quickly came to understand that the BA system rewarded longevity and passivity, not customer service and risk taking, key requirements for the mission's success. Changing the performance appraisal and reward systems became a key ingredient in changing BA into a successful world-wide competitor. Chapter 14 ("Implementation") returns to this important topic.

Some important questions in this analysis of systems resources relates to the evaluation of the organization's present structure: Is the present organizational structure likely to be supportive of the achievement of the new mission and LOBs? Does the form fit the function? Peters (1984) strongly argues that strategy follows structure, rather than the other way around. Nevertheless, regardless of which is cause and which is effect, it is clear that there must be a congruence between the two and the performance audit is the place to check for that congruence. One approach to this problem is to reach outside the planning team and, for example, ask a sample of management and rank-and-file employees what they see as the strengths and weaknesses of the present organizational structure. Small samples may allow the use of individual interviews, whereas larger samples may require the use of a short, written survey or some type of specifically prepared questionnaire.

In addition to the likely discovery of previously unidentified issues involving organizational structure, a fringe benefit of these data from employees is the identification of patterns of belief regarding the internal resources, which may point to areas of relatively greater strength and weakness. In the case of a written survey, if the survey is properly introduced and results are fed back to employees, the employees will probably feel more closely identified with the strategic planning process and its outcomes. This topic also is further addressed in Chapter 14.

Organizational Culture

The performance audit is the point at which the planning team has an opportunity to examine the organization's culture, warts and all. By this time, there probably has been a good bit of discussion of both organizational culture in general and the culture of this organization in particular. The task then is for the planning-team members to knit together the fabric of their understanding into a comprehensive understanding of the culture of this organization. As was the case in the review of the performance appraisal and reward system, the basic question to be answered is how the organization's culture helps or hinders it in the execution of its mission.

One method for organizing the many impressions of the organization's culture is to use the Harrison and Stokes (1992) model for four organizational cultures, those primarily based on *power, role, achievement,* and *support.* These are discussed in some detail in Chapter 3. If further information about the organization's culture is necessary and the Harrison and Stokes instrument has not been previously used as part of the strategic planning process, this is an appropriate time to use it. In any event, the Harrison and Stokes four culture model is a reasonable one for the planning-team members to use to organize their thinking about the culture of their organization and to help them decide on its appropriateness.

Implementation Considerations

Rather than merely identifying strengths and weaknesses as a means of establishing a current picture for the strategic planning process, the Applied Strategic Planning team begins immediately to use this information. While the planning process continues, the organization is encouraged not to accept weak elements, but to begin to shore them up immediately. For example, if the internal fiscal-reporting system is considered weak because of slowness in getting monthly MIS reports in the hands of management, immediate efforts must be made to speed up the accurate processing and distribution of these critical data. With organizations that are increasingly functioning in unforgiving environments, it is necessary but not sufficient to identify relative strengths and weaknesses. Historically, planners accepted these as planning realities without action. Today most organizations cannot afford the luxury of allowing this exposure to continue without action for months or longer as planning progresses.

Taking prompt action on the identified weaknesses also transmits to the organization a powerful message, namely, that top management is taking the Applied Strategic Planning process seriously and that this is not just another exercise in pushing paper. It also indicates that the organization is committed to spending the time necessary to analyze and learn from its prior mistakes. In this connection, we often point out how Joe Montana, the star quarterback of the San Francisco 49er's, views each of his game films over one hundred times in order to catch his errors and correct them. If America's premier quarterback can learn from his mistakes, any organization that expects to succeed in today's turbulent environment cannot afford to do less.

Additional Analytic Tools

A number of concepts and analytical tools can help the planning team understand the current state of the organization and how business is being done. It is unlikely that any organization can or should use all of these in the performance audit, but several should be in the consultant's and planning team's tool kits to be used if needed. These include the product life-cycle analysis, portfolio analysis, distinctive competencies, and total cycle time.

Product Life Cycle. Lines of products or given services progress through a series of stages identified as a life cycle. Basically, the stages are emergence, growth, maturity, and decline (see Figure 10-5). The concept of life cycle is useful in several aspects of the internal-business-analysis portion of Applied Strategic Planning. It is especially helpful in identifying what stage of the cycle each LOB is in and what stage key products or services are in.

The position of an LOB in its life cycle can be analyzed by using a format shown in Figure 10-6. Essentially, the relevant output data (sales, clients served, etc.) are examined to determine historical pat-

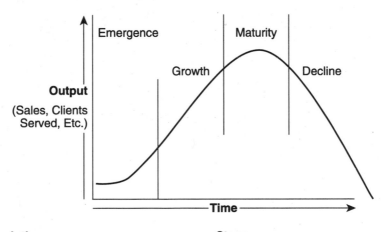

Descriptions	Stage			
	Emergence	**Growth**	**Maturity**	**Decline**
Growth Rate	Accelerating	Faster than GNP	Equal to or Slower than GNP	Declining
Nuber of Competitors	Increasing Rapidly	Increasing; then Shakeout	Stable	Declining
Market Shares	Volatile	Movement Among Top Players	Fixed	Fixed (Except for Exits)
Customer Behavior	Naive Trial	Trial Based on Product Attributes	Price-Conscious; Knowledgeable	Price-Conscious; Knowledgeable
Profitability	Low	High	High	Usually Low
Cash Flow	—	—	+	Varies

Figure 10-5. Stages and Implications of Product Life Cycle

Instructions: Complete a copy of this work sheet for each line of business (LOB). As you work, keep in mind that some stages may occur quickly, that is, a given LOB may proceed from "Emergence" through "Growth" and "Maturity" very quickly.

Line of Business: _____

Output (Sales, clients served, etc.) is:

_____ **Building**

_____ **Stagnant**

_____ **Declining**

If output is building, is it doing so rapidly or slowly?

What patterns in output describe the history of this LOB?

What is the current position of this LOB in its life cycle?

_____ **Emergence** (new LOB/low level of output/output building

_____ **Growth** (output building rapidly)

_____ **Maturity** (output rate of growth decelerating/ stable output/slight decline in output)

_____ **Decline** (output reducing with each time period)

Figure 10-6. LOB Life Cycle

terns. Members of the planning team should answer the questions independently and then work toward a consensus on where in the life cycle each product or LOB is. There may well be variance among LOBs. It may be helpful to seek assistance from an outside marketing consultant if significant disagreement results from team discussions. Often an outsider can help identify patterns that are difficult for insiders to see.

One of the goals of strategic planning should be to develop strategies to extend product life cycle, most typically through innovative enhancement of existing products as well as developing new products. Consider the bathroom-fixture business, surely a mature business. What possibly could be done to enhance that product line? The answer is the "smart toilet," already widely available in Japan. This toilet keeps the seat warm in winter, sanitizes itself after each use, includes a built-in bidet, and is able to perform a series of standard medical tests! Or consider the "smart bathtub," already available from American Standard—a computer-controlled tub that awaits you with warm water as you return from a particularly tense strategic planning session. While these product enhancements are clearly not for everyone, they suggest that applying proactive futuring through vision can change what is typically thought to be the decline of products following their mature phase.

Portfolio Analysis. Several tools have been developed to enable an organization to analyze its various lines of business. The earliest and simplest model is that developed by the Boston Consulting Group (BCG) (see Figure 10-7). In this model, the circles represent business units, and the size of the circles correspond to the volume of sales. The vertical axis represents the growth rate of the overall market in which the unit competes. The horizontal axis signifies the relative market share (the unit's market share divided by the share of the largest competitor). Therefore, only the units that are market leaders will have a relative share greater than one. A product that is low in both existing

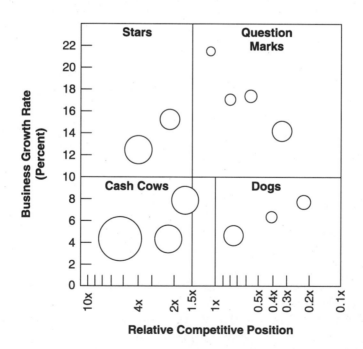

From "Strategy and the Business Portfolio" by B. Hedley in *Long Range Planning* (February 1977), p. 12. Reprinted by permission.

Figure 10-7. The BCG Portfolio Matrix for a Sample Company

market share and potential for future growth is called a "dog," and what one should do with an aged and ailing dog is put it out of its misery. Products that are low in potential but are doing well currently are called "cash cows," and obviously one feeds them to sustain their ability to produce milk or milks them until they run dry! Products that aren't doing well but have high potential need to be developed; these are the "question marks" or "problem children." Those products that both are doing well currently and have high potential are "stars." Obviously we need to celebrate our stars and work to make stars of our problem children.

Figure 10-7 actually represents a modification of the BCG model developed by the planning staff at the General Electric Company. They substituted the gradations on both axes for a simple high-low dichotomy and also the relative sizes of the circles are proportional to the relative sizes of the industry. The BCG model or its GE-amended version is useful in helping an organization understand how to focus its energies, especially its marketing.

Distinctive Competency. Almost all organizations function in competitive environments. To succeed—especially in comparison to others operating in the same marketplace—an organization must develop a distinctive competency or set of competencies that differentiate it from the others. Identifying that distinctive competency or set of competencies is part of formulating the organization's mission.

As part of the performance audit, however, it is necessary to determine how that distinctive competency or set of competencies can be helpful to the organization in executing its strategic business model. Organizations that have clarity about their distinctive competencies and attempt to build on them stand a much better chance of succeeding in their mission than those that are inattentive to those competencies. For example, Marriott's clarity about its distinctive competencies allowed it to rid itself of its cruise-ship and airline-catering businesses and thus to free up both capital and management resources to exploit its distinctive competencies in building and running hotels and other residence units.

Total Cycle Time. Speed is becoming a critically important competitive criterion—speed of product development, product launch, and product delivery. This concept is now identified as *total cycle time* (TCT) (Blackburn, 1990; Thomas, 1990). There are both external and internal benefits from reducing TCT. The external benefits include competitive products that are not easily copied, increased market share, being seen as an innovator, an opportunity to lock up distribution channels, and using new technology. The internal benefits include reducing the learning curve, allowing for more new-product introductions, decreasing inventory costs, and increasing information flow across functional units. As an example, the Buick Division of General Motors can produce a car manufactured according to the buyer's specifications in less than five working days from the time that the buyer enters his or her choices in the dealer's salesroom. This ability to meet promptly a buyer's needs or wants provides Buick with a distinct advantage over its competitors. This capacity to reduce TCT is seen as one of the important emerging competitive factors for the 1990s. The McKinsey organization holds that TCT is one of the "mega strategies" for the twenty-first century. Even if this enthusiastic evaluation is somewhat overblown, TCT is still a strong competitive factor and its importance will increase over the next decade. Examining the organization's total cycle time would thus be worth considering in most performance audits.

External Opportunities and Threats

The performance audit must also include information about outside forces that may impact the organization's goals. These outside forces are the *opportunities* and *threats* of the SWOT analysis. The planning team must study competitors, suppliers, markets and customers, economic trends, labor-market conditions, and governmental regulations on all levels that can affect the organization positively or negatively. This information should include a consideration of both current and future trends—a longitudinal perspective. In chess, this perspective is called "down-board thinking"; in business, the down-board thinkers say, "If I do this, my competitor (or customers, or supplier, or governmental agency, or whoever) will do that, then I will need to..."

Thus, the second major aspect of the performance audit is an examination of the organization's external world. No organization functions in a vacuum; no organization can succeed without customers, clients, or consumers of its efforts. No organization functions without some impact from other organizations in the form of competition, collaboration, or regulation. Although this has always been true, it has never been so painfully obvious to organizations as it is today. At the same time, managers in most organizations are internally focused and have more understanding of the organization's strengths and weaknesses than they do of the opportunities and threats facing the organization. Therefore, these managers must be gently led to broaden their scope of vision through the Applied Strategic Planning process.

Normally, changes in the market have required internally focused organizations to become market driven. Seemingly impervious organizations like utilities, hospitals, universities, and automobile manufacturers are finding their whole futures dictated by forces outside their own structures. For most government agencies, competitors—which formerly were exclusively other government agencies—are now equally likely to be private enterprises.

The Applied Strategic planner must devote significant energy to the examination of pertinent forces in the external environment. No plans should be developed without careful study of these external forces, such as deregulation, demographic shifts, and changing markets. Few plans will work if they do not address both the threats and opportunities that exist in the environment within which the organization must function.

External Threats Should Be Examined

In the Applied Strategic Planning process, the examination of the external forces should be a part of the work of the planning team. As was the case with the internal view, the team may need help. However, unlike the internal process, in which the planning team could actively involve the organization employees in gathering data, it is less clear whom to involve in gathering data on the external environment. Organizations usually have fewer data—and less of a grasp—on the external environment than on the internal environment; and like internal data, external data may well be fraught with bias.

Some organizations put a great deal of energy into tracking external environmental issues such as customer needs, market trends, and relevant legislative activity. If this is the case, these data offer an excellent starting point for the external view. The individuals tasked with such data gathering will become real assets in the planning process; they may be rich sources of data in areas beyond those with which they normally deal. Similarly, organizations with significant customer contact may have a rich source of data with which to work. What is typically needed is a systematic way to organize and regularly review these data—to convert data to information. In most organizations, too much of this organizing and review is left to informal contacts. A system is what most organizations need!

An effective marketing group within the organization may be most helpful to the Applied Strategic Planning process. This group may already be tracking competitor activity, identifying client desires, and accumulating data on products or services that sell well for the organization. Unfortunately, in many organizations marketing people are not involved in the strategic planning process. Although we are not advocating that strategic planning is to be driven by marketing, we definitely are advocating the use of all the expertise available to maximize the quality of decision making. Overlooking potentially pertinent data is not prudent.

Organizations that lack current resources to gather useful data from external sources will need to quickly build, borrow, or buy this talent. Our strong preference is for internal people to maintain control of the process, understand it, and interpret the results of data gathering (with consultant help, if necessary). The development of skills in and orientation toward monitoring the environment should become part of the organization's policy.

A change in the external environment can be either an opportunity or a threat to an organization, depending on its own particular strengths and weaknesses. The bankruptcy of a competitor, for example, can be an opportunity for a financially strong, market-driven organization that sees the loss of an existing competitor as a wonderful opportunity to increase market share by picking up the competitor's customers. A financially troubled, insecure organization could see the same situation as a threat; its lack of resources to increase its own customer base could encourage a stronger competitor to move in and obtain these customers, further weakening the insecure company's competitive position. The bankruptcy might also herald tighter credit controls by banks, squeezing even further the organization's cash position.

In considering changes in the environment, therefore, planners cannot simply divide them into opportunities and threats, because many changes can be either or both. If the organization can quickly regroup and develop an immediate strategy for rising to the challenge of the change, it can turn a perceived threat into an opportunity. Thus, rather than discussing opportunities and threats separately, this section considers several different and concurrent environments in which organizations operate and how these environments provide both opportunities and threats. These environments include the following:

1. The industry environment;
2. The competitive environment;
3. The general environment; and
4. The organization-specific environment.

The Industry Environment

An organization needs to track what is occurring in the environment of its particular industry. By "industry" we mean a group of organizations producing products or services that are close substitutes for each other (Porter, 1980). Understanding these industry trends allows an organization to understand what is happening elsewhere in that industry that may affect its continued vitality and success. For example, a telecommunications company needs to know what is going on in the communications industry; a school system, what is occurring in the field of education; and a restaurant chain, what is happening in the food-service industry. As organizations offer goods or services that can substitute for each other in the same market or to the same potential clients and customers, other organizations become competitors. The competitive environment, however, is dealt with later in this chapter. The present section is concerned with how organizations maintain surveillance over the trends that are likely to affect their industry as a whole.

The factors that can be considered in tracking the industry environment include potential modifications in the industry structure, changes in the industry technology, changes in the presence of the government in the industry, the introduction of new products or services, the development of new applications for existing products or services, the opening of new markets, changes in the methods of industry financing, changes in the availability of raw material or parts, and the possible unionization of a nonunion industry.

To understand how a few of these factors could impact an organization, consider how the structure of an industry would change if franchising became a strong factor in that industry, as it has in the lodging industry and the fast-food-service industry. Also consider how mass utilization of bank debit cards could affect both the financial-service industry and most retail trades. If, for example, income tax laws in the United States and the United Kingdom did not permit personal income-tax deductions for interest payments except for primary dwellings, consider the impact on the vacation-home market and real estate in general. Or, as a real example, consider how the rising price of oil has affected the automobile industry, the petroleum industry, the price of products that have to be transported long distances to the retailers, and the general pattern of consumer behavior.

Galbraith and Nathanson (1978) offer an interesting example of how changes in the industry environment affected the aerospace industry. Through the 1960s technical performance was the criterion on which U.S. defense contracts were awarded, and the price was typically on an actual cost-plus-fixed-fee basis. By the middle sixties, however, the environment began to change. Strong pressures to reduce defense costs began to develop, and the Secretary of Defense insisted that technical performance could be maintained at a reduced cost. Cost effectiveness then became a primary criterion, and contracts were granted on the basis of fixed costs with various incentives for cost reduction. Over the next few years the entire pattern of management in the aerospace industry changed; and project managers who were charged with cost control gained power in the organization over the traditional engineering managers who focused on technical requirements, a trend that is sure to continue with the recent decreased emphasis on defense-related spending.

Data Sources. Because the aspects that need to be monitored in the industry environment are so industry specific, we do not attempt to list specific guidelines for tracking particular industry environments. What is important is that the planning team realize that the industry environment must be monitored both as part of the strategic planning process and as part of management's general responsibilities.

In each industry a variety of journals, magazines, and newsletters provide useful information about what is happening in that industry. Trade shows and conventions are another useful source, particularly to pick up the rumors, guesses, and hypotheses that rarely find their way into industry publications. Federal bureaus (e.g., Census, Economic Analysis, and Domestic and International Business Administration, all under the U.S. Department of Commerce; and Labor Statistics, under the U.S. Department of Labor) issue many reports containing useful industry data. A variety of private research groups, such as the Conference Board, publish occasional papers on various industries. Since there is no shortage of information about the industry environment, the important issue is to develop the organizational commitment to monitor such data in a systematic fashion.

Various electronic data bases (such as Economic Information Systems, a subsidiary of Control Data Corporation; Dataquest, which focuses on the computer industry; and Investex, published by Business Research Corporation of Brighton, Massachusetts) provide information on competitors' dollar revenues, market shares, number of employees, industrial facilities, and so on. These services charge fees but are legal sources of information. One such source is the PIMS program, developed by the Strategic Planning Institute of Cambridge, Massachusetts, which compares an organization's strategic indices with those from a two-thousand-company data base, thus providing comparative data on strategic strengths and weaknesses.

The Competitive Environment

Of special importance to organizational viability and success is the monitoring of the competitive environment, that is, keeping track of those organizations that do or can provide substitute goods and services to the same marketplace. Without systematically and thoroughly monitoring this competitive environment, organizations are at direct risk. Competitors typically attempt to increase their shares of the market by taking customers away from other organizations. Without an early-warning system to detect such competitive strategies and without skills to develop adequate countermoves, organizations may lose significant market shares and resources for continued health or even survival.

One of the most important sets of data is the competitor analysis, which profiles organizations that are in the same business or aiming for the same market segment of clients or customers. The competitor analysis should include *creative crossovers*—items that are sold or services that are delivered for similar reasons. For example, one of the chief competitors of Cross pens during the holiday seasons is not another pen manufacturer but the billfold industry, because both pen-and-pencil sets and billfolds are frequently purchased as holiday gifts for men. Movie theaters compete against cable TV and video rental shops (Robert, 1990). Because the competitor analysis usually requires some research and—as an additional benefit—an increased awareness of the marketplace, we recommend that each member of the planning team have responsibility for conducting an analysis of one to three competitors. An *overall* competitor analysis could hide more than it revealed; therefore one *must* be done for each of the organization's LOBs, both current and potential. As Robert (1990) points out, it is extremely important to take a broad view of one's potential competitors and their strategies and then to manage one's own strategy accordingly.

Michael Porter (1980), America's foremost analyst of competitive strategy, argues that there are five basic competitive forces that determine the intensity of competition in any industry:

1. Intensity of rivalry among existing competitors;
2. Threat of new entrants;
3. Bargaining power of buyers;
4. Bargaining power of suppliers; and
5. Pressure from substitute products or service.

Although all five forces should be considered in monitoring the competitive environment, most organizations tend to consider only one or two. Because an understanding of these forces is essential to a successful monitoring of the competitive environment, each will be briefly examined.

Competitive Rivalry. Competition among existing organizations, the most easily recognized and understood of the five forces driving competition, typically takes the familiar form of price wars ("Special this week only: new lower prices!"), competitive advertising campaigns ("Quality is Job 1!"), new product introductions ("The computer you already know how to use"), and increased customer service or warranties ("Only our cars have a 7-year/70,000-mile protection plan"). As competitive rivalry increases and customers become more and more sophisticated, customer service has become more and more a factor in that competition. British Airways initially learned to its sorrow that its poor quality of customer service was a major factor in its deteriorating market share but was able to increase that service so that it is now a competitive advantage for BA (Goodstein & Burke, 1991). Measuring customer service and satisfaction must be part of every performance audit, even in nonservice industries like manufacturing. In fact, customer service has become so important today that *every successful* business is in the service business (Ross & Shetty, 1985).

Rivalry increases because one organization feels pressure to improve its position or sees an opportunity to do so. In most cases, a competitive move by one organization precipitates a countermove by the other(s) most threatened by this action. This in turn sets off an escalating pattern of moves and countermoves that often leaves all the organizations in the industry worse off than had previously been the case.

This negative effect of increased rivalry is especially true when the principal competitive strategy is pricing. Price cuts are typically matched by the competitors (consider the price wars in the deregulated industries, e.g., long-distance telephone service, interstate trucking, and airlines). Advertising wars and the other competitive strategies, contrariwise, often produce increased customer demand and benefit the entire industry.

Another example of price wars is seen with great regularity in the airline industry. One airline—usually one that is experiencing financial difficulties—announces a new discount pricing structure. Newspapers carry full-page advertisements by that carrier and, for a few days, it has an advantage over its competition. While the competitors can change their own prices immediately, it takes several days before they can mount their own competitive response. Although this is industry knowledge and the short-term advantage is often more than offset by the reduced margins, this almost suicidal practice occurs with great regularity.

Potential Entrants. The second competitive force is that posed by potential entrants into the industry. New entrants bring new vigor, new resources, and a strong desire to gain a market share. They may be new organizations, but more often they are large organizations that are seeking new opportunities for growth in a related business (such as Procter & Gamble when it entered the frozen-citrus-juice industry with its new brand, Citrus Hill) or in an unrelated business (such as Mobil Oil when it acquired Montgomery Ward). What is important to recognize is that a competitor may enter the scene from some unexpected quarter, and the planning team needs to consider potential sources of new entrants into the industry.

In considering such potential entrants, the planning team needs to recognize that there are barriers to entry (see Figure 10-8) that may make the industry resistant to incursions by outsiders. These include economies of scale, capital requirements, product differentiation, switching costs, access to distribution channels, cost disadvantages, and governmental policy. In general, economies of scale for manufacturing, operation, and so on, are possible only during the mature phase of the product's life cycle. Thus getting started is expensive and unprofitable, requiring not only capital requirements but also perseverance. Product differentiation is opposed by established brands and consumer brand loyalty that may be difficult to change. Other barriers to entry are the additional costs that potential buyers would incur if they switched to an entrant's products or services. For example, consider the time and psychological costs in switching one's personal physician, dentist, or accountant.

Still another barrier to entry is access to distribution channels. Nowhere is this more apparent than in most retail businesses, where prime

Exit Barriers

	Low	High
Low	Low, stable returns	Low, risky returns
High	High, stable returns	High, risky returns

Entry Barriers

Figure 10-8. Barriers and Profitability

shelf space is the continual object of fierce competition. There are also cost disadvantages that can outweigh any economies of scale. The most important of these is the learning or experience curve in operating a particular kind of organization in a particular kind of industry. Costs decline as both workers and managers gradually become more efficient, but the lack of this experience is one of the costs of entry. Another entry barrier may be governmental policy, especially in those businesses that are regulated to some degree by government.

In addition to entry barriers, there are exit barriers—obstacles that keep organizations in competition even when they would prefer to leave the industry. These exit barriers include specialized assets, such as factories or equipment that have low liquidation value; fixed costs of exit, such as long-term labor contracts or long-term subscriptions that must be fulfilled; strategic interrelationships between the business unit and other units in the company that provide parts or raw materials, image, financing, and so on; emotional barriers, which include pride or loyalty; and governmental or social restrictions to closing down.

Although entry and exit barriers may be independent, they combine to affect the level of threat from potential entrants. Where both entry and exit barriers are low, there will always be a high risk of potential entrants. With low entry barriers and high exit barriers, there will be fewer potential entrants but not as few as with high entry and low exit barriers. The risk of potential entrants is lowest, of course, with high entry and high exit barriers.

Bargaining Power of Buyers. As Porter (1980) points out, buyers compete with the industry by attempting to drive down prices, by demanding concessions, by insisting on higher quality or additional services, and by playing suppliers off against one another. All of these activities impact the profitability of the industry. This form of competition is typically not recognized by organizations, yet it becomes very important when there is a large-scale buyer or group of buyers that represents a significant portion of the organization's revenues.

In the United States, the Federal government is attempting to increase its bargaining power as the largest purchaser of health care through Medicare. Sears is noted for its strong control over those manufacturers who produce for Sears' private-label merchandise. Porter's analysis strongly suggests that environmental monitoring should include a close look at the organization's customers, especially changes in customer patterns.

Bargaining Power of Suppliers. Not only do buyers compete with an industry, but so do the suppliers. They can impact an industry by raising or threatening to raise prices or by reducing the quality or availability of goods or services. Such moves, of course, dramatically impact profitability, especially when the industry cannot raise prices enough to cover the increased cost. The potential impact of suppliers on an industry is increased when the supply is dominated by a few vendors, when there are few substitutes for what is provided, or when the industry is not a major customer of the supplier group. The impact of the OPEC cartel on those businesses producing petroleum-based products, such as plastics, is an example of the importance of suppliers as part of the competitive environment. The behavior of suppliers also requires routine surveillance as part of the ongoing environmental monitoring.

Substitute Products or Services. All organizations compete to some degree with organizations offering substitute products or services. The degree to which there are clear alternatives to the offered products or services puts a ceiling on the prices that an organization can set for those goods or services. The increased sales of poultry and fish when the price of beef becomes "too high" is a case in point. The determination of what are reasonable substitutes from the consumers' point of view and the relative availability and price of those substitutes should be considered in monitoring the competitive environment.

Understanding how substitute products or services can impact an organization often requires using human sources as well as the usual printed ones. The customers, vendors, and distributors of one's competitors are often excellent sources of information about competitors' current and future strategies, as are their advertising agencies. Another prime source of information is ex-employees. Some organizations actively recruit new employees from their major competitors primarily as an information source about the competitors' future plans. One major competitor of IBM is proud of its reputation as a home for IBM "retreads" and is always actively recruiting new transfers from "Big Blue."

"Shopping" the competition is another useful, informal source of information; and this may include purchasing goods from a competitor and engaging in reverse engineering to learn more about the competitor's material and methods of production. For example, U.S. military forces have purchased captured Russian military equipment from the Israeli defense forces in order to conduct such reverse engineering studies and field trials with the Russian equipment. Obviously, many companies are unlikely to cooperate with sharing strategic information with their competitors, and many may actively attempt to prevent their competitors from learning about their present and future strategies. Nevertheless, there are ways to obtain a good deal of useful and pertinent information without resorting to unethical or illegal practices.

Monitoring the competitive environment is a complex task, and there are aspects of this environment that are frequently overlooked. A comprehensive, in-depth monitoring of the competitive environment is a task that should be high on the management's list of tasks, both for planning and for everyday management.

The General Environment

Organizations function in an environment that can be readily divided into two:

1. The general economic, social, and political environment; and
2. The organization-specific environment.

Both are critical to understanding external forces impacting the organization.

Although it is important to be aware of national economic and political trends, it is also valuable to focus on regional economic or sociocultural trends. For example, an organization can find itself functioning simultaneously in a national economy in which interest rates are moderate, business good, and the outlook optimistic and in a region where—because of its agricultural focus—the economy is down, unemployment is high, and loans are hard to obtain.

In the performance audit, the examination of the general environment is purposeful: It is an attempt to understand which important forces impact the organization today and which may significantly impact the organization in the future. The strategic planning team should artfully address these forces and use them effectively in the planning process. These actions can occur only if the forces have been clearly identified.

The Organization-Specific Environment

Porter (1980) identified three distinct ways in which the organization can compete: through differentiation, cost, and focus (or segmenting the market). As the performance audit progresses, it is important to identify how the organization has met the competition. Figure 10-9 illustrates some key components of the five-pronged competitor analysis framework developed by Porter. The questions it poses can form the

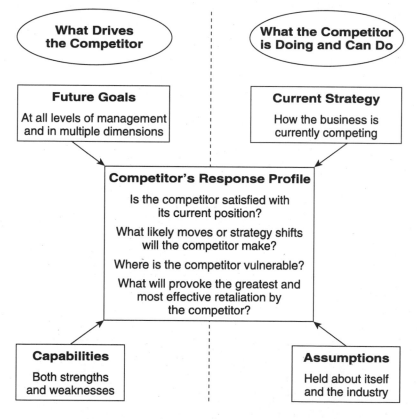

Reprinted with permission of The Free Press, A Division of Macmillan, Inc., from *Competitive Strategy: Techniques for Analyzing Industries and Competitors* by Michael E. Porter. Copyright © 1980 by The Free Press.

Figure 10-9. The Components of a Competitor Analysis

basis for an analysis that can be tailored to a particular organization's competitive universe.

Understanding the competitive environment is critical to success in Applied Strategic Planning. It provides the basis for the identification of opportunities and threats; it also provides the basis on which the plan can be built, and it represents a constantly changing backdrop against which the plan must be adjusted. Particular conditions in the competitive environment dictate the success or failure of certain tactical moves.

Using Porter's model to determine where to look for competition, the planning team can identify current and potential competitors. It is critical for the planning team to focus beyond the current state and to begin to identify the competition two, three, and four years into the plan.

When the current and potential competitors have been identified, they should be sorted into high, medium, and low threats. This sorting enables the organization to put more energy and resources into the study and tracking of the most important of all the potential competitors. Those classified as medium or low may still be tracked to keep data current and to catch competitive changes that may cause a competitor to grow in importance.

Noncompetitive Aspects of the Industry Environment

Although it is critical to constantly track competitors and new entrants into the marketplace, analysis must go much further when dealing with the industry environment. Among the things that should be studied as part of strategic planning are the following:

1. The customer;
2. The availability of key raw materials;
3. The current marketing mix; and
4. The industry life cycle.

As the planning-team members study competitors, customers, economic trends, and governmental regulation, they must keep in mind that they are trying to identify both threats to the organization and opportunities on which the organization might capitalize. Opportunity identification has demonstrated itself to be difficult for many planning teams. Typically they are more adept at identifying threats in the environment than opportunities. One might speculate why this is the case, but what is more important is that the planning team may find itself most in need of assistance from the consultant at this point.

Ease of Exit

Earlier in this chapter we discussed the varying degrees of difficulty in entering or leaving a given market with regard to competitors. The planning team should also look at its own organization with regard to the ease or difficulty of exiting its particular markets. This will provide important information for the performance audit. Pertinent questions would include the following: Is the organization in markets that would be difficult to exit? How deeply entrenched in current markets is the organization? If the organization exited a given market, what might the consequences be on the image of the organization—its perceived reliability, stability, competence, and so on?

END PRODUCT

The performance audit and subsequent analysis are some of the most detailed and time-consuming aspects of the strategic planning process. However, without this important, detailed information, the basis for planning is incomplete and shaky. In addition, the need for candor, openness, and nondefensiveness during the performance audit cannot be overestimated. An organization that fools itself during the performance audit is almost certain to find itself with an unworkable plan. Obviously, under such circumstances, the time and effort put into the strategic planning process will result in a travesty.

The end product of a quality performance audit is an overall review of all systems from a macro perspective. Creating this will take time, energy, patience, and commitment, but without grounding the strategic planning process in the organization's current reality, the future will not be built upon a solid foundation. Figure 10-10 provides a convenient checklist to verify that all the necessary steps in the performance audit have been taken.

SUMMARY

Before any detailed plan for an organization's journey into the future can be implemented, the organization must accurately determine its present location. The performance audit is intended to provide the exact coordinates of the organization's location on the important, relevant dimensions, including its internal strengths and weaknesses and its external opportunities and threats—the traditional SWOT analysis. The external environment in this case includes the general economic environment, the industry environment, the competitive environment, and the organization-specific environment.

_____ Determination of how the performance audit will be conducted in terms of data types, responsibilities, and schedules.

_____ Identification of organizational strengths and weaknesses relative to direct competitors, to be considered in validating the strategic business model.

_____ Identification of opportunities and threats within the environment, to be considered in validating the strategic business model.

_____ Measurement of the current performance of the organization relative to its performance targets, establishing a performance gap.

Figure 10-10. Checklist of Necessary Outputs from Performance Audit.

The performance audit is frequently difficult, because it involves taking a hard look at the current status of the organization, including the success of its current LOBs (as well as its resources for new or different LOBs), the quality of its tracking systems for its CSIs (as well as the organization's current performance on each of these CSIs), its strategic profile, and its current organizational culture.

REFERENCES

Blackburn, J.D. (1990). *Time-based competition: The next battle ground in American manufacturing.* New York: Dow Jones-Irwin.

Caminiti, S. (1991, July 15). Sears need: More speed. *Fortune,* pp. 88-90.

Galbraith, J.R., & Nathanson, D.A. (1978). *Strategy implementation: The role of structure and process.* St. Paul, MN: West.

Goodstein, L.D., & Burke, W.W. (1991). Creating successful organization change. *Organizational Dynamics, 19,* 5-17.

Harrison, R., & Stokes, H. (1991). *Diagnosing organization culture.* San Diego, CA: Pfeiffer & Company.

Peters, T.J. (1984). Strategy follows structure: Developing distinctive skills. *California Management Review, 26*(3), 111-125. Reprinted in J.W. Pfeiffer (Ed.). (1991). *Strategic planning: Selected readings* (rev. ed.). San Diego, CA: Pfeiffer & Company

Porter, M.E. (1980). *Competitive strategy: Techniques for analyzing industries and competitors.* New York: Free Press.

Robert, M.M. (1990, March-April). Managing your competitor's strategy. *Journal of Business Strategy,* pp. 24-28.

Ross, J.E. & Shetty, Y.K. (1985, February). Making quality a fundamental part of strategy. *Long Range Planning,* February, 53-58. Reprinted in J.W. Pfeiffer (Ed.). (1991). *Strategic Planning: Selected Readings* (rev. ed.). San Diego: Pfeiffer & Company.

Thomas, P.R. (1990). *Total cycle time: An overview for CEOs.* New York: McGraw Hill.

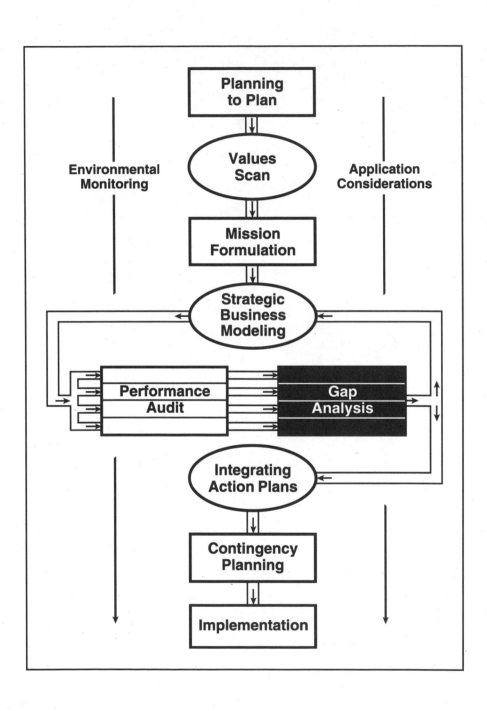

Chapter Eleven

Gap Analysis

An error is more the dangerous the more truth it contains.

Henri-Frederic Amiel
Journal, 1883

Although generally there are difficult moments in every phase of Applied Strategic Planning, the gap analysis is typically the "moment of truth," a moment that can upset and dishearten even the most hard-boiled members of the planning team. After the performance audit is completed, it is necessary to identify gaps between the current performance of the organization and the performance required for the successful realization of its strategic business model.

This gap analysis is a *reality test,* that is, a comparison of the data generated during the performance audit with whatever is required for executing the organization's strategic plan. Furthermore, the gap analysis requires the development of specific strategies to close each gap identified. In fact, if the gap analysis reveals no disconcerting discrepancies between the organization's future goals and its present performance, then the planning process thus far has been inadequate; the planning team simply did *not* reach *far* enough in its visioning and strategic business modeling. Thus, every gap analysis will have its difficult moments.

Gap analysis is the truly critical step of the Applied Strategic Planning process, when the probability of successfully implementing the plan gets assessed. Gap analysis is an active process of examining how large a leap must be taken from the current state to the desired state—an estimate of how big the "gap" is. The "analysis" provides the answer to the question of whether the skills and resources at hand are sufficient to close the gap—to achieve the desired future within the proposed period. If this analysis suggests that the gap is not bridgeable, then appropriate action must be taken to reduce that gap. The consultant's role is to make certain that the data are adequately analyzed and appropriate action plans are created to close the gap.

Gap analysis is a time for careful, considered decision making. If the gap between the current state and desired state seems too large to close, then either the desired future must be redefined, with a refocus on those aspects of the strategic business model that are accomplishable, or creative solutions for closing the gap must be developed. For each gap that cannot be closed by a readily apparent strategy, the planning team must *return* to the strategic business modeling phase and rework the model until the gap can be closed. Several repetitions of this process may be necessary before the observed gaps can be closed. The mission statement may also have to be modified in this process. This cycle is graphically illustrated in the Applied Strategic Planning model with an arrow that leads from gap analysis back to strategic business modeling or, when the gaps are finally manageable, on to the next steps of the planning process.

CONSULTANT'S ROLE

There are essentially two general approaches to reducing gaps in an organization's strategic business model: One is to modify or reduce the goals—the transactional solution; the other is to reduce the identified obstacles that are responsible for the gap—the transformational solution. As a colleague in strategic planning consultation is fond of pointing out, "Transformational solutions require letting go of the trapeze bar." Organizations generally bring their habitual preferences for either a transformational or a transactional approach to the gap analysis, and the consultant may need to remind the planning team of the other option.

The gap analysis tends to be a relatively straightforward process. However, as the planning team compares its proclaimed "business we want to be in" with its current state, there is a tendency for *group think* to develop; that is, the team members may become overly positive and collude to overlook significant gaps between current and desired states, gaps that may indeed not be closable. On the other hand, the team may see gaps that it concludes are not closable, whereas creative thinking could determine ways to close them. An important role for the consultant at this point is to help the planning team avoid either or both of these planning traps.

When the planning team has set goals that are too optimistic—goals that are well beyond the organization's ability to achieve—recycling to strategic business modeling becomes necessary. This recycling, how-

Closing the Gap May Require a Transformation

ever, can be frustrating to team members. A strong feeling can develop that "We've done all that before, and it didn't work; so why will it work this time?" Nonetheless, reworking the strategic business model is critical until all the detectable gaps are closable. Therefore, this is a time for the consultant to be firm in moving the team back to the issues it needs to resolve.

OUTCOME OF GAP ANALYSIS

The expected outcome of the gap analysis is a strategic plan that has a reasonable probability of success. The purpose of the gap analysis is to bring the test of today's reality to the dreams of tomorrow. Priorities must be based on the normal limits of available resources. In any organization, the equipment, people, dollars, and other resources are finite. As the result of gap analysis, these resources should be properly committed to the pattern of activity that has been determined to have the highest organizational payoff.

Resource limitations are not the only factor to consider. Elements of the strategic business model will fit the organization to varying degrees. Some will readily be assimilated into the organization, its historical mission, its lines of business, and its culture; others will not. The gap analysis must consider each of the elements of the strategic business model for both resource availability and fit with the existing organization. While we are not suggesting that only those elements of the strategic business model that are easily integrated be retained, neither are we suggesting that we can transform organizations overnight. Actions that stretch both the available resources and organizational fit are what are required, not kamikaze heroics.

ANALYZING THE GAP

Gap analysis is the detailed examination of the distance between each element of the strategic business model and the current state of the organization as revealed in the performance audit. Specifically the gap analysis asks the following questions:

1. How does our desired strategic profile compare with our current one?
2. How do our planned LOBs fit with our existing ones and with our resources, both current and planned, to bring them on line?
3. Where do we stand on our current CSIs and what does that tell us about our capacity to meet our new ones?
4. What are our current strategies and what do they tell us about our capacity to execute our new ones?
5. How different is our existing culture from the required one?

The gap analysis must also answer those questions, not simply ask them.

A Hypothetical Example

Gaps may be observed in response to each of these questions. Consider the hypothetical case of the Epsilon Company. During strategic business modeling, the Epsilon planning team might have described the desired state in the following, measurable terms:

> In five years Epsilon will have annual sales of $30 million spread across four lines (two of which will be new). We will have a pretax profit of 15 percent with an annual growth rate in sales of 30 percent. To accomplish these goals, we intend to display a strong orientation to risk, which is necessary as we shift from the development of scientific equipment for the professional field to more consumer-oriented electronic product lines, an area just beginning to grow. We intend to succeed by becoming a low-cost leader. We will reduce costs of manufacturing and institute tight controls to assure our goals of cost competitiveness.
>
> Our priorities are as follows: (1) growth (increased market share), (2) ultra-effective internal cost-control systems, and (3) profitability.

As the Epsilon planning team completes its performance audit, it must examine its current position on each of the key dimensions of the plan. Assume, for example, that the quick (and incomplete) "current state" of Epsilon indicated the following:

- Current annual sales, $13.9 million,
- Pretax profitability, 4.6%.
- Current growth rate, 25%.
- Family-owned firm with conservative history of manufacturing select, professional, scientific equipment.
- Current product sales, based on excellent quality, to a select group of physicians' offices, hospitals, and scientific laboratories.
- Current product lines in mature and declining stages of their life cycles.
- Strong loyalty among current customers, who trust Epsilon and its products.
- Strong R&D group fairly free to explore/develop new products.
- Company weakness: Products take longer to produce and cost more than initially planned.

The Epsilon planning team would need to identify and analyze a series of gaps. It would need to consider the following factors, among others:

- Time available to meet the CSIs: five years.
- Overall goal: to move company from specialty R&D/manufacture of quality scientific equipment to competitive manufacture of consumer-oriented science-related products.
- Increase in sales: from $13.9 million to $30 million.
- Improvement in pretax profitability: from 4.6% to 15%.
- Improvement in growth rate: from 25% annually (unadjusted for inflation) to 30% annually.
- Other moves: from conservative to high-risk style of operation; from competitive stance typified by "differentiation" to a stance of "low-cost leader."

Although these lists do not constitute all the dimensions of the strategic business model nor all the aspects of the performance audit, the flavor is there. The strategic planning team would proceed to esti-mate the dimension of each gap, trying to identify whether it could be closed in the time and with the resources available. If a gap could be bridged, the planning team would carry it into the strategic plan as stated in the strategic business model and then move on to consider another gap. If it appeared that a particular gap was too large to close or that no clearly apparent strategy to close it was available, then the planning team would, by necessity, move back to the strategic business modeling phase for an adjustment of that particular element of the model.

In the Epsilon example, several of the gaps pose serious problems. The intention to move from a conservative to a high-risk profile is likely to collide with the core values of this family-owned firm. Unless the fear of decline in the current LOBs was strong enough to override these traditional values, it is unlikely that such a shift in Epsilon's basic orientation to the marketplace would occur.

The Gaps Can Pose Serious Problems

The proposed improvement in profitability also seems unlikely. To triple profitability while switching to a new—probably more cost-conscious—market is difficult. While striving for an annual growth rate of 30 percent and, at the same time, relegating it to a third priority, Epsilon would find the increase impossible to achieve. There are costs of learning a new market—products that will not succeed, competitive pressures that were not anticipated, etc.—that are not factored into the team's projections. If the 15-percent profitability were important for funding growth, this element would be even more dangerous to the overall success of the Epsilon plan.

One might argue that the Epsilon example is too extreme to be realistic. However, the enthusiasm and optimism of planning-team members during strategic business modeling could enable them to generate an ideal future like the one outlined here—one fraught with large, perhaps even massive, gaps that could not be closed. Too often the planning group becomes overly optimistic—especially when considering entering a market that it does not yet understand. While the Epsilon executive could wax eloquent for hours about why a 4.6-percent profit was reasonable in their present market, they simply know so little about the consumer market, that 15 percent looks likely! Our experience indicates that the Epsilon case clearly and credibly illustrates the pitfalls to avoid through gap analysis.

To simply agree that this outcome is achievable, especially in light of the issues we raised, could lead to a disaster for Epsilon. The consultant's role is to raise these questions and help the planning group address these issues. A skilled consultant will help the planning-team members to maintain their enthusiasm while rethinking their future until each of the gaps can be closed and necessary action plans developed.

Key Considerations

Several key considerations exist at this point. When a gap is being examined, the question of whether it can be closed must be asked realistically. The question is really "Can this gap be closed, given all the other things we are seeking to do?" Also, it is possible that insights gained during the gap analysis will cause the planning team to recycle all the way back to the mission statement. In addition, a gap in one area may lead to the identification of gaps in other areas.

Another significant issue in the gap analysis is whether or not there is alignment between the strategic business model and the values scan. Such a comparison is necessary in order to ascertain that the actions the organization is proposing are consistent with its culture. As already noted, plans that do not take into account and build on the organization's culture are not likely to succeed. This portion of the gap analysis requires the same degree of openness, candor, and confrontation that should have typified the original values scan. The gap analysis is important in this regard, because it contrasts the organization's wants against reality; in effect, it is the anchor that keeps the plan from floating off in an unguided, or misguided, direction.

One element that typically arises in planning for organizational growth is how that growth is to be attained. Chandler (1962) identified four approaches to growth that arise sequentially in the development of the organization:

1. Expansion of volume;
2. Geographical dispersion;
3. Vertical integration; and
4. Product or service diversification.

Chapter 14 ("Implementation") describes these in greater detail. Nevertheless, it is important to identify in the gap analysis which of these approaches has been adopted, explicitly or implicitly, and then to determine if the present structure of the organization is adequate to successfully execute that approach as part of the strategic business model. In other words, does the form fit the function? Without such a fit, it is highly improbable that the organization can successfully carry out its plan. For example, the dynamic growth that was part of Epsilon's strategic business model would require a less hierarchical structure, a separate marketing function, and less reliance on the family as a source of expertise. Epsilon's form clearly did not fit its newly planned function.

Gaps also occur in the strategic plans of not-for-profit organizations. For example, Regis University, a small Jesuit school in Denver, was on the brink of financial ruin when its new president saw the need for strategic planning. The gap analysis quickly revealed that its typical market segment, recent high-school graduates, was in decline and would not increase in the near future. However, the gap could be closed through developing a new market: adult education. Regis developed a highly successful niche-marketing strategy, one that involved segregating the adult students from the typical younger students, who tended to be less serious, and bringing accelerated-degree programs to community centers, close to concentrations of businesses. This successful strategic closing of the gap has enabled Regis to increase its enrollment from one thousand students to over eight thousand and to have an annual budget surplus, despite a serious and costly effort to upgrade its campus facilities.

ADDITIONAL ASPECTS OF GAP ANALYSIS.

As an organization examines the feasibility of the goals it set during strategic business modeling, several conceptual tools can be applied effectively. Though simple in concept, they are useful in estimating the amount of risk in a particular move—a critical aspect of gap analysis.

These tools are the "Y" model, the "Z" model, and the analysis of entry/exit barriers.

The "Y" Model

The first such tool—the "Y" model—is a variation of the simple "who, what, how, and why," model (see Figure 11-1) initially discussed in Chapter 8 ("Mission Formulation"). During the mission formulation phase of Applied Strategic Planning, the planning team develops a mission statement by using this model to describe its desired future. During gap analysis, the planning team should develop a "who, what, and how" diagram for each major LOB in the strategic business model, but there is no reason to re-examine the "why," the organization's reasons for existence.

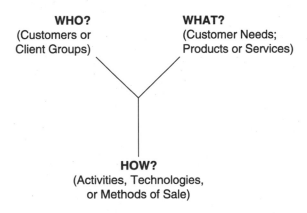

WHO?
(Customers or
Client Groups)

WHAT?
(Customer Needs;
Products or Services)

HOW?
(Activities, Technologies,
or Methods of Sale)

Figure 11-1. The "Y" Model

Having completed the "Y" model for each LOB in the business plan, the team compares each of these to the one developed during mission formulation as a test of how far that LOB is from the overall mission. The projected LOBs should be compared with each LOB in the current business so the team can determine how many of the three dimensions have changed. Changing only one dimension (with whom business is done or what is sold or how business is done) carries the least risk. Changing two dimensions at once is more risky and, in most cases, is imprudent. A three-dimensional switch generally turns out to be foolhardy even if the organization has massive resources to learn simultaneously about new customers, new products, and a new delivery system. Changing all three is equivalent, in effect, to a new-business start-up.

The "Y" model is a quick test for conceptually identifying a potential gap. It should be used to identify potential problems, to give the team direction regarding areas requiring further investigation, and to help the team plan the reduction of a potential gap. This application will be discussed later in this chapter in conjunction with ways to close the gap. However, the planning team should be cautioned to use this tool carefully, because there clearly are situations in which changing only one dimension could be a disaster, whereas there are other very selected cases in which simultaneously changing all three dimensions could succeed. Convincing another person that the changes will be less traumatic than they actually will be is sometimes easy. The consultant's role is critical in maintaining careful and open discussion that leads to the exercise of good judgment. Applying the "Y" model to the Epsilon plan suggests how this could occur. The Epsilon plan involved changing the product (what) and the market (who)—from scientific products for professionals to consumer electronics—and the approach (how)—from a technology leader to a low-cost provider. Thus, using the "Y" model suggests that adopting Epsilon's strategic business model would involve a high degree of risk, even if all the other elements of the gap analysis raised no serious issues.

There are also rare instances in which the product is of such high quality, the market so ready, and the new delivery system so well suited, that it is possible to change all three dimensions at once and still find success. The entry of IBM into the minicomputer market in the late 1970s with the introduction of the IBM PC is an outstanding example of such a success. A new product (a personal computer) was introduced to a new market (individual users rather than organizations) by a new method of sale (through retail stores rather than sales representatives). Again, an alert planning team may be able to spot such an opportunity regardless of warnings posed by the model. Such situations are very rare—far more rare than most excited champions of new products would admit. Any such dramatic move must be carefully examined for flaws. Before such an approach is adopted it is necessary to determine whether the payoff is commensurate with the risk. While the IBM-PC venture entailed risk, IBM saw the risk as moderate because of the corporation's enormous resources. A smaller, less well-endowed organization would have to see the risk quite differently.

The "Z" Model

Another useful model is illustrated in Figure 11-2 (the "Z" model). Essentially, this model classifies customers and products according to

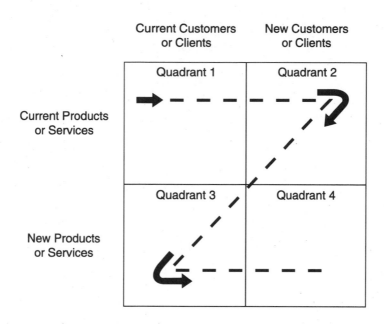

The "Z" model of increased risk was developed by John M. Simonds of Martin-Simonds Associates, Seattle Washington. The Matrix of "current clients-current services" originally appeared in "Strategies of Diversification" by H.I. Ansoff in *Harvard Business Review,* September-October, 1957, pp. 113-124.

Figure 11-2. The "Z" Model for Business Expansion

the same two dimensions: current and new. According to this model, there is least risk in concentrating organizational efforts in Quadrant 1, that is, in selling more current products or services to current customers. The next in magnitude of risk is Quadrant 2 (selling current products or services to new customers), and the next most risky is Quadrant 3 (selling new products or services to current customers). The most risky is Quadrant 4: selling new products or services to new customers. The "Z" comes from drawing a line through each of the quadrants according to the degree of risk. The farther an organization travels down the Z, the higher the risk.

Applying the "Z" model to the proposed Epsilon strategy reveals that their proposal lands them in the lower right quadrant of the "Z," indicating the highest possible risk. If such a risk is unavoidable, the organization must clearly recognize the risk involved and be willing to take a bet-the-organization approach.

The risk in delivering new products or services to new customers is one of the reasons for the high failure of new businesses—which, by definition, are using this strategy. On the other hand, a new product line that appeals to a new customer base could present such an attractive market niche that pursuing the high-risk course would be desirable. The model enables members of the planning group to sort risk factors and gives them a chance to compare the organization's risk orientation with the desired subcomponents of the strategic business plan. To enter into a strategy of higher risk, the organization should have both a style of willingness to take risks and the availability of resources to support this style.

Another dimension that should be examined at this point is the degree to which LOBs are interrelated and how they are related to the types of business they do. Developing LOBs that have a common theme is frequently a valuable strategy. This common theme can enhance profitability by providing opportunities for economy of scale through procurement of goods or services across LOBs. Organizations tend to be more successful when operating with related—or interrelated—parts. Organizations with LOBs that fit a common theme have an enhanced possibility of achieving synergy across the LOBs.

Entry/Exit Barriers

As Chapter 10 ("Performance Audit") noted, different businesses have different degrees of difficulty in starting and liquidating a business. These are typically known as entry and exit barriers (see Figure 10-8). In the gap analysis, attention needs to be paid to both of these in order to prevent the organization from being overly attracted to opportunities that have prohibitive entry requirements or that might be difficult to abandon if they do not meet expectations.

There are many entry barriers in regulated businesses; for example, one cannot simply start up a radio or TV station. A governmental license is required and there are many hoops to jump through before one is ever issued. Even in deregulated industries there are entry barriers. While anyone with sufficient resources, itself a significant barrier, can now start an airline in the United States, the lack of landing slots at most major airports poses another significant barrier to entry. The availability of certain resources, facilities, equipment, trained personnel, and capital also can be entry barriers.

The difficulties in leaving an LOB cannot be ignored. For example, when the American Psychological Association purchased the now defunct magazine, *Psychology Today,* the issue of barriers to exit was never raised. When the financial burden of supporting the magazine became excessive, the financial obligation posed by the prepaid subscriptions, over $8 million dollars, was an exit barrier. Unless the Association was able to find a willing buyer, closing down the publication would have entailed repaying the subscribers for their unfulfilled subscriptions, an unacceptable burden. Thinking through the exit barriers prior to entering into this LOB would almost certainly have led to a different decision about acquiring the magazine in the first place.

In analyzing the gap, the planning team needs to understand and apply the entry/exit barrier paradigm to both any new LOB that they are considering and any existing LOB they want to abandon. Such an analysis will enable the planning team to evaluate the potential risks involved in these actions and also the potential financial return.

MEANS OF CLOSING THE GAP

There are multiple ways to close the gap between the organization's current state and its desired future state. Generally, these options will fall into either a growth or a retrenchment category, depending on the relationship of the current organization and its desired future. If growth is necessary to achieve the goals of the strategic business model, options are internal expansion, a new business start-up, an acquisition, a merger, or a strategic alliance. If the strategic business model calls for retrenchment, options are divestment, phase-out, phase-down, or turnaround.

At this point a division may emerge as team members who are tied to role-driven, turf-protection efforts see implications for their areas of responsibility. The consultant should work to acknowledge and manage this tendency as much as possible. Focusing on this problem may be helpful if it does not promote dishonesty or abuse, because it can contribute to later commitment to the plan, which can come only with an honest belief in the feasibility and desirability of the plan.

Closing Gaps Resulting from a Growth Orientation

There are several ways to close gaps resulting from a growth orientation.

Internal Expansion. Internal expansion is often typified by reasonable risk and steady growth. Significant growth from within requires a good deal of financial and other resources. These may be internally identified and committed, or they may come from outside the organization—often at significant costs. Internal expansion is a reasonable way to close the gap if products or services are strong, market share seems to be subject to expansion, and resources are at hand. Products or services offered should be desirable in their marketplace and—if possible—technologically superior to those now available. Planners must keep in mind that current competitors will not view expansion of market share as favorable and will tend to respond aggressively. This factor must be a key consideration in selecting this strategy.

New Business Start-Up. A new business start-up is a growth strategy with a relatively high risk attached to it. On the "Z" model, it is Quadrant 4—selling new products or services to new customers. If the new business is completely separate from current lines of business, risk is highest. If it is in tune with current business, risk may be reduced, because current products or services may help presell the new business. For example, when Sears, Roebuck & Company, which traditionally had been a chain of retail stores, added a giant new business, the Sears Financial Network Centers, it believed that its experience with its Allstate Insurance subsidiary put it in tune with its current business. It thus added Coldwell Banker Real Estate and Dean Witter, a major stock brokerage, to go with its already existing insurance operation. While there was considerable doubt about the wisdom of this strategy on the part of many, the past decade has proven that it was a wise decision indeed. In fact, the Financial Network Division of Sears is currently its most profitable, while its retail outlets, as noted earlier, are in decline.

Knowledge of the interests and needs of customers or clients may also help lessen the risk. For example, Sears knew that many of its middle-class, middle-aged customers were interested in purchasing stocks, bonds, and other securities but were reluctant to approach the brokers who sell these. Sears quite correctly believed that their customers would approach brokers in the more familiar Sears stores. Despite the original disbelief of the financial community, the Sears-Dean Witter connection has been a highly successful one, the general disarray of the U.S. financial industry notwithstanding. Nevertheless, the planning team should show care in selecting this growth strategy. If selected, creative effort should be placed into the means of reducing the risk. The new business should be run by an individual who understands start-ups and who has the freedom to make decisions necessary for success; and there should be a carefully designed, supportive relationship with the parent organization.

Acquisitions and Mergers. Acquisitions or mergers are techniques that often accelerate the attainment of growth goals. Used properly, these approaches can quickly close a gap. Concern must be shown, however, in examining the value of these modes of growth. It is possible to close one or two gaps through an acquisition but to fail in other areas of identified gaps. For example, it is possible to grow in total sales while failing to achieve profitability goals defined in the strategic business model. Care and creativity typify the fully successful acquisition or merger. This move should be made with a specific view to the high priority goals of the strategic business model.

Special attention must also be given to the match of organizational cultures between the two parties. The majority of business acquisitions and mergers do not turn out well, and more than half are reversed within three years. The primary reason for these commercial divorces is the incompatibility of the cultures of the two organizations. The merger of the Fireman's Fund and American Express made all kinds of business sense, but the incompatibility of the values of the two organizations, discussed in detail in Chapter 7, led to an early and unhappy divorce. The planning team must examine acquisition and merger proposals carefully, both from business and compatibility points of view.

Strategic Alliances. One of the major changes in today's strategic environment is the changing view of an organization's relationships with competitors, vendors, and customers. At one time these relationships were seen as necessarily adversarial. Organizations are now much more open to considering a variety of alternatives, especially strategic alliances. A strategic alliance is a mutually beneficial relationship between two or more organizations to share information and resources in order to advance and develop all parties involved. Badaracco (1991) suggests that the traditional view of the organization as a medieval fortress that invents, owns, controls, and finances all its strategic assets is now outmoded. Instead, he offers the Renaissance Italian city-state as a more appropriate metaphor in these equally turbulent, dangerous, and confusing times. These city-states, like Milan, Venice, and Florence, had open and porous boundaries, very different from the fortress. Such boundaries require a complex, changing network of strategic alliances for survival. This new perspective helps managers understand that collaboration is now the name of the game and that they must develop skills in developing and sustaining these alliances; that is, they must develop diplomacy rather than implements of war.

One of the biggest surprises of the early 1990s was the strategic alliance between IBM and Apple Computers, once hated rivals in the microcomputer segment of the computer industry. While it is far too early to determine the viability or the benefits of this alliance, the question of how this could have happened remains. While Apple pioneered the microcomputer and IBM extended it into the business world and turned it into the enormous business it is today, both IBM and Apple have fallen upon difficult times. In the organizational marketplace, buyers insist that PCs work together in networks, regardless of the make or

A Strategic Alliance Is a Mutually Beneficial Relationship

model. This has hurt Apple with its proprietary software, but it has hurt IBM as well, as buyers chose to buy IBM clones at a much-reduced cost. The new strategic alliance is intended to develop a new generation of operating software that will drive both IBM and Apple PCs, allowing them to be part of the same network in an organization. While there are many who doubt that anything important will come from this alliance, its very creation suggests the potency of such alliances as another way of closing a gap.

A different set of strategic alliances have been established by Procter & Gamble, long known as a tough bargainer, even sometimes a bully, in its relationships with its retail-sales outlets. Recognizing the mutual advantage of just-in-time inventories, P&G has changed its posture and formed partnerships with several of the major retail chains, like K-Mart and Wal-Mart, in an effort to cut costs in the long pipelines that connect manufacturers to consumers. Cross-functional teams from P&G and the other organization—teams composed of data-processing experts and marketing and sales people from both sides—work collaboratively to automate and integrate both order and financial records, enabling warehousing and shipping costs to be substantially reduced. Procter & Gamble estimates that such a partnership can save it over one billion dollars annually and just as much for its major customers.

Organizations do not need to be the size of IBM, Apple, P&G, or Wal-Mart to develop strategic alliances. In Washington, D.C., nine downtown, highly competitive, up-scale restaurants combined their resources to develop the A la Carte Express. The Express allows people to make one call to a central number to arrange home or office delivery of food from one or more of these restaurants, reducing the costs of order taking and delivery service for the seller and allowing a wider variety of choice for the user.

The opportunities for strategic alliances are becoming more numerous as organizations seek to shrink their support services that are not value added. For example, Commodore Computers turned its postsales customer-service function over to Business Logistics Services, a subsidiary of Federal Express (Fed Ex), which provides a twenty-four-hour help line for Commodore. If the customer's computer needs service, Fed Ex drops off a replacement, picks up the broken computer, and often repairs it at its Memphis hub. The customer, impressed by the prompt, reliable service, never knows that he or she is dealing with Fed Ex, except when the delivery person arrives. Commodore is saving 50 percent of its prior service costs. IBM has developed a similar relationship with Fed Ex to handle its small spare parts in order to both provide better service and contain costs. In both of these cases, a threat to one organization provides an opportunity to another. Kanter (1989) provides a theoretical model and numerous additional examples of such alliances, which the interested reader can use for an additional resource on this important topic.

There are additional options for potential relationships between an organization and the others in its environment. The planning team, in considering how to close the gaps in the strategic business model, needs to be both aware of such possibilities and creative in attempting to develop them.

Tactics for Closing the Gap

Four highly specific tactics for closing gaps between the organization's current and desired state should be considered when the planning team identifies gaps that need to be closed and when the plan is clearly in the growth mode:

1. Lengthen the time frame for accomplishing the objective. This tactic should be considered if the current allocation of resources is appropriate and if it will take more time to achieve these aggressive goals than initially planned.
2. Reduce the size or scope of the objective. This tactic applies when the vision was appropriate but lesser or somewhat modified objectives are more achievable and less risky.
3. Reallocate resources to achieve goals. This tactic is appropriate if the goals can be achieved only by rallying existing resources that have been spread too thin.
4. Obtain new resources. This tactic should be considered when new talent, products, markets, or capital are necessary to achieve desired goals.

Decisions regarding the ease of closing a gap should not be taken at face value. It is easy to say, "Well, we'll just find the resources," or "We'll just go out and hire the talent we need." Delivering on these airy promises is more difficult. Therefore, these difficulties *must* be factored into the decision-making process.

Down-Board Thinking

All movements to expand must be done with down-board thinking—examining the impact on the market and on competitors who share the marketplace. Since it takes time to accomplish a change in market share, many things can happen during the process—not the least of which might be the emergence of a competitor that is planning to expand its own market share. Down-board thinking enables the planning team not only to identify the current state, but to anticipate the condition of the market as it will exist in the future.

Porter (1980, 1985) stresses the need to plan strategy carefully around competitive realities. He encourages planners to anticipate the important factors of tomorrow and stresses that retaliation should be expected. He also coaches his readers in the tactics necessary to meet each of the varied potential challenges.

Closing Gaps Resulting from a Retrenchment Orientation

The markets in which all organizations, both profit and not-for-profit, operate are constantly changing. Although these changes sometimes mean growth and opportunity, at other times they may mean decline in size of market and potential sales. It is as critical to properly identify a market that is losing its potential and to respond as it is to spot a new market and leap into it. The natural optimism of most managers and planners often interferes with the identification and early response to such downturns. Indeed, one constant feature of business life is the "expansion trap" (Thomsett, 1990), the belief that "bigger is always better and the market will never head South, certainly not on my watch"; the belief that there is no downside to any market, any deal, or any industry.

If the gap dictates retrenchment as part of the strategy, an entirely new set of tactics must be considered, such as *downsizing* (more properly called *rightsizing*), *divestiture*, and *shut down*. These tactics are frequently seen in a highly negative light, because often they are tied to failure. This mind-set could lead to serious delays in acting on necessary information. Managers shy away from taking clear, direct actions to resolve these issues, and consultants need to be aware of this tendency and do whatever is necessary to push for resolution.

Shrinking markets call for tactics of planned withdrawal or reduction of effort to maintain profitability and to free resources for investment in more promising markets. Tactics may be gradual, such as phase-out or phase-down. Both are a series of moves to reduce overhead to align it with decreasing sales in order to maintain profitability in the market as long as possible. When phase-out of a product line occurs simultaneously with an overall growth strategy, a unique opportunity is presented. The human, physical, and fiscal resources committed to the LOB that is being phased out may be carefully transferred to a growing LOB, thus reducing losses, layoffs, and disruption.

Divestment of lines of business—selling them off—is more dramatic. Although such a move can cause much internal disruption, it may mean a sale while there still are resources to sell. This may be an astute tactic if barriers to exit (such as those that are due to capital invested or labor contracts) are very high, making phase-out a potential disaster, as was the case with *Psychology Today*. Divestment also quickly frees up critical management time and other resources for commitment to markets with higher potential.

Other Gaps

Sometimes gaps are related to the leadership style and culture of the organization, but leadership and culture are changeable. The British Airways (BA) example cited in Chapter 3 demonstrates the importance of change in both the leadership and the culture of a declining organization. While this clearly may become part of a strategic plan, changing the leadership is easier than changing the culture. At BA it required a high level of commitment from the new leadership and almost five years to achieve real, measurable cultural change.

If a gap is identified in risk orientation, the planning team must examine the feasibility of change in that orientation, and it must base the examination on the root cause of the present orientation. Risk orientation may be restricted either by lack of resources or difficult market conditions. These causal factors may or may not be subject to change. When risk orientation is more clearly related to the style of the CEO, the question becomes, "Can this person change or must a new leader or leaders be brought in?" Regardless of desired direction of change (from conservative to risk oriented or vice versa), these styles are often not easy to change. If you cannot change the person, you must change the person!

The planning team must analyze each gap individually, and some ways of closing the gaps must be found before the team can move on to other matters. This is another time for candor and honesty. Collusion on the part of the planning-team members to overlook reality at this stage can be costly. After each individual gap has been closed, the team must then re-examine the overall gap between the organization's current state and the desired state. It is quite possible that all gaps can be closed if analyzed individually but that the organization will lack sufficient resources to close all gaps simultaneously.

WHEN THE GAPS CANNOT BE CLOSED

If it appears unlikely that an individual gap can be closed, the planning team must recycle to the strategic business model and re-examine the goal set in this area. This review may identify a creative way to close the gap. If not, the goal in this area must be reworked to a level at which the gap can be closed. Profitability or growth goals may have to be more conservative—a relatively easy readjustment. For example, a goal of 25 percent annual growth may have to be reduced to 20 percent—the rate that is achievable. Other goals that are not achievable, such as changing risk orientation, may not only need to be rewritten, but may significantly impact several or all of the remaining dimensions of the strategic business model.

If it appears that each gap can be closed individually but that realistically all gaps cannot be closed simultaneously, choices must be made. These choices should be relatively easy, given the earlier work to prioritize the various aspects of the strategic business model. Since these priorities were set in direct congruence with a values-driven mission statement, care should be taken to adhere to the results of this previous work. In the hypothetical Epsilon case, growth was given top priority. Therefore, if tactics to achieve profitability would reduce the company's growth, efforts would need to be made to maintain the growth goal. This could mean looking for more profitable ways to achieve growth goals or reducing the profit target.

Recycling between gap analysis and reworking the strategic business model should continue until a strategic business model emerges that clearly lends itself to successful accomplishment. When this happens, two things need to occur:

1. Action plans must be developed to carry the carefully defined strategic plan to the operational level.

2. Contingency plans need to be developed to prepare the organization to adjust to potential significant changes in the internal or external environment.

These two major steps will occur next in the Applied Strategic Planning sequence. Figure 11-3 provides a checklist for verifying that the necessary steps have been completed in the gap analysis phase.

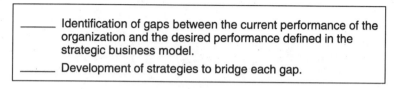

_____ Identification of gaps between the current performance of the organization and the desired performance defined in the strategic business model.

_____ Development of strategies to bridge each gap.

Figure 11-3. Checklist of Necessary Outputs from Gap Analysis

SUMMARY

Gap analysis is a critical phase of the Applied Strategic Planning process. During the gap analysis the desired future developed during strategic business modeling is compared with the current state of the organization. Generally, the options for closing gaps will fall into either a growth or a retrenchment category. If the gap between the current state and the desired state seems too large to close, then either the desired future must be redefined or creative solutions for closing the gap must be developed.

REFERENCES

Badaracco, J.L., Jr. (1991). *The knowledge link*. Cambridge, MA: Harvard Business School Press.

Chandler, A.D., Jr. (1962). *Strategy and structure: Chapters in the history of the industrial enterprise*. Cambridge, MA: M.I.T. Press.

Kanter, R.M. (1989). Becoming PALs: Pooling, allying, and linking across companies. *Academy of Management Executive, 3*(3), 189-193. Reprinted in J.W. Pfeiffer (Ed.). (1991). *Strategic planning: Selected readings* (rev. ed.). San Diego, CA: Pfeiffer & Company.

Porter, M.E. (1980). *Competitive strategy: Techniques for analyzing industries and competitors*. New York: Free Press.

Porter, M.E. (1985). *Competitive advantage: Creating and sustaining superior performance*. New York: Free Press.

Thomsett, M.C. (1990). *The expansion trap: How to make your business grow safely and profitably*. New York: AMACOM.

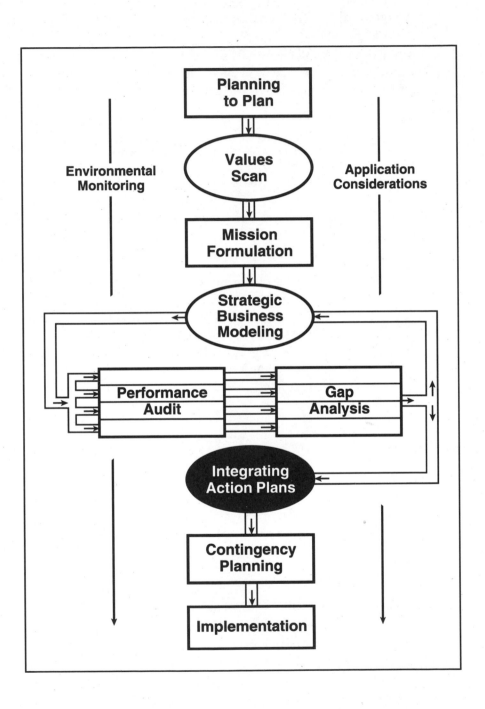

Chapter Twelve

Integrating Action Plans—Horizontally and Vertically

One of the greatest pains to human nature is the pain of a new idea.

Walter Bagelot
Physics and Politics, 1867

Once the strategies for closing the gaps revealed in the gap analysis phase of the planning process have been developed and initiated, two important issues need to be addressed. First, each of the various constituent units of the organization—business and functional—need to develop detailed operational or tactical plans based on the overall plan of the organization. Each of these plans should reflect the grand strategy and needs to involve budgets, marketing plans, and timetables. Second, after these unit plans have been separately developed, they need to be integrated into a comprehensive whole. In other words, the first task is to develop a specific operational plan for each organizational element, then the second task is to knit them together into a seamless whole.

Prior to developing action plans, the organization needs to establish priorities. Typical questions include the following:

1. Which LOBs get more attention early in the implementation and which can wait until later?
2. Are some CSIs more important than others?
3. Will some strategies be emphasized during the next year or two while others are held until later?

The major reason to extend the planning horizons (e.g., to five years into the future) is to give the organization the ability to use time to its advantage. This means that not everything can or will be done during the first year or two. Aggressive managers, until otherwise directed, often try to do exactly that: they attempt to do everything at once.

To avoid this—and the resultant disruption and greatly enhanced likelihood of failure—the planning team should set the priorities across each dimension of its plan and transmit them clearly to each manager tasked with developing an action plan. The strategic planning-team members should also insist on clarity in their assignments. The length, format, and expected content of each action plan should be clearly specified in advance.

DEVELOPING VERTICAL OPERATIONAL PLANS

A comprehensive, detailed operational plan now needs to be developed for each of the LOBs—both new and existing—that survived the gap analysis. The combined thrust of these separate plans represent the newly established strategic direction of the organization. Developing such operational or business plans will be relatively straightforward in those organizations with separate strategic business units (SBUs). See Figure 12-1 for a graphic portrayal of the SBU and other typical organizational structures. (Flamholtz, 1990, provides a simple and potentially useful approach to understanding the appropriate relationship between these various organization structures, on one hand, and organizational development and size, as measured by annual sales revenues, on the other.) Each of these SBUs typically has an infrastructure, including the human resources function, that has considerable experience in developing such business plans. The major difference in this case is that there may be some new LOBs assigned to the SBU with which it is relatively unfamiliar, indeed with which the entire organization is unfamiliar. These are the new LOBs that were developed in the Applied Strategic Planning process. The development of business or operational plans for these LOBs will require a fair amount of research on the part of those assigned the task.

An issue emerges, however, in the case of developing operational or business plans for organizations that are still centralized without an SBU structure. It is usually too great an overload to require the existing support staff of an organization to take on the task of creating detailed operational plans for the actions emerging from the strategic planning process in addition to their other ongoing responsibilities. This is especially true when new LOBs are involved—LOBs that require considerable research. Using special task forces for this purpose, one for each LOB—both existing and new—works quite well. These task forces should be chaired by one of the champions of that particular LOB and should include sufficient technical expertise in the way of budgeting, manufacturing, marketing, sales predictions, and so on. These task forces should not be expected to reinvent the wheel or do anything else that is already part of the organization's repertoire.

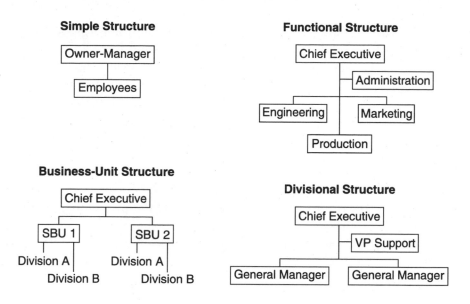

Figure 12-1. Four Basic Organization Structures

Operational Plan Content

The business plan for a new LOB should be a clear, easy-to-understand scenario of how the organization will move from point A to point B, that is, the necessary steps involved in launching this new LOB. While such plans will vary enormously, depending on the actual LOB involved, the following elements should be present:

1. A clear description of the product or service to be offered.
2. The intended target market.
3. The resources necessary to develop, produce, and deliver this new product or service. These resources will ordinarily include the facilities and machinery necessary to produce the new product, the people—engineering, production, sales and marketing, management, and others—and the capital.
4. A detailed and realistic financial analysis, including revenue projections and fixed and variable costs. The assignment of overhead allocation should be left for the integration phase and not attempted at this juncture.
5. A timetable for the entire process, from initiation to full operational status.
6. A comprehensive marketing plan.

Obviously, the size, detail, and complexity of such operational plans will depend on the nature of the new LOB. In a law firm that created a new LOB of environmental law, the plan was short and simple. It involved recruiting two senior attorneys with environmental-law expertise, allowing each of them to hire several junior associates and support staff, enlarging the office to accommodate the newcomers, buying office furniture and equipment for the newcomers, adding several on-line data-retrieval services to the existing ones, and marketing this new LOB to existing clients. Implementing the plan from start to full operational status would involve ten months, and the LOB was projected to make a significant contribution to profit within eighteen months.

Contrast that example to the development of a new LOB for a major chemical manufacturer, where acquiring the plant site, developing the environmental-impact statements, raising the funds for construction of the plant through an additional stock offering, building and outfitting the plant, recruiting, hiring, and training the production force would take more than five years and no contribution to profit was expected for four additional years. It is difficult to regard these two plans as comparable in any ways other than intent and format.

In the not-for-profit world, developing such implementation plans is equally important. For example, an international agency for population control decided to add a nonsurgical implant (NorPlant) to its already existing strategies for contraception. NorPlant is inserted in a woman's upper arm to prevent pregnancy for five to six years. The organization focuses its contraception activities in developing countries, where any procedure needs to be simple and easy to explain, with little or no follow-up required of the patient. The living conditions of the clientele precludes the use of birth-control pills, diaphragms, and other contraceptive devices of the more industrialized world. In planning this new LOB, the issues involved in the operational plan were the availability and cost of the NorPlant inserts, training the necessary personnel in their use, developing marketing strategies and materials in several different languages, obtaining permission of the health ministries in the affected countries, and so on. All these were accomplished in ten months from initiation to full operational status.

Marketing Plans

One of the elements of the operational plan that is easiest to overlook is the development of a marketing plan for the particular LOB. Kotler (1980) notes that the two major activities required for organizational survival are the evolution of a strategic plan and the creation of a marketing process. The marketing process should always be derived from the strategic plan and should reflect the organization's decisions about which LOBs will be built (the stars), maintained (the cash cows), force fed (the problem children), or terminated (the dogs). Within this strategic context, the marketing process involves four distinctive steps:

1. Identifying and analyzing market opportunities;
2. Segmenting and selecting target markets;
3. Developing a marketing-mix strategy; and
4. Designing and implementing marketing management-control systems.

Identifying and Analyzing Market Opportunities

While the first of these steps—identifying and analyzing market opportunities—is properly part of the strategic business modeling and performance audit phases, the other steps in Kotler's analysis are critical aspects of the integration phase. Despite the fact that the identification and analysis of marketing opportunities should have been completed in earlier phases of the strategic planning process, it is worthwhile to recapitulate Kotler's points about this first step in the context of his overall position. Kotler makes an important distinction between *environmental* and *organizational* opportunities: The former become the latter only when there is a match between the opportunities afforded the organization and its distinctive competencies. In other words, finding opportunities in the environment that are incompatible with what the organization does best is simply a waste of time; but if the organization's distinctive competencies exceed those of its competitors, it will have a *differential advantage* over those competitors. Thus, for the Epsilon Company (the example in Chapter 11) to determine that there was a market need for certain types of consumer electronics was not helpful, because producing or marketing such products was not one of Epsilon's distinctive competencies. On the other hand, had Epsilon determined that there was a strong need for some new scientific instrument in its existing market, the reverse would have been the case.

Segmenting and Selecting Target Markets

Target-market selection involves developing a clear and detailed identification of the potential customers whose needs the company plans to meet. Market selection invariably involves market segmentation and subsegmentation to determine which products are most likely to appeal to which segments or subsegments of the marketplace. For example, in the banking industry, Citicorp, America's largest bank, segments its market into three major divisions: international, institutional, and retail. Within each of these segments, and the many subsegments into which each of these can be divided, there are a number of products that have differing appeals. In order to clarify how segmentation can assist the planning team in determining the target market, Kotler suggests using a product/market grid similar to Figure 12-2. In the hypothetical analysis for large, international banking in Figure 12-2, long-term loans for developing a nation's infrastructure are clearly intended for the international division, whereas credit cards are offered to the bank's institutional and retail customers. Building-construction loans appeal to both the retail and institutional segments, lines of credit appeal across the board, and so on.

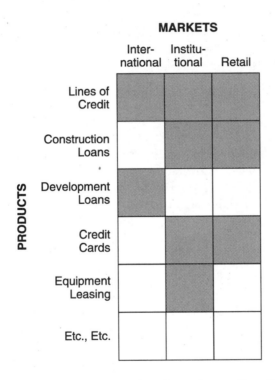

Figure 12-2. Product/Market Grid for an International Bank

In a similar fashion, the Marriott Corporation divides its market into four subsegments, based on a multitier classification system developed by corporate travel managers for employees, from back-office workers to the CEO. Marriott offers four levels of lodging, varying in amenities and price ranges:

1. Fairfield Inns, with the fewest amenities and the lowest price;
2. Courtyard Inns, with a few more amenities and a slightly higher price;

3. Residence Inns, a bit more luxurious at a higher price; and
4. Marriott Hotels, Suites, and Resorts, the most luxurious and highest priced.

Marriott intended to serve different travelers with different needs and with different-sized billfolds. When such subsegmentation is warranted, a customer-level/customer-need grid (as shown in Figure 12-3) should be developed for each identified market segment. The hypothetical example in Figure 12-3 shows how various customer needs can be considered as a function of the level of the business customer in his or her organization. Similar grids can be constructed for customer-size/customer-use, and so on.

CUSTOMER LEVEL

	Senior Executive	Manager	Manager	Other
24-Hr Restaurant				
Health Club				
Price				
Valet Parking				
Indoor/Outdoor Swimming Pool				
Room Size				
Etc., Etc.				

CUSTOMER NEED

Figure 12-3. Customer-Level/Customer-Need Grid for Business-Travel Segment of the Hospitality Industry

These analyses allow the planning team to decide which of the following five market strategies is most likely to produce success for new LOBs:

1. *Product/market concentration,* which involves targeting one product in one market niche (e.g., in the banking industry, providing equipment leasing for the institutional market segment only).
2. *Product specialization,* which consists of providing one product for all market segments (e.g., providing construction loans for all customers).
3. *Market specialization,* which involves meeting a variety of needs in a particular market segment (e.g., completely covering the retail market and ignoring the others).
4. *Selective specialization,* in which the organization exploits individually attractive market subsegments without regard to whether they relate to each other, thus offering products on an *ad hoc* basis whenever a need is identified.
5. *Full coverage,* which involves meeting all needs for all segments of the market. This is the Citibank market strategy, or at least it was prior to the close of the 1980s, when its international division suffered enormous losses because of defaults in many of its loans to developing countries. Its marketing strategy for the 1990s appears to be a concentration on its other two market segments and a greatly reduced international focus, except for its institutional and retail efforts outside the United States.

In the integration phase of Applied Strategic Planning, the planning team must clearly identify which of these marketing strategies is involved in each LOB. When the overall integration of the several LOBs occurs later in this phase, it is imperative for the several marketing strategies to be integrated into some kind of cohesive whole.

Developing a Marketing-Mix Strategy

The third step in the marketing process involves developing an effective *marketing-mix* strategy based on the competitive position that the organization wants to occupy in its target market. The market mix is determined by choosing the product, price, place, and promotion—the so-called "four Ps": what products are to be offered at what price, where, and through what vehicles. For example, a hotel chain can offer facilities similar to those offered by its competitors but at a cheaper price—a "me-too product" that competes on the basis of price—or it can develop a unique product that will meet market needs until its competitors duplicate it. The development of "guest quarters," which allowed hotels to offer suites rather than single rooms, provides an example of a unique *product.* Then the question of where they would be built (place), how they would be advertised (promotion), and what the rates would be (price) had to be determined. These kinds of detailed questions need to be addressed for each new LOB.

Designing and Implementing Marketing Management-Control Systems

Finally, a comprehensive marketing-control system must be designed and put into place. This system needs to include a marketing planning-and-control system, a marketing-information system, and a marketing-organization system. The planning team may decide that these information and control mechanisms would be developed best after the various LOB plans are completed, or it may turn this issue over to the marketing group as part of the integration of its functional plan. In any case, it is essential for these control mechanisms to be in place to assure the development and implementation of an appropriate marketing process for each new LOB.

Grand Strategies

A grand strategy is a comprehensive, general approach that guides the actions of an LOB. Grand strategies (more than one can be adopted simultaneously) indicate how the strategic plans of each LOB are to be accomplished. Pierce and Robinson (1991) identify twelve grand strategies, some of which are more appropriate for existing LOBs and some for new ones. These are the following:

1. *Concentrated growth,* or focusing on a single product that has been a profitable mainstay of the organization. The Wrigley Company has successfully followed this grand strategy for over ninety years. Chewing gum is its only product, and Wrigley controls almost half of America's $2.5 billion retail chewing-gum market, double that of its nearest competitor.

2. *Market development,* that is, adding new customers in related markets. Geographic expansion, through branch operations or franchises, is the most common approach to market development. Witness the phenomenal success of Domino's and other nationally based fast-food operators.

3. *Product development,* that is, creating new but related products that can be sold to existing markets. MCI and Sprint, in direct competition with AT&T, offer slightly improved long-distance telephone service at a slightly better price and have grown tremendously since their founding.

4. *Innovation,* or creating products that are so new and superior that existing products become obsolete. It is difficult to find a better example of this grand strategy than at 3M, where 25 per-

cent of all its products are less than five years old and developing innovative products is a primary requirement of its managers.

5. *Horizontal integration,* that is, acquiring or merging with a similar organization to reduce competition. The recent string of mergers and acquisitions in the American banking and airline industries, as well as the acquisition of American Motors by Chrysler, are examples of this grand strategy.

6. *Vertical integration,* that is, either developing an internal supply network (backward vertical integration) or developing an internal distribution system that puts the organization closer to its end users (forward vertical integration). Amoco's acquisition of Dome Petroleum is an example of vertical integration, whereas Pepsico's acquisition of Kentucky Fried Chicken, Pizza Hut, and Taco Bell is an example of combined horizontal and vertical integration. By these acquisitions, Pepsico assured itself of an enormous number of retail outlets for its soft drinks (forward vertical integration) and expanded in the general fast-food business (horizontal integration).

7. *Joint venture,* or teaming up with another organization to develop a new product or market. The Apple-IBM joint venture, discussed earlier, is an example of this grand strategy.

8. *Concentric diversification,* that is, acquiring or merging with organizations that are compatible with the organization's technology, markets, or products. The Sony acquisition of Columbia Motion Pictures and Records exemplifies such a strategy.

9. *Diversification,* that is, acquiring or merging with an organization that counterbalances its own strengths and weaknesses. The acquisition by Time of a pulp and paper company represents this strategy.

10. *Retrenchment,* or reversing the negative trends in profits through a variety of cost-cutting methods. Given the recession of the 1990s, most large companies in the United States are relying on this grand strategy, at least to some extent.

11. *Divestiture,* that is, selling off or closing down a segment of the organization. The American Express divestiture of the Fireman's Fund Insurance Company (discussed in Chapter 3) is an example of this approach.

12. *Liquidation,* or selling off the organization for its tangible assets and closing it down. The examples are so numerous and obvious that no specific illustrations seem necessary. They range from the giant Eastern Airlines to the unending series of failures in any neighborhood shopping strip.

Selecting the grand strategies that best fit the individual LOBs and the organization as a whole in meeting its goals is an important part of

Applied Strategic Planning. For each LOB, the question is, "What mix of grand strategies will allow this LOB to become viable?" When the overall vertical action plans are finally integrated by the planning team, it is especially important that a coherent grand strategy be clearly understood and articulated. The relationship between the overall grand strategy and two additional factors—rate of market growth and the strength of the organization's own competitive position—is illustrated in Figure 12-4. Once an organization locates itself in one of the four quadrants of the matrix, the preferred overall grand strategies become apparent, that is, those that pose the least risk and the highest pay-off—at least according to Pierce and Robinson (1991). In any event, the matrix provides a convenient way of initiating an in-depth discussion of the organization's overall grand strategies and their appropriateness.

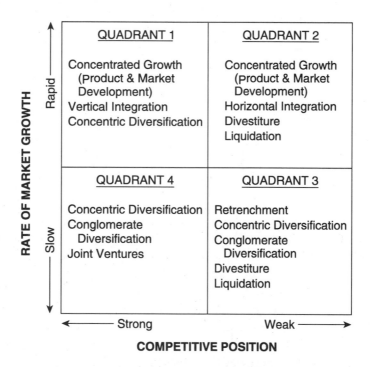

Figure 12-4. Grand Strategy Choice Matrix (After Pierce & Robinson, 1991)

DEVELOPING HORIZONTAL FUNCTIONAL ACTION PLANS

In addition to the vertical action plans that involve the LOBs, action plans for the usual organizational functions need to be developed and integrated. This step commonly occurs after the vertical action plans for the LOBs have been developed. On the functional level, the action plans typically need to include financial plans, sales and marketing plans, human- and capital-resource plans, and so on. These generally cannot be developed until there is clear agreement by the planning team about the shape of the overall vertical action plan.

For example, in a human resource plan, current and future needs for staffing on the managerial, supervisory, technical, production, and administrative levels would be developed for the time period of the plan, based on the agreed-on vertical action plan. Such a plan would take into account employee turnover, staffing needs, recruitment and training programs, and costs and would include contingency plans.

Each plan developed by a functional group or business unit in the organization also must be understood and agreed to by each of the other functional groups in the organization. This process often is difficult, because once the model is developed and plans are made, each part of the organization begins to compete for limited resources in order to attain its objectives, achieve the planned growth, and so on. Several departments may simultaneously require the services of the graphics department, need a new computer program, or produce something that requires the support of the sales staff or the mailing department. All these actions have timing and budget implications as well. It is imperative that each of the functional units within the organization understand the impact of such competition and agree to the planned allocation of resources both to itself and to the other functional units.

The process of integration changes considerably over time. During the organization's first attempt at Applied Strategic Planning, integration most often involves a kind of cut-and-paste process. However, the process smooths out over time as the planning team and others begin to understand the integration process and to realize that it involves setting out responsibilities, resources, timetables, and so on. Once the operating managers in the organizations develop this understanding, they usually become enthusiastic supporters of the process and view it as a help in doing their day-to-day jobs. It creates a context for what they do and clearly establishes their priorities, resources, and timetables.

The planning team will identify the gaps in and between these combined functional plans and determine how these can be closed and what the impact of the gaps might be on the successful execution of the strategic business model. The integration of the horizontal functional plans with the vertical plans (i.e., LOB, SBU, divisional, or other plans) involves putting together *all* the pieces to make certain whether and how the overall action plan will work and where the potential trouble spots are. Most of these integration issues must be resolved during the budgetary process.

Each constituent plan must be checked against the organizational values scan and mission statement to determine whether the proposed actions and directions are consistent with what the organization said it wanted to be. This check may reveal a need for further clarification of the values, culture, mission, and strategic business model of the organization, so that all plans are developed with the same overall objectives and assumptions.

Resource Allocation

Functional plans are integrated with one another and into the organization through the time-honored practice of resource allocation (budgeting) among the various functional areas. The translation of Applied Strategic Planning into near-term dimensions is the two-step process of functional planning and budgeting—which are simply different aspects of resource allocation. The test of the effectiveness of these aspects is the degree to which they support the strategic business model. If the managers who are responsible for the various functional areas understand and support the strategic goals, their respective functional plans will demonstrate that understanding and support.

Prior to the planning-team meeting on integrating functional plans, all functional managers should prepare plans similar to those shown in Figure 12-5. These largely narrative plans must be integrated by the planning team and specifically approved prior to the initiation of the budgeting process.

Each functional unit, such as engineering, marketing, finance, and human resources (see Figure 12-6), is then required to develop detailed plans for that function that take into consideration the identified constraints on the human or financial resources of the organization. These narrative statements will provide the rationale for the detailed budget plans that will be presented later in the process. Particular attention needs to be given to integrating marketing plans and human resource plans because these are the two areas in which most organizations too quickly reach or exceed their existing capacity. It is essential that these functional plans be completed and integrated before the fiscal-year budget cycle begins.

At this point a shift in the way in which the planning team functions is desirable, as was discussed in Chapter 5 ("Planning to Plan") and which is also presented in Figure 12-7. It is fairly predictable (and natural) for functional managers to shift from the organization-wide

Publications Fulfillment:

Our emphasis has been on streamlining the systems and learning to work as a team so that an expected increase in orders can be handled with existing staff. To that end, data-entry and customer-service clerks are being trained in order-entry programs; several people from inside can post the mail; warehouse personnel can do receiving and fill out inventory-change requests; etc. A real work team has started to come together, and communication is improving every day. (Another advantage is to avoid crises when employees are sick or on vacation.)

A positive sign of how people are feeling about working for this company is that three productive members of our department have found opportunities for career growth by *staying,* because of lateral transfers, so we are not losing their expertise and we are not having to hire and train outsiders for new positions that have been created.

Several of our people are interested in learning more about the personal computers, and some will be trained in word processing.

More key operators for the photocopy machine have been trained, and some people have been sent to courses on office organization and business-letter writing.

A part-time position has been created for dealing with catalog and other inquiries, which now average XXX per week, up XX percent from last summer.

The publication-fulfillment staff members are more skilled and more willing to expand their capacity than they have had a reputation for being in the past.

Customer Service:

This whole area is in such a *reactive* mode that it is hard to find time to make changes or set up systems. Computer support seems inadequate, so we have recently used help from the Computer Department to fix programs. This last function is crucial, because all records were being kept by hand and updating was becoming impossible. Up to 20 hours a week are being spent with the photocopy machine, making it look as though we are understaffed. Those hours can be spent *much* more profitably by keeping files up to date and keeping the books in the customer room in alphabetical order.

Facilities:

With a division between *tenant* responsibilities and *owner* responsibilities now clear, we plan to start a system for handling minor repairs; to delegate responsibility for such things as the forklift and mailing-machine repair to the warehouse manager; to maintain good key control; to check and monitor the telephone costs; and to set up files so that the next employee can tell what has happened previously.

Miscellaneous:

With half-time secretarial help, the department manager should be relieved of many routine chores and be able to concentrate more on major aspects of operations. We want to keep the Operations Department open to change but always working on streamlining systems. We are attempting to be flexible and not to spend more money and time to get things done.

**Figure 12-5. Sample Functional Plans for the Operations
Department of a Publishing House**

Functional Managers Shift to Constituency-Based Approaches

view they held during earlier planning sessions to more constituency-based approaches that manifest themselves in comments such as "I can't meet my commitment if I am not allowed the necessary resources." Assuming the strategic business model is at least moderately aggressive, we find that competition is inevitable among the various operational functions for the scarcer resources of the organization. Although this competition should be viewed as both natural and healthy, the CEO needs to manage it carefully.

Figure 12-6. Blending Functional Plans into Company-Wide Plan

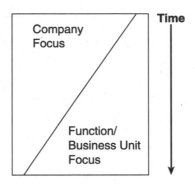

Figure 12-7. Constituency Ratio for Applied Strategic Planning

The Role of the CEO in Integration

The role of the CEO at this stage is to monitor the functional plans and budgets to ensure that they have a high degree of fidelity with respect to strategic goals. Additionally, at this stage it is relatively common to have functional plans that are in conflict with one another or, as mentioned, that are in direct competition for finite organizational resources. It is the CEO's responsibility to see that all conflicts in functional plans or budgets are resolved, that is, to set the priorities in the integration of these functional plans. This is a process that often involves making hard choices, choosing between several important and worthwhile enterprises where the resources of the organization simply preclude doing them all at the same time. Equally important, functional plans and budgets must be implemented. It should be an absolute rule that functional managers cannot alter plans and budgets that directly or indirectly support strategic goals.

In most organizations, managers are experienced in some form of budgeting process that works more or less satisfactorily for the organization. This means that, from the consultants' perspectives, there may be limited need for their involvement in this phase of the planning process. There are, however, two recommendations about budgeting that should be made to most organizations: One is focused primarily on monitoring profit goals established in the strategic business model; and the other is more focused on meeting growth goals, particularly if they are moderately aggressive ones (i.e., 15 percent or more).

Aside from the obvious limits on financial resources faced by most companies, the major constraint to planned (or even happenstance) growth is inadequate human resource planning. To help avoid this planning pitfall and also to provide a model for all functional-level planning, we offer the following approach to human resource planning.

AN APPROACH TO HUMAN RESOURCE PLANNING

"Effective human resource planning is a process of continually analyzing an organization's human resource needs under changing conditions and developing the activities necessary to satisfy these needs" (Walker, 1980). Human resource planning is basically a two-part process. The first part consists of forecasting what human resources the organization has and what resources it is going to need on a year-by-year basis to meet the goals outlined in the strategic plan. The second part, in its most simplistic terms, is to develop a functional plan to close the gap identified in the first part in a timely and cost-efficient manner.

Human Resource Planning Is a Two-Part Process

A model for human resource planning is presented in Figures 12-8 through 12-11. It starts with "The Human Resource Forecast" (Figure 12-8) in which the human resources necessary for the execution of the various aspects of the strategic plan are carefully identified on a year-by-year basis. Although a five-year planning cycle is common in this kind of functional planning, the actual cycle might be shorter or longer than that. The identified yearly needs must then be corrected by adding to the human resource requirement the replacements necessitated by losses from retirements, turnovers, promotions, and other changes in staffing patterns.

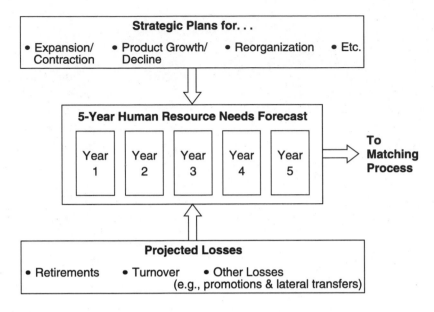

Figure 12-8. The Human Resource Forecast

The next step (Figure 12-9) is to carefully inventory the current human resources of the organization on an individual-by-individual basis: what each person's career and work interests are, especially as these impact the organization, and how each person's actual performance compares with his or her interests and aspirations. These comparisons should be the focus of regular performance/development discussions between employees and managers with the involvement of human resource specialists.

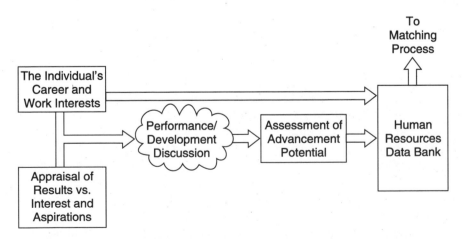

Figure 12-9. The Human Resource Inventory

These discussions need to focus on the potential opportunities that exist for the individual, stemming from the strategic planning process, and what the individual and the organization need to do in order to have these plans come to fruition. These steps may include training courses, mentoring, cross-training, and so on. All of these are intended to facilitate and enhance the assessment of advancement potential, which needs to be stored in the human resource data bank. Information from the data bank would be more readily accessible if computer technology were used.

Once the organization identifies its human resource supply and demand for the strategic planning time frame, the supply and demand need to be matched and the imbalances identified (see Figure 12-10). The supply of current human resources may not be adequate to meet the organization's demand, especially in periods of rapid growth, or it may be too large in periods of *right sizing* or retrenchment. There are circumstances in which both conditions exist at the same time; for example, when old products and services are being phased out, new products or services are being introduced, and the delivery of the new requires new and different skills that cannot be learned by the present work force. Clearly, the introduction of robotics in manufacturing organizations and of computers in service industries are creating this type of condition. The matching process identifies the imbalances that must be addressed and resolved.

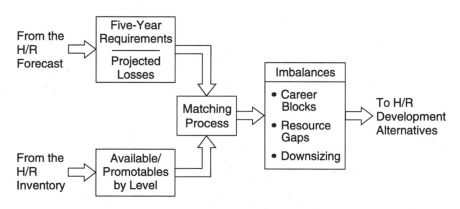

Figure 12-10. Matching Human Resource Supply and Demand

Figure 12-11 suggests some alternatives to consider on a systems basis when the organization's human resource demands exceed its supply at any level of the organization. Similar plans need to be developed for technical staff and for other human resource needs. The potential

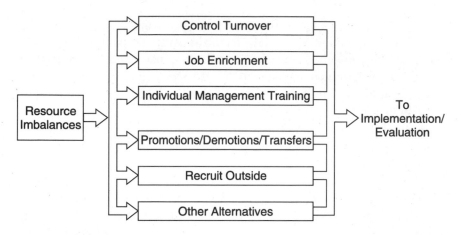

Figure 12-11. Human Resource Development Alternatives

for filling these needs by these several development alternatives must be realistically evaluated if the organization's human resource needs are to be met.

The human resource requirements for executing this element of the strategic plan are too often given short shrift. When there is inadequate capital or equipment for execution, the plans will be re-evaluated, but frequently too little attention is paid to the human resource requirements for execution. Such requirements must be thought through carefully.

Succession Planning

The most difficult portion of this process, and one that is often neglected or avoided, is succession planning at senior levels of the organization. Succession is a topic frequently avoided in many organizations; or—to the degree that it is discussed—it tends to have a more casual, conversational orientation than befits such an important concern.

The inevitable test for promoting someone consists of two questions. The first is "Can the person proposed for the promotion do the job, given some traditional reservations?" The answer is usually yes. The second is "Has the proposed person groomed someone to take his or her job?" Very often the answer is so emphatically negative that the potentially successful candidate cannot be promoted.

Although succession in case of the unforeseen is typically covered in the contingency planning phase, it is a rare small-to-medium sized company that links succession planning to career development. Nevertheless, a functional human resource plan must include specific succession plans for all senior managers, especially the CEO. If the succession cannot come from within, as is often the case with chief financial officers and senior data-processing managers, a succession plan can nevertheless be prepared through the establishment of a well-written job description and a clear plan of where to look for the prospective new employee.

The most complex dimension of this compelling problem is the succession for the CEO, particularly in closely held companies in which the CEO is either the entrepreneur/founder or the son or daughter of the entrepreneur/founder. Bennis and Nanus (1985), in a detailed summary of in-depth interviews with ninety top leaders in all aspects of American life, conclude that "the almost-universal common failing of entrepreneur/founders is that they fail to make a successful plan for their succession."

INTERNAL SCANNING

During the integrating action plans phase, the focus should shift substantially from external scanning to internal scanning. In the first instance (i.e., regarding the monitoring of profit goals established in strategic business modeling), all managers who have responsibility for budget lines—either income, cost of goods, or expenses—generally need to meet monthly to review, line-by-line, budget versus actual figures for both the preceding month and for the fiscal year to date.

Effective Applied Strategic Planning needs to be monitored frequently to assure that the implementation of the plan is synchronized with the specific goals manifested in the strategic business model and the CSIs that were developed to track their progress. The monthly monitoring of the operating statement (profit and loss) should also be carefully checked against any triggering levels established in the contingency-planning process, which will be discussed in greater detail in Chapter 13 ("Contingency Planning"). Generally, this monthly accounting function should be done within the first ten working days of the following month. If it takes longer than this recommended time, managers are faced with an exasperating delay in being able to make necessary decisions to stay on the course established by the strategic business model.

As consultants, we sometimes recommend—particularly when moderate-to-high levels of growth are targeted—the establishment of a rolling quarterly budgeting process. This process typically calls for (a) a revision, if necessary, of the next three quarters' budget and (b) a new budget for a fourth quarter that is a year ahead of the quarter just completed. Assuming moderately good budgeting skills and a business that is not unreasonably complex, we recommend that this process be done within a month of the close of the quarter, that is, within ten working days of the actual-to-budget monitoring meeting for the end of the quarter. Additionally, we routinely recommend quarterly balance-sheet meetings in which all assets and liability accounts are fully reviewed. In the absence of an unusually complex process that can be designed to monitor both original and updated budgets, the trade-off depends on which of the following is more important to the organization: (a) to know how accurate the managers are with respect to the annual budgeting cycle or (b) to know what is the most accurate picture that can be developed with respect to where the organization will be eight to eleven months in the future. We strongly believe that the latter view is more important, although we urge doing both if possible.

Managers who are fully involved in monthly operating-statement monitoring and rolling quarterly budgets see the pragmatic value of the process when compared to the typical annual budget ritual. Because these monitoring/budgeting skills are kept focused, the quarterly budgeting process takes only about 50 percent more time than the traditional once-a-year, "I-cannot-remember-how-we-did-this-last-time" method.

When, on occasion, changes in external conditions force adjustments in action plans or budgets, all managers responsible for major functions must meet to realign their positions with respect to the shifting external conditions and the corresponding responses from others with functional responsibilities. Additionally, predetermined response patterns occasioned by the triggering of events covered by contingency planning will require immediate functional realignment. It is the CEO's absolute responsibility to ensure that adjustments by functional managers are synchronized with the organization's strategic goals.

Most typically near-term functional goals should be planned with a minimum three-year horizon and updated annually. Budgeting should be done on a one-year basis, and we highly recommend rolling quarterly updates. Organizations should adopt time frames that are consistent with their businesses. Functional plans must be fastidiously synchronized with one another and absolutely integrated into the strategic plans. Near-term functional plans, often referred to as tactical (or operational) plans, should, at a minimum, be required to be translated into *pro forma* profit-and-loss statements; and these should be checked against the overall strategic business model. Additionally, translation into *pro forma* balance sheets may provide an additional check against the templates of the strategic plan.

Dimensions that may be included are products, pricing, sales programs, manufacturing methods, warehousing and distribution facilities, equipment, location and space requirements, organization and personnel, finance and control procedures, data processing, record keeping, and purchasing. New-product development, marketing, acquisitions, and required capital expenditures may also need to be included.

Depending on the nature of the business, an individual function will often drive others. For example, marketing often drives (or dictates) production and personnel needs, and production may drive purchasing and capital expenditures. In capital-intensive companies, facilities (or capacity) may be the central point from which other functional plans are developed. Because of the intensely complex nature of the interaction among the various functional plans, it may be desirable or necessary for the CEO to approve a master script that is built in consultation with the functional heads.

A decision that needs to be made is the degree of tightness required between the overall strategic plan and the various action plans. This includes planning time horizons and level of detail. If too much detail or tightness is required, the process may become too burdensome and may dull the thrust of planning and execution. Conversely, if the relationship is too loose, the process may become meaningless. Only key functions may need to be integrated. Plans should be kept relatively simple, short (a few pages), and limited to high-priority actions, thereby avoiding the pitfalls of mere linear extrapolation.

Figure 12-12 provides a checklist for making certain the key elements of integrating action plans have been addressed.

_____ Consideration of an appropriate organizational structure to support the strategic direction.

_____ Identification of functions that must submit supporting plans.

_____ Collection, review, and integration of action plans by functional and line managers.

_____ Collection, modification, and acceptance of budgets consistent with action plans.

Figure 12-12. Checklist for Outputs from Integrating Action Plans

SUMMARY

Integrating action plans is that aspect of Applied Strategic Planning in which detailed action plans are developed first for each of the new and existing lines of business and then knit together in a cohesive whole. Then the traditional horizontal organizational functions develop their detailed action plans stemming from the vertical action plans. It is especially important to attend to the development of marketing processes and human resource plans, the two aspects of strategic planning most likely to be neglected. The CEO often will have to make a series of hard choices between competing priorities.

References

Bennis, W.G., & Nanus, B. (1985). *Leaders: The strategies for taking charge.* New York: Harper & Row.

Flamholtz, E.G. (1990). *Growing pains: How to make the transition from entrepreneurship to a professionally managed firm.* San Francisco: Jossey-Bass.

Kotler, P. (1980, May-June). Strategic planning and the marketing process. *Business,* pp. 2-9.

Pierce, J., & Robinson, E. (1991). *Strategic management.* Homewood, IL: Irwin.

Walker, J.W. (1980). *Human resource planning.* New York: McGraw Hill.

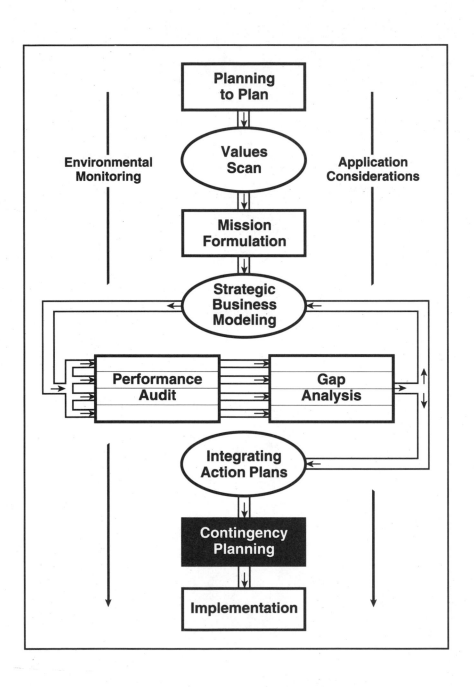

Chapter Thirteen

Contingency Planning

The best laid schemes o' mice and men oft go astray.

Robert Burns
"To a Mouse," 1785

The ability of humans to control their own destiny has not changed much since Burns' observation of over two centuries ago. Events never quite work out as anticipated; nevertheless, strategic plans need to be developed. The typical planning process focuses, appropriately, on the highest-probability events, but this focus can result in an incomplete set of plans. As George Steiner (1979), one of the fathers of strategic planning, puts it, "Contingency plans are preparations to take specific action(s) when an event not planned for in the formal planning process actually does take place." Contingency planning involves the development of specific action(s) when lower-probability events occur, but only those lower-probability events that would have important consequences for the organization.

IMPACT AND PROBABILITY

The two key concepts in contingency planning are probability and impact. In other words, contingency plans involve potentially high-impact events that do not have the *highest* probability of occurring. Figure 13-1 graphically shows how contingency planning fits in with the other planning processes. Applied Strategic Planning is primarily focused in Quadrant 2, while contingency planning focuses on Quadrant 1. Obviously no serious strategic planning should focus much of its time in the

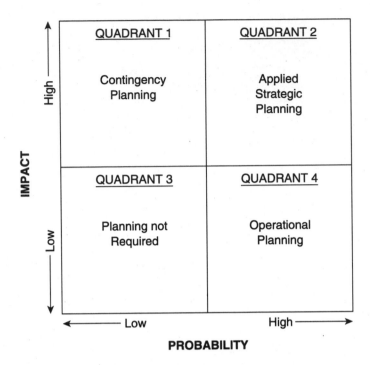

Figure 13-1. Impact-Probability Matrix

other quadrants, unless there are special circumstances that would justify such an investment.

The most important contribution that contingency planning can make to an organization is the development of a *process* for identifying and responding to unanticipated or less-likely events. It is impossible for any organization to sort out all the lower-probability events that might have a significant impact on the organization and develop detailed plans for responding to them. Any organization attempting to do so would spend all its time in such planning and never get around to accomplishing its mission. Nevertheless, a serious and thorough contingency planning process should assist the organization to develop a more thorough tracking system (which would provide early warning signs of changes) to monitor changes in internal strengths and weaknesses and external threats and opportunities. The contingency planning process should also provide a model of how to use a planning process to develop a prompt response to those emerging changes, either internal or external. In this connection, most planning teams come to the table with an understanding of the need for some contingency planning to meet *threats*, but rarely have they thought of a similar need for planning for *opportunities*.

ORGANIZATION-SPECIFIC CONTINGENCIES

Aside from "universal" external threats such as war or economic collapse and "universal" external opportunities such as the collapse or disappearance of a major competitor, each type of organization is subject to a specific set of organization-specific contingencies that must be planned for. For example, producers of building materials are heavily influenced by new housing starts, which are, in turn, a function of interest rates and general economic conditions. In developing its strategic business model, a producer of building materials may identify several alternative futures, each based on different volumes of housing starts. Scenarios may be developed for each major possibility. Housing starts, in turn, are influenced by a variety of governmental actions. For example, the elimination of mortgage deductions from personal income taxes (which are now permitted in both the United States and the United Kingdom) would pose a threat to housing starts, whereas a large governmental program to subsidize single-family homes would offer an opportunity. The strategic business model of the building-materials producer would assume that neither of these two events would be highly likely to occur, placing these events in Quadrant 1, but contingency plans should be developed in any case.

The SWOT analysis done as part of the performance audit provides the basis for contingency planning. The SWOT analysis should have identified the organization's internal strengths and weaknesses and the opportunities and threats that loom in the organization's external environment. Building on that earlier SWOT analysis, contingency planning involves (a) identifying the most important internal and external threats and opportunities, especially those involving other than the most-likely scenarios; (b) developing trigger points to initiate action steps for each contingency; and (c) agreeing on which action steps will be taken for each of these trigger points.

The internal threats that are often identified by planning teams are the death or severe disability of an "irreplaceable" key staff member— the director of research and development or the orchestra's principal soloist; the destruction of a key facility—such as a manufacturing plant or the computer room; a prolonged strike; and so on.

Internal opportunities would include an unanticipated opportunity to commercialize a chance invention or a cash infusion by the settlement of long-standing litigation, whereas external opportunities would include a sudden opening of new markets—witness what occurred in Eastern Europe—or the availability of new technology and equipment. Certainly not all of these contingencies could have been anticipated, but careful attention to the early warning signs of such critically important changes can alert the organization to the need for effective contingency planning.

Contingency planning is based on the assumption that the ability to forecast accurately the significant factors that will affect the organization is somewhat limited, especially in terms of variations in those factors. However, the planning team should be able to identify the factors themselves, such as interest rates, employment, housing starts, postal rates, and foreign-currency exchange rates, and develop alternative plans based on possible variations in these factors. Thus, contingency planning should provide the organization with a variety of business modeling strategies that can be used with a variety of scenarios, each of which can be evaluated and planned for.

TRIGGER POINTS

Contingency planning should also identify a number of key indicators that will trigger an awareness of the need to re-examine the adequacy of the strategy currently being followed. A *trigger point* could be an actual or anticipated increase in the price of a critical raw material or fuel or in the interest rate, or it could be a sharp, unexpected positive turnaround in the economy that offers the possibility for expansion and growth. When a trigger point is identified as having been reached, two levels of response should be generated:

1. *Higher-level monitoring.* No precipitant action should be taken; in fact, no immediate action may be required. However, the possibility of a need for a change in main-line assumptions should be noted, and indicators should be watched.

2. *Action.* At this level, the decision is made that conditions are different, and some contingency plan is implemented or some aspect of a strategy is modified.

The end of 1990 and the early months of 1991 saw a rapid increase in the price of oil and the threat and then the reality of war in the Gulf while the world economy was experiencing a recession—all of which had profound consequences for airlines, both domestic and international. Had the airlines had adequate contingency plans with any or all of these variables as trigger points, they might have taken earlier and more functional actions, saving several of them from having to seek the protection of bankruptcy.

The 1991 problems of financier Donald Trump have been interpreted as stemming, at least partially, from his failure to have developed a contingency plan. It was only when he determined that he was not able

**Contingency Plans Should Include
Trigger Points**

to meet the current interest payments to his creditors did he begin to attempt to develop a contingency plan. By then he had lost control over the planning process and perhaps, in the long run, his financial empire. The lesson is a clear one—think about what might go wrong with your plan. It really might!

Similar needs for contingency planning are present in the not-for-profit and public sectors. The changing demographics of Los Angeles County (especially the influx of families with many young children), the fiscal crisis impacting the county, and the constant need to readjust the capacity and focus of its nearly one hundred community-based libraries were all part of the contingency planning by the Los Angeles County Public Library. One of the major obstacles to effective contingency planning in the not-for-profit sector is the general unwillingness of too many senior-level bureaucrats to take seriously the notion that any such changes could occur; or that even if such changes did occur, that they would impact their agency. This may be even more true in such organizations when they are organized around a profession like library science or medicine.

Appropriate contingency planning significantly enhances the continued viability and growth of every organization. It is the spare tire, jack, and lug wrench of Applied Strategic Planning. Contingency planning puts managers in a better position to deal with the unexpected by forcing them to explore scenarios other than the most probable. We often say that a problem is "a muddled opportunity." Because it involves down-board thinking, contingency planning dramatically reduces time delays in responding to threats or emergencies and/or rapidly opening windows of opportunity. These turbulent times require a great deal of such thinking.

Planners must keep in mind that contingency planning is an integral part of a comprehensive Applied Strategic Planning process. Inasmuch as contingency planning equals preparation for alternative futures, the more turbulent the economic environment, the more attention that needs to be given to contingencies. For example, the microelectronics and fashion industries need to and do pay more attention to contingency planning than do the furniture or automotive-parts industries.

THE CONTENT OF CONTINGENCY PLANNING

While it is not frequently necessary to develop highly detailed plans in contingency planning, it is necessary to identify the primary environments that need to be monitored and to make certain that the trigger points are established, that adequate monitoring systems are operational so that information to trip the trigger points will be available, and that a broadly defined process for responding to the tripping of the trigger points is in place, even if it is nothing more than promptly calling a meeting of the management team. More detailed contingency planning, however, may be necessary if the nature of the organization involves long lead time or serious risk, such as nuclear power, heavy industry, or the military. Generally, in the initial attempts at Applied Strategic Planning, contingency planning is very much of an afterthought, but as the planning process is repeated over time, more and more time and attention is devoted to contingency planning as the planning team begins to see the importance of this "what if" thinking.

THE TECHNOLOGY OF
CONTINGENCY PLANNING

In doing contingency planning, the following five key concepts or procedures are useful.

1. *The contingency-planning matrix,* which will help an organization to ensure that adequate attention is paid to its vulnerabilities and opportunities from both internal and external perspectives during the contingency planning phase of the planning process;

2. *The organizational-status taxonomy,* which allows an organization to develop a single indicator that is most descriptive of the fiscal viability of the organization;
3. *The macroeconomic indices* that are available from the environment and that are determined to be most significant to the organization or—where applicable—to the composite lines of business (LOBs);
4. *Expanded-business indices,* which are to be monitored by the various LOBs, SBUs, departments, divisions, and so on; and
5. *Composite budget-variation indicators,* which provide a single-figure indicator for the cumulative accuracy of the current year's budget, with a weighted variance indicator that can be keyed to both opportunity and vulnerability triggers for plans identified in contingency planning.

The Contingency-Planning Matrix

As in the SWOT analysis, contingency planning can be divided into two major categories: internal strengths and weaknesses and external opportunities and threats. Most organizations are more attuned to planning for internal contingencies than for external contingencies. They may have plans for succession, fires, and other disasters, but few have plans for new technologies, sudden changes in interest rates, and the like. Similarly, when managers consider business contingencies, they over-emphasize vulnerabilities and underemphasize opportunities.

Figure 13-2 depicts both the foci and emphases to be considered in contingency planning. If all four cells are evenly addressed during the contingency planning phase, the planning team can be assured that mutual blind spots will be avoided.

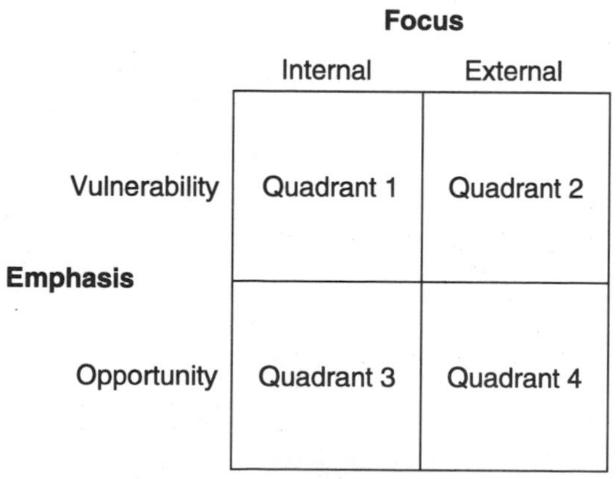

	Focus	
	Internal	External
Vulnerability	Quadrant 1	Quadrant 2
Opportunity	Quadrant 3	Quadrant 4

Emphasis

Figure 13-2. Contingency-Planning Matrix

Internal Weaknesses Need Contingency Plans

Nowhere in strategic planning literature or practice is "the conventional wisdom" less wise than it is with respect to contingency planning. A series of interviews with fifty-eight executives (O'Connor, 1978) indicates that the typical organization plans for a half-dozen critical events or contingencies. Steiner (1979) suggests that an equal (or smaller) number be planned for in order not to "generate excessive pessimism on the part of the planning team."

Our experience indicates that typical contingencies examined by a planning team include mundane possibilities such as:

1. The computer "eats" all the data;

2. The warehouse/facilities burn down;

3. Key employees leave to work for competitors; and

4. A key manager is hospitalized for an extended period.

One can easily see that these contingencies are vulnerabilities, and—with reference to Figure 13-2—probably belong in Quadrant 1 (i.e., internal vulnerabilities). As we will detail later, there is much, much more to contingency planning than simply identifying Quadrant-1 concerns.

The Applied Strategic Planning base plan builds an organizational model on a series of the highest-probability outcomes. Therefore, if the world behaves as the planning team thinks it most probably will, the planning is optimal. However, contingency planning goes farther: It examines times when the world behaves other than as expected in the base strategic plan. Given the relative low accuracy of most base-plan assumptions, the organization can come to a point at which the contingency planning supersedes the base plan. A *trigger point* is a set of observable circumstances that indicate that the base plan is not proceeding as anticipated and that the contingency plan should be put into action. Trigger points need to be carefully *predefined* to determine when the assumptions of the base plan are no longer valid and when new assumptions are required. Contingency plans (along with trigger points) should be established for each of the quadrants of Figure 13-2.

Quadrant-1 contingencies should include developing backup strategies for the loss of key personnel, reduction of productive capacity or storage facilities, and similar problems. Quadrant 2 should include alternative plans for securing critical resources, the arrival of unanticipated competitors, and the like. Quadrant 3 involves consideration of a new application of an existing product, the unexpected development of a new product, the development of new and strikingly significant cost-reduction processes, and so on. Quadrant 4 should involve consideration of potential acquisitions and mergers, the sudden availability of raw materials and other resources, and the like.

Once a contingency element has been identified, it is essential that (a) timely data be generated and monitored and (b) specific trigger points be established. One of the traps of managing in good times is that relatively high profits can mask eroding levels of productivity. If, for example, in monitoring the ratio between revenue and total employee compensation, a CEO discovers that total employee compensation equals $2,000,000 on annual sales of $10,000,000 (a ratio of .20), then the trigger points for the compensation-to-revenue ratio might be set at two levels: An erosion to .21 (+5 percent) may indicate an alert status (e.g., all managers should emphasize their monitoring of productivity concerns), but at .22 (+10 percent) specific action plans should be established (e.g., a hiring freeze). At .23 or .24 (+15 or +20 percent) an emergency would exist and the action plan should call for more drastic actions, such as layoffs.

Similar trigger points can be established around other key indices, such as the revenue/marketing ratio or revenue/scrap-costs (rate) ratios. The key indices generated in the strategic business modeling phase should all be bounded by specific contingency actions related to specific, preset trigger points.

It is equally important for the other cells in Figure 13-2 to be emphasized. For example, if sales of a new product or service exceed projections by 15 percent, the contingency plan may call for accelerated marketing, introduction into new geographic areas, or a crash introduction of spin-off products or services. It is as important to have specific plans for external opportunities as it is for internal vulnerabilities.

The number of key issues to be monitored should be between eight and twelve (two to four in each quadrant), with at least two in all four cells. It is the CEO's function to see that accurate and timely data are generated so that he or she can personally monitor all indices. Although it is acceptable to delegate preplanned actions to managers, it is not acceptable to delegate the monitoring of the indices.

The Operational Status of the Organization

It is an important aspect of contingency planning to be able to define the operational status of the organization at any point in time. To this end we have found it helpful to establish a definition for a seven-level operational taxonomy, as is shown in Figure 13-3. Although Figure 13-3

Level	Definition	Current Status
7.	*Extraordinary Performance:* Outperforming industry, long-term; profitable contracts; outstanding commitment from quality key staff; cash rich; etc.	———
6.	*Outstanding Performance:* Industry leader; several substantial contracts; highly motivated and competent staff; excellent cash and lines of credit; etc.	———
5.	*Very Good Performance:* Solid performance, reasonable future prospects; well-trained and interested staff; good cash and access to lines of credit; etc.	———
4.	*Good Performance:* Average performance; balanced strengths and weaknesses in products, services, customer base, and staff; mixed cash and credit line status; etc.	———
3.	*Fair Performance:* Below average performance; more weaknesses than strengths in products, services, customer base, and staff; unclear access to cash and credit necessary to survival and growth; etc.	———
2.	*Weak Performance:* Well below average performance, obvious weaknesses in almost all areas; serious difficulties in recruiting staff; serious cash and credit problems; etc.	———
1.	*Crisis Performance:* Grossly inadequate performance, insolvent; operating on guts and credit; can operate less than three months without cash infusion or major contract; etc.	———

Figure 13-3. Operational-Status Rating Sheet

details the recommended procedure for the planning team to define the taxonomy levels, it is important at this point to grasp the potency of a single organizational-status indicator that is prominently displayed in the offices of managers, meeting rooms, and—one would hope— employees' lounges and/or work areas.

It is important to distinguish this organizational-status indicator from the budget-variation indicators of Figure 13-5. It is conceivable that the accuracy of the budgeting process can be very high while the organization is simultaneously hurdling pell-mell toward failure. It is equally true that profits can be considerably below budgetary expectations while the company is solvent, profitable, and cash rich. The organizational-status indicator reflects basic organizational health, whereas the budget-variation indicators (which will be reviewed in more detail shortly) reflect the accuracy of the budgeting process.

Senior management, under the direction of the CEO, should be able to reach consensus on the organizational-status mode of the organization and invoke actions related to trigger points established for each mode. This will help monitor the expansion-contraction behavior necessary to avoid the overexpansion and survival modes as defined in Chapter 6 ("Environmental Monitoring and Application Considerations") and illustrated in Figures 6-2 and 6-3.

Macroeconomic and Expanded-Business Indices

The macroeconomic indices (such as changes in the gross national product or the money supply) and indices of inflation should be defined as relevant indicators for each organization or, where relevant, for each LOB. For example, a general economic downturn may be defined as a decline of two or more percentage points in gross national product for three consecutive quarters. This indicator should serve as a predictor of short-term future buying patterns of an organization's customers, and the organization should adjust accordingly.

Additionally, it is important to monitor inflationary pressures that may be defined as three quarters with annualized consumer-price-index increases of 8 percent or more. This pattern may trigger a move from quarterly (or even annual) to monthly pricing reviews. Perhaps annual reviews were adequate at one time and monthly reviews were seen as a time-consuming nuisance, but the times are changing and old solutions may no longer be adequate.

The indices relevant to any particular organization will, of course, vary widely. For example, construction-related organizations may monitor housing starts; labor-intensive industries may monitor the labor pool through the local unemployment rate; and credit-oriented consumer sales may be monitored through the prime interest rate.

Composite Budget-Variation Indicators

The budget-variation indicators are intended to be a key triggering point of the contingency-planning matrix. Although Figure 13-4 shows a basic business model for a sample manufacturing company, it can easily be adapted to any organization. Figure 13-5 shows composite budget-variation indicators (for the sample company of Figure 13-4) for the most recent month and cumulative figures for the fiscal year. By our definition, an organization is outside its strategic plan boundaries (Applied Strategic Planning base plan) when the weighted variation for a three-month period exceeds 10 percent. This should be a trigger level for some contingencies in the budget-variation alert matrix, as shown in Figure 13-6.

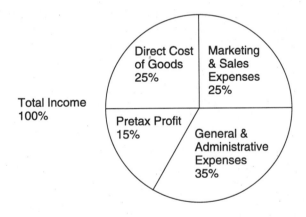

Figure 13-4. Basic Business Model (Manufacturing Company)

Weighted variations for a three-month period that exceed the 10-percent trigger levels should, at different levels of urgency, be triggers for other planned contingencies in the matrix. Although these alert levels are expressed in three-month horizons, we do not mean to imply that the process requires only quarterly attention. The CEO must monitor them on a monthly basis in order to direct tactical/operational interventions that can ameliorate or enhance monthly trends. Our point is that the three-month horizon removes the issue from the tactical/operational domain, and through the budget-variation alert guidelines it forces the issue into the strategic arena.

	Budget	Most Recent Month (June)	Variation	Last 3 Months (Apr.–June)	Variation	Weighted Average for Fiscal Year to Date (Jan.–June)	Variation
Total Income	100%	96%	-4%	91%	-9%	89%	-11%
Direct Cost of Goods	25%	27%	+8%	26%	+4%	24%	-4%
Marketing & Sales Expenses	25%	30%	+20%	28%	+12%	29%	+16%
General & Administrative Expenses	35%	36%	+2.8%	38%	+8.6%	38%	+8.6%
Pretax Profit	15%	7%	-54%	8%	-47%	9%	-40%

Figure 13-5. Sample Composite Budget-Variation Indicators

3-Month Cumulative

Alert Level 3 (> ± 10%, < ± 15%)   Some action required.

Alert Level 2 (> ± 15%, < ± 20%)   Immediate action required.

Alert Level 1 (> ± 20%)   Emergency action required.

Figure 13-6. Budget-Variation Alert Guidelines

Figure 13-7 provides a checklist for making certain the key elements of contingency planning have been addressed.

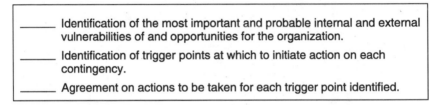

_____ Identification of the most important and probable internal and external vulnerabilities of and opportunities for the organization.

_____ Identification of trigger points at which to initiate action on each contingency.

_____ Agreement on actions to be taken for each trigger point identified.

Figure 13-7. Checklist for Necessary Outputs from Contingency Planning

SUMMARY

Contingency plans are preparations for specific actions that can be taken when unplanned-for events occur. Five key concepts should be considered in planning for contingencies: the contingency-planning matrix, the organizational-status indicator, macroeconomic indices, expanded-business indices, and composite budget-variation indicators. However, contingency planning is almost worthless unless it is an integral part of a good Applied Strategic Planning process. Contingency planning can be divided into two major categories: internal vulnerabilities/opportunities and external vulnerabilities/opportunities. Although most companies are more aware of internal contingencies than external contingencies, contingency plans should be established for each quadrant of the contingency-planning matrix. It is important to be able to define the operational status of the organization at any point in time. The budget-variation indicators are intended to be a key triggering point of the contingency-planning matrix.

REFERENCES

O'Connor, R. (1978). *Planning under uncertainty: Multiple scenarios and contingency planning.* New York: Conference Board.

Steiner, G.A. (1979). *Strategic planning: What every manager must know.* New York: Free Press.

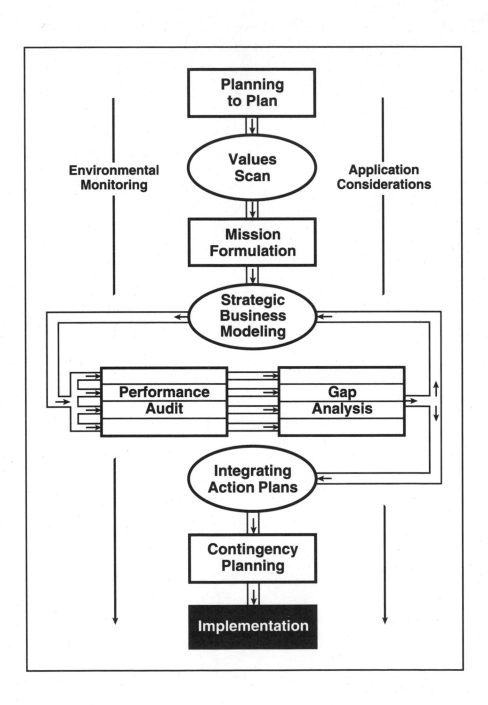

Chapter Fourteen

Implementation

Planning has to be a part of the company's mind set. Our people think about these things all the time. They don't hold a meeting once a year to dream up ways to plan for the future. It's part of the company's identity, values, and vision which can be recited by every Apple employee.

John Sculley
1987
(*Odyssey: Pepsi to Apple... A Journey of Adventure, Ideas, and the Future*, p. 296)

S trategic planning, in and of itself, is an academic pursuit, of little direct use to any organization. The payoff of strategic planning is in its application, in the execution and implementation of the strategic plan. It is here that we begin to see the long-term, systemic impact of Applied Strategic Planning. Galbraith and Nathanson (1978) emphasize the implementation aspects when they define strategy as "specific actions deriving from the 'strategy formulation process.' " The aim of strategic planning is to develop a better road map to guide the organization, and the planning process fails unless this road map actually does guide organizational decision making. This chapter is concerned with the decisions made to implement the strategic plan.

STRATEGIC MANAGEMENT

The management of an organization according to an explicit strategic plan is *strategic management*. All organizations have a strategy, but this strategy is often implicit and has not been thoughtfully examined. In such instances, one should not use the term strategic management to identify the management processes used by that organization. Strategic

The Aim Is to Develop a Better Road Map

management involves the execution of an explicit strategic plan that has captured the commitment of the people who must execute it; that is consistent with the values, beliefs, and culture of those people; and for which they have the required competence to execute (Peters, 1984).

In a study of ninety-four CEOs of a wide range of businesses, Reid (1989) found that this integration of strategic planning into the operations of their organizations occurred rarely, making the strategic planning process sterile. Reid identified three major reasons for these failures to implement the outcome of the planning process:

1. These CEOs and their direct subordinates were insufficiently involved in the planning process;
2. The planning process was not continuous and was seen as a sometime, semiacademic exercise unrelated to the operations of the business; and
3. The planning process did not adequately stimulate strategic thinking.

Although the Applied Strategic Planning model reduces or eliminates these reasons for failure, the important point to note here is that fewer than half of the CEOs in this study had even attempted to implement the plans that had been developed. Truly, for these CEOs, it was an academic exercise.

The acid test for any strategic planning process is the degree to which it impacts the ongoing behavior of the organization. The heavy emphasis on process considerations and concrete action steps in the Applied Strategic Planning model is intended to raise the probability that organizations that follow this model will find obvious behavioral consequences throughout the organization, especially at the managerial level. For example, "quality" is a key component of the Hoechst Celanese Corporation's strategic plan. Employees, including the top managers, wear HCQ (Hoechst Celanese Quality) lapel pins, posters about quality are everywhere in their plants, quality statistics are known by all, and all employees are evaluated against quality criteria as part of their routine performance appraisals.

The need for ownership, at least psychological ownership, is paramount for implementation. Consider the following simple, but true, metaphor. Have you ever rented a car from a car rental agency? Of course! But have you ever personally had that rental car washed at your own expense, even when it badly needed it? Probably not. Our informal survey on this matter has turned up only a handful of people who have taken this step, even though virtually all of them agreed that they regularly washed their own cars or had them washed. What's the difference? Ownership! If a planning team wants its strategic plans implemented, it should make sure that the people who are expected to implement them have a real sense of ownership *before* the implementation phase begins.

The final implementation of the strategic plan involves the initiation of the several action plans designed at the unit and functional level and their integration at the top of the organization. This may, for example, involve new construction, initiation of management development or technical training, increased research and development, or marketing of new products or services. All parts of the organization should feel that there is activity on all levels of the organization that will bring about the successful completion of the organization's mission. In the implementation phase all stakeholders need to be informed that the strategic plan is now being implemented and to agree to support that implementation.

This implementation of the strategic plan involves the *concurrent* initiation of several tactical or operational plans at a variety of different levels of the organization and in different segments. It is imperative that these changes be carefully managed at the top of the organization. In order to accomplish this, the changes in the management-control system, the information system, and the organizational culture that are needed to monitor and support the implementation of the strategic plan must be in place. If this is not the case, then a postponement of the implementation phase should be seriously considered.

A key challenge during implementation is keeping the strategic planning team involved and interested, yet not allowing them to take over the managing function of the organization. The planning team cannot and should not replace the properly constituted decision-making structure of the organization. If that structure is judged to be incapable of properly managing the implementation of the strategic plan, then, of course, the appropriate changes must be made. However, these changes should be made by the CEO, cleanly and with full awareness of what is being done and why. The risk is that the planning team can slowly and imperceptibly take over the management functions of the organization if this team is not managed properly. At this junction, the CEO should meet with the planning team and discuss the issues involved in implementation and clearly, but gently, assure the team that the implementation process will and must be handled by the management of the organization. The planning team's role will continue to be the oversight of the entire planning process. One important task that can be delegated to the planning team is to meet periodically and assess the progress of implementation. Their progress reports can then be shared with the management team and the rest of the organization. Such feedback is not only informative, but it also can motivate the organization to strive harder with the task of implementation. In other words, the planning team is responsible for formulating the strategic plan; the management team, for executing it.

The most important test of implementation, however, is the degree to which organizational members, especially managers, integrate the strategic plan into their everyday management decisions. A strategic plan is being implemented when the initial response of a manager confronted by a problem is to consider whether an answer is found in the organization's strategic plan. Although guidelines for every decision will not be provided by the planning process, consideration of the plan as the first step in decision making is the best evidence of the plan's implementation. Again, at Hoechst Celanese it is rare to attend a business-planning meeting where those in attendance do not refer to their division's or operating unit's strategic plan as the template against which to test a decision that is being made.

An organization that is driven by a strategic plan solidly based on environmental monitoring can be said to be *aligned* with its environment. Without such a strategic plan the organization is *misaligned* with its environment, as shown in Figure 14-1. The figure schematically shows that, without a common mission, neither the organization nor its members know where they are going and thus are incapable of moving in a cohesive, integrated fashion. Figure 14-2 schematically shows what happens when an organization has a strategic plan that attempts to align it with its environment but has not been successful in communicating this plan to its members. In Figure 14-2, while the energy of some of the members is directed to a common goal, other members are pursuing other goals. This lack of internal alignment limits the organization's progress in attaining its goals. Figure 14-3, however, suggests what can happen when there is an alignment both of the organization and of all its members. This means that there is widespread understanding and acceptance of the organization's mission and strategy, as well as commitment to it, and that major decisions made by the organization are derived from that strategy. The goal of Applied Strategic Planning is that kind of alignment.

THE STRUCTURAL ASPECTS OF IMPLEMENTATION

In the strategic planning of almost all organizations, the long-term survival of the organization is either an explicit goal or a given. That survival depends on the organization's positive response to the opportunities for appropriate growth to meet the increasing demands of the marketplace. It is impossible for an organization to maintain a steady state over any extended period of time; as the demands for the organization's products or services wax and wane, the organization must grow or shrink in response to those changes. Furthermore, not only must the size of the organization change, but its structure must also change. The structure that served the organization well at a certain size may no longer be appropriate for its new or planned size.

One of the seminal thinkers on strategic planning, Alfred D. Chandler (1962), identified four key growth strategies (see Figure 14-4) that typically are sequentially used to ensure survival, and he suggested appropriate structures for each state in the organization's development. Chandler's four strategies are (1) expansion of volume, (2) geographic dispersion, (3) vertical integration, and (4) product or service diversification. Chandler demonstrated that each of these strategies posed different administrative problems and, therefore, tended to lead to different organizational structures. Chandler was the first to both argue and prove that there needs to be a "fit" between an organization's strategy and the organization's structure if that strategy is to succeed. Therefore, one of the important ways to implement a strategic plan would be to design the organization to "fit" that plan; that is, to make certain that structure followed strategy.

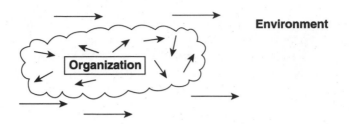

Figure 14-1. A Misaligned Organization Without a Strategic Plan

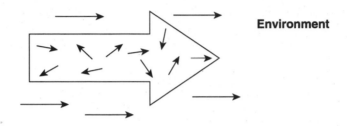

Figure 14-2. An Organization that Has a Strategic Plan but Does Not Have its Members Aligned with the Plan

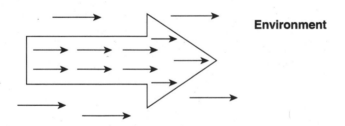

Figure 14-3. An Organization that Has both a Strategic Plan and its Members Aligned with the Plan

In fact, without attending to these structural issues, it may be impossible to implement the strategy. Consider each of Chandler's key growth strategies in the light of what organizational-structural issues emerge for each. The first strategy is *expansion of volume* or increasing sales to a single new market or in existing markets. In most cases an organization starts as a single unit—a plant, a hospital, a store, a warehouse, or a school. As growth occurs, it requires the single unit to develop an administrative arm to handle those functions that are not directly involved in the major organizational processes. As the factory

> 1. Expansion of Volume
> 2. Geographic Dispersion
> 3. Vertical Integration
> 4. Product or Service Diversification

Figure 14-4. Key Growth Strategies

produces more and more widgets, as the hospital treats more and more patients, and so on, there is more and more need for record keeping, financial management, supply ordering, and the like. Thus, volume expansion creates the need to develop separate administrative services; and when an organization's strategic planning process leads to a principal focus on volume, adequate attention must be paid to having the necessary administrative structure in place to support the increased volume. Otherwise, the plan will fail.

The second growth strategy is that of *geographic dispersion*, which creates multiple field units in the same function or industry but in different geographic locations. Such expansion can provide closer contact with the organization's customers or client base, enhance the delivery of goods or services, increase production volume and market penetration without committing the organization to a limited resource or customer pool, and so on; but problems of interunit coordination, specialization, and standardization arise and need to be solved, typically by the development of functional departments, such as manufacturing, marketing, and sales. These problems often come as a surprise to those involved, and—because of inadequate planning—the organization lacks the understanding or the resources to develop the functional departments that can solve such problems. The development of these functional departments adds to the overhead expense of the organization, often in unforeseen ways. Failure, however, to solve these problems of coordination would prevent the successful implementation of a strategic plan based on geographic expansion.

The third growth strategy is that of *vertical integration;* that is, the organization stays in the same business but develops or acquires related functions. These functions can precede the organization's current function—*backward integration*—or follow it—*forward integration*. For example, in backward integration a computer manufacturer might develop the capacity to produce its own chips—as Digital Equipment has done, at least partially. Such backward integration might even extend to the raw materials required for its primary products; for example, paper mills may buy forests. In forward integration, manufacturers may develop their own distribution centers or their own sales forces, as Boise Cascade once did with its home-improvement centers.

The problems that emerge in the vertical-integration strategy concern balancing the sequential movement of goods, services, and people through the various interdependent functions of the organization. For example, an organization may need to deal with a subassembly manufacturing unit that produces more than the main plant needs in the immediate future. The management of such a problem is typically accomplished through the development of accurate forecasting procedures, scheduling, and capacity-balancing techniques. Any organization contemplating a vertical-integration strategy needs to determine how these coordinating mechanisms will be developed. During the end of the decade of the 1980s, vertical integration fell into disfavor as a growth strategy as organizations discovered the diseconomies of scale—the cost and slow response times of large bureaucratic systems that develop as coordinating mechanisms. Recall the cases of Commodore Computers and IBM detailed in Chapter 11 ("Gap Analysis") regarding divesting their service and warehousing functions, respectively.

Chandler's fourth growth strategy is that of *product diversification*. In this strategy, organizations move into new businesses to utilize their existing resources, including physical, human, and capital resources, as their primary markets mature or decline. The problems that emerge in this strategy are those of appraising and evaluating new product divisions, each of which must be treated as an investment decision that requires time to make. At the same time, the organization must continue to serve its existing markets. The typical solution to these problems has been the development of the multidivisional structure, wherein each division reports to a corporate headquarters. This structure is based on temporal considerations; the general office is concerned with long-term, strategic decisions, and the product divisions tend to be concerned with short-term, operational decisions. Also typical in this structure are general managers, usually titled group executives, who are expected to tie the strategic direction set by the general office to the internal management of the product divisions.

Regardless of which strategy is selected, extensive attention needs to be paid to these issues of organizational structure. If these issues are not considered earlier during Applied Strategic Planning, they must be dealt with during the implementation phase.

A Case Example

Chandler (1962), Kotler (1980), and others have provided strong empirical support for the concept that the successful execution of an organization's strategy requires that an organization either have in place the appropriate structure for that strategy or quickly develop such a structure. For example, Galbraith (1971) traced the changes over a decade in the structure of the commercial airplane division of the Boeing Company as a function of changes in the division's strategy. At the beginning the 707, the civilian version of the military KC-135 transport, provided Boeing with a vehicle to enter the commercial aircraft market.

Boeing "made a market" for commercial jet aircraft where there had previously been only propeller-driven aircraft. Boeing built a prototype, demonstrated it to the airlines, and took the resulting orders from the impressed airline officials. The success of the 707 resulted in the development of competition (DC-8 and Convair 880) for the intercontinental aircraft market. Boeing next "made a market" by introducing the 727 for intermediate-length flights. The strategy was the same as it had been for the 707. Boeing carefully developed and tested a model that resulted in orders before production began. All of this was accomplished with a traditional functional organization.

The commercial aircraft business changed dramatically in the mid-1960s. Douglas, rather than developing a competitor to the 727, developed the DC-9, a short-haul aircraft. This further subdivided the market and soon there was a host of competitors. Rather than being able to "make a market," Boeing then had to face the fact that the market existed and that it had to be entered quickly. Boeing's initial strategy (i.e., slowly and carefully developing a new model and expecting to monopolize the market temporarily as a consequence of its technological innovation) was no longer functional. It had to develop new models quickly (new versions of the 727, the short-haul 737, and the jumbo 747) and market them in the face of competition. The combination of competition, internal demands for various resources, and a shortened time frame produced serious internal problems that made it clear to Boeing's top management that the earlier functional organization was not adequate to solve these emerging problems.

Boeing's response was to reorganize its commercial-aircraft division into a multidivisional structure. One division was created for each of its major product lines together with a central fabricating division. Once this structure was firmly in place, Boeing was able to solve its internal problems successfully and resume its profitable course. A divisional structure enabled Boeing to adapt more promptly to its new market, its diverse product lines, and the increased competition.

Total Cycle Time

More recently, increased competition and reduced market share have forced many other organizations to reconsider how their present structures impede promptness in responding to the market—promptness in product development, product release, customer service, and so on. The December, 1990, issue of the journal, *Planning Review*, was devoted to "TIME: The New Strategic Frontier," and a series of articles by prominent strategic planners argue that time has become a strategic weapon and that a time-based strategy can give an organization a competitive advantage. Chapter 10 ("Performance Audit") introduced the concept of Total Cycle Time (TCT) as a competitive advantage that should be assessed as part of the performance audit (see Thomas, 1990).

Total Cycle Time Has Become a Strategic Weapon

The examples of time as a competitive advantage are multiplying almost too quickly for most of us to keep up with. As one example of this growing trend, Toyota, by decreasing its model-development time from five to three years, has been able to both offer more styles and incorporate the latest technological developments into its cars. Buick, discussed in Chapter 11, is still struggling to reduce the time it takes to move a new model from conceptualization to production to four years. Toyota's reduction in TCT has earned it both increased market share and customer loyalty as a technology and quality leader. As another example from quite a different industry, Citibank has been able to cut the approval time for its home mortgages from one month to ten days. Since all the parties to this transaction—the mortgage broker, the buyer, the seller, and their realtors—value this reduction in approval time, Citibank had been able to use time as a competitive weapon and carve out a 10-percent market share in the national home-mortgage market. In a more general example, Procter & Gamble (one of America's most successful marketing organizations) was able to speed up its product-development and release cycle. Procter & Gamble rolled out several of its new products, such as Ivory Shampoo and Liquid Tide, from test market to nationwide distribution in less than four months, rather than the three or four years previously required.

In Japan, Panasonic is able to produce custom-made bicycles overnight. To do this, a customer walks into a shop that sells Panasonic bicycles and sits on a special bike that is adjusted to "fit" the customer. Once the fit is accomplished and the color and other choices are made, the clerk activates the internal modem in the special bike, which flashes the measurements to the Panasonic factory where it is scheduled for production the next day. What is interesting about this example is that Panasonic has had to "age" their bicycles for several weeks, because customers simply refused to accept the next-day delivery as possible for a truly customized product. Apparently TCT takes some external market preparation as well as changes in the internal structure of the organization. The Panasonic story is an example of how quickness of response, the key ingredient of TCT, can send the wrong message to the customer.

Nevertheless, in all these examples, the companies have used TCT—in either product development or delivery—as a competitive advantage to take market share away from their competitors. Making this happen is not easy; it typically requires a dramatic change in the structure and function of the organization. In the case of Toyota, it required greater integration of its marketing with both its design and its production-engineering groups. In the case of Citibank, it required the development of multifunctional teams and the delegation of decision-making power to lower levels of the organization. In the case of P&G, it required a realignment of its marketing and product-management structures and staff. Clearly, any organization that tries to use TCT as a competitive tool will need to examine its structure and work processes to ascertain where blocks to prompt response exist and then to move to eliminate them.

These blockages to TCT can be categorized into three major groupings:

1. The organizational culture;
2. The existing structure and systems; and
3. The existing pattern of work flow.

Insofar as the organizational culture is involved, the central question is to what extent speed has ever been part of the culture of the organization. We can all think of organizations that prize precision over promptness, where one could perish while waiting for an organizational response. To now insist on a dramatic shift in that approach may represent too large a gap to close, at least in some reasonable time frame.

With respect to structural and systems issues, the planning team must consider how hierarchical the structure is and where decision-making power resides. Greater empowerment of the lower levels of the organization is required for TCT to work as a strategy. Similarly, multifunctional work teams, in which all the necessary expertise and skill are present, are essential for TCT to work effectively.

Finally, most organizations spend a good bit of time and energy in the simple handing off of work from one person to another, from one team to another, and so on. For example, in the case of Citibank's mortgage-processing operation, one group handled the credit-rating information, another the appraisals, another the title information, and so on. Each group did its portion of the work in a sequence and a holdup anywhere in the sequence simply stopped the movement of the case through the system. This differentiation of effort produced highly efficient technicians in the various phases of mortgage handling but severely slowed down the output of the completed application. This kind of task differentiation, so powerful a force in the development of the industrial model, has now become obsolete. As we noted in the previous paragraph, the use of multifunctional work teams who accomplish most, if not all, of a task is an essential ingredient of TCT.

Time-based strategies have become a critically important part of the strategic options for organizations in the 1990s. Implementing them, however, will not be easy. The issues that we have touched on as impediments to adopting TCT as part of an organization's approach to implementing strategy, or as part of its core strategy, need to be directly addressed and resolved—resolved with the same degree of vigor that should have characterized the rest of the organization's Applied Strategic Planning efforts.

Time can provide a competitive advantage, however, only if a time-based differential is sustained and if time is valued by the customer. That means that the goal must be one of continual reduction in TCT; the time-based leader can never stop watching the clock. In the words of the baseball immortal, Satchel Paige, "Never look back. They may be gaining on you!" Furthermore, a time-based competitive advantage can be sustained only in an organizational culture that prizes innovation, nimbleness of action, and speed of response, coupled with the technology that allows these values to be implemented—combining the soft and hard aspects of management.

Some Research Evidence

If we examine in greater detail the nature of the mechanisms used by organizations to implement strategic plans, the research of Galbraith (1973) is instructive. He compared three industries that differed dramatically in the introduction of new products over two decades. The container industry introduced no new products during that period, but new products introduced by the food industry accounted for 15 percent of all its products and the plastics industry's new products accounted for 35 percent. All three industries used four common integrative/control mechanisms: rules, hierarchical authority to resolve disputes, goal setting, and direct contact among diverse elements for problem solving. The food industry, however, also used cross-functional task forces and product managers who served an integrative product-development function; the plastics industry used multilevel, cross-functional integrative teams as well as a higher percentage of integrative product managers.

Galbraith concludes that these additional mechanisms for coordination enabled the food and plastics industries to be innovative and develop new products. He notes that these product managers serve a general management function that is necessary to coordinate the cross-functional work required to develop new products. This added structural element was required to execute the strategic plans for product innovation that typified the plastics and food industries. It was not re-

Announce the Plan with Pomp and Ceremony

quired for the more predictable and less diverse container industry; however, changes in the highly innovative container industry since the Galbraith study indicate that this is no longer true.

It should be clear by now that any Applied Strategic Planning process must involve an in-depth analysis of whether or not the organization's structure fits its strategic plan. If it does not fit, either the structure or the plan needs to be revised. Structure alone, however, is not sufficient to guarantee that the strategic plan will be implemented; a number of functional factors need to be considered.

THE FUNCTIONAL ASPECTS
OF IMPLEMENTATION

Once a strategic plan is in place, together with an organizational structure that fits that plan, it needs to become the road map by which the organization travels, the template against which organizational decisions are made, the scale on which resource allocations are made, the focus of organizational energy, and so on. However, if these descriptions of the strategic plan are seen simply as cliches, the plan will never be implemented. On the other hand, even if the planning team and top management are committed to the plan and its success, there is still the question of how a strategic plan becomes part of the lifeblood of an organization.

If the Applied Strategic Planning process has been followed, then the organization is more than casually aware of the planning process. This awareness will be heightened if the planning team has been making periodic reports to the employees about planning developments and where it stands in the process. The final announcement and presentation of the plan needs to be accomplished with the pomp and ceremony that signal an important event in the life of the organization. All-personnel meetings, special issues of newsletters, and videotape presentations are several ways to alert and involve the rank and file of the organization. Figure 14-5 provides a list of ideas for communicating the final strategic plan to the rest of the organization at this stage of the planning process. The effort in this roll out is to celebrate the creation of a plan with broad ownership—it is the organization's plan, not the planning team's plan!

The process by which employees buy in and commit to the strategic plan does not stop with the introduction of the plan. A strategic plan is not an event; it is a process, and for most organizations it must be an

---

- Printed plan distributed with a cover letter.
- Organization-wide managers' meeting to hear directly from the chief executive and other members of the planning team.
- Divisional all-employee meetings to hear questions and answers and concerns about the plan.
- Two-day workshops to learn about strategic planning, discuss the strategic plan, and build supporting plans at a unit or individual level.
- Posters with planning themes.
- Individual cards with statement of values, mission, and CSIs.
- Videocassettes of the chief executive or others as they explain the organization's vision and strategies to achieve that vision.
- Internal-newsletter stories or memos/letters introducing the plan (overall, and then later one piece at a time).
- News releases and special public feature stories.
- "Report cards" each quarter.
- Copies of information available to all employees at convenient locations.

Figure 14-5. Ideas for Communicating Strategic Plans

ongoing process. For this process to "take," managers, especially top managers, need to be clearly committed to the strategic plan and need to use it in obvious ways. When a decision based on a strategic consideration is made, the basis for that decision needs to be explicitly and fully communicated to those involved. When a decision is requested by subordinates, managers need to discuss how the organization's strategic plan can guide that decision. Even with operational decisions that have no bearing on the execution of the strategic plan, management's commitment to the plan enhances its credibility throughout the organization.

The Role of the CEO in Strategic Management

The role of the CEO in the implementation of the strategic plan cannot be overemphasized. The CEO must lead that effort and must be totally committed to it. This commitment goes far beyond annual talks to employees and reports to shareholders or to the board of directors. The implementation of an organization's strategic plan requires an emotional *internalization* of the plan on the part of the CEO. The chief executive officer has to want to effect the changes that the strategic plan requires; and his or her actions have to indicate that there is a deep, strong belief in what he or she is doing. Once the strategy is internalized by the CEO and by those who report directly to the CEO, it guides every operating decision and becomes the driving force for the organization.

The importance of the role of the CEO is further documented by a recent report by Sellers (1991). Sellers asked the CEOs of America's ten best-managed companies what they viewed as the critical elements of their job. There was widespread agreement on three such elements:

1. Setting the corporate strategy;
2. Aligning the employees with it; and
3. Developing a successor.

The first of these does not mean that these CEOs believe that they should personally set the corporate strategy but rather that they need to make certain that a strategy-formulation process is initiated and that they participate in that process. Aligning the employees behind that strategy is what we have been highlighting throughout this chapter and this book. Having a strategy without aligning the members of the organization with that strategy (see Figure 14-2) is an exercise in futility. The final task of developing a successor is a topic for a different book, but certainly an important one. What is clear from Sellers' work is that if the best-managed companies in America see a need for setting and implementing a strategy, should others try for less?

The Role of Budgeting in Strategic Management

Several supporting functional elements help incorporate the strategic plan into the workings of an organization, the most important of which is the budget. As Chapter 12 ("Integrating Action Plans") noted, the budgets of the functional units of the organization need to be integrated into a single organizational budget that is the personification of the organization's strategic plan. The process by which the organization's management reviews the variances from budget, positive and negative, is the most obvious and clear-cut way of identifying the degree to which the strategic plan is being executed. The budget may be considered as the navigator's tactics for arriving at the ship's destination; and budgetary variances, especially serious ones, suggest that arriving at the intended port may be delayed or may never even occur.

At this juncture it is worthwhile to remember that it is typical to underestimate the true costs of implementing the strategic business model. Chapter 9 ("Strategic Business Modeling") pointed out how the cost of strategic thrusts such as globalization and automation are underestimated. When these costs are underestimated, the budget can be quickly exceeded and the implementation process may have to be placed on hold, with negative consequences for both the integrity of the planning process and the development of the organization. In order to prevent such delays, proper budget planning and close monitoring of the budget are mandatory.

The use of the budget to operationalize the strategic plan and the use of the budget-review process as a constant measure of the organization's success in executing its strategic plan not only give life to the organization's budgeting processes, but also demand a strong commitment to the use of the budget on an ongoing basis. When forecasts of revenues are not met, when expenditures exceed budgetary limits, and when resources are allocated off-line, we have clear evidence that the strategic plan is not being executed.

CSIs and Strategic Management

Other indices also need to be included in the evaluation of the degree to which the strategic plan is being implemented. The Critical Success

Indicators (CSIs) developed in strategic business modeling should be those indices. The CSI should have set the standards of performance in each of the strategically important areas of organizational functioning. These CSIs should drive the process of implementation; the task of management is to measure actual performance continually in these areas and to identify any deviations from these predetermined standards of performance. An organization that has increased market share as an important aspect of its strategic plan should have developed a CSI about market share in its strategic business modeling process. The executive staff of the organization should monitor this CSI on a regular basis and initiate corrective actions if the CSI is not being attained or provide rewards to those involved in the successful attainment of the CSI. In a similar fashion, an organization that holds quality as part of its strategic plan needs to include a variety of quality CSIs, such as scrap rate, in-warranty service calls, and customer complaints. None of these, however, should take the place of the budget as the main measure of the success of the organization in executing its strategic plan.

Nevertheless, the implementation of the strategic plan requires more than adherence to an adequate budgetary system and the emotional and psychological commitment of management. The strategic plan needs to be embedded in the performance-management and performance-appraisal systems of the organization. The strategic-focused performance-management system is one of the key tools of strategic management. In such a plan, the performance appraisals of all members of the organization include a test of how their work since their previous reviews has helped carry out the strategic plan of the organization. In other words, each member of the organization should have a personal set of CSIs that were derived from the organization's CSIs. Thus the performance of an operator on a production line is not measured simply on the basis of output, but also on the basis of how that output (or quality, etc.) has helped the organization accomplish its objectives.

One of the important reasons for the success of British Airways in achieving its mission of becoming "the world's favorite airline" was the inclusion of customer service as a factor in the performance-appraisal system. All BA employees, from top management to cabin crew and reservation clerks, are evaluated on their attitudes toward and performance in customer service. Installing such a performance-management system is not easy; it takes both some imagination and a high degree of commitment to the full implementation of the strategic plan.

Accountability

For the Applied Strategic Planning process to continue to be seen as vital to the future of the organization, the various approaches used by the organization to hold units and people accountable *must* reflect the elements of the strategic plan. A process for doing this involves, first, developing specific strategically based CSIs for each member of the top-management team; then each member of that team does the same for his or her subordinates, and so on, cascading throughout the structure of the organization. The organization's performance-management system should then hold every member of the organization accountable for the achievement of his or her CSIs, thus ensuring that the strategic plan will be implemented or, at least, that there will be serious effort expended toward that goal.

For example, if a bonus plan exists, it should be tied to the strategic plan. Bonuses should be based on the achievement of CSIs established by the strategic planning process. If a management-by-objectives program is in place, the objectives should be selected from the CSIs of the strategic plan. If a pay-for-performance system is used, the performance that is "paid for" should spin out of the strategic plan. In other words, there should be a close alignment of the pay system and the organization's strategy (Lawler, 1990). The bottom line of this discussion is that for the strategic planning process to have the required impact on the organization, it must hold people accountable for the effort that is necessary for implementation.

This accountability needs to occur in the not-for-profit sector as well. At the County of Los Angeles Public Library, the strategy and CSIs for the next year are tied to the pay-for-performance goals of the CEO, the County Librarian. These CSIs then cascade down through the several management levels as each person is assigned his or her part of each critical success indicator.

Acknowledgments, Recognitions, and Celebrations

Each time a significant milestone is reached in implementation, a celebration is needed. Organizations that regularly attend to such accomplishments with verbal praise, recognition pins, company picnics, bonuses, and the like are clearly demonstrating to their employees two things: the organization's commitment to the accomplishment of its

A "B" Quality Plan Implemented in an "A" Manner Will Outperform an "A" Quality Plan Implemented in a "B" Manner

strategic plan and the organization's awareness that the accomplishment of the plan requires everyone's involvement and hard work.

The successful implementation of a strategic plan is no small accomplishment. It requires the initial creativity and energy to develop the plan, the courage and commitment to introduce it, and the persistence and thoroughness to see it through to its implementation. Without a strong process for ensuring its implementation, there is little or no reason for developing a strategic plan. An unidentified student of strategic planning expressed it this way: A "B" quality plan executed in an "A" manner will always outperform an "A" quality plan executed in a "B" manner.

ENVIRONMENTAL SCANNING

The fact that the "final" strategic plan has been rolled out and the beginning steps of implementing that plan are underway does not relieve the organization from continually monitoring its environments, both internal and external. The world in which the organization exists *continues* to change; and management needs to be alert to any changes in its external environment, its industry, or its competitors and in its internal environment that threaten the successful implementation of its strategy. This monitoring is especially important during the early stages of implementation, when the organization is preoccupied and may neglect its environmental monitoring and then fail to resume it—hoping, if not believing, that everything that needs to be done has been done.

In this connection, the strategic decisions are based on assumptions—about markets, products, internal resources, and so on—and it is necessary to verify that the assumptions made during the planning process are holding true. For example, one of our clients assumed as part of its planning process that a new manufacturing facility would be fully operational by the middle of the upcoming budget year, and many of the new LOBs depended on this increased capacity. Shortly after the beginning of the budget year, it was discovered that some of the new equipment for the plant would not be available from the manufacturer, because of an unexpected labor stoppage. The assumption about capacity was no longer viable and the client was forced to move to one of its contingency plans. Without monitoring the possibility of this event and moving promptly to take the change in assumption into account, the negative impact on the organization no doubt would have been much greater than it was.

An example of the consequences of this process can be found in the case of General Motors, which in the late 1970s designed a highly ambitious, very sophisticated strategic plan to restore the automaker to its former preeminence. Using the best data available, GM developed complex computer models to make it comparable to the Japanese. GM committed forty billion dollars and several years to a plan that would retool their manufacturing facilities by advanced technology while simultaneously redesigning both the corporation structure and the vehicles it produced. By 1990, over sixty billion dollars had been spent, but GM's quality was still uneven, its sales were weak, it was hemorrhaging money despite closing many plants, and for several years during the end of the 1980s, Ford was both outselling GM and making more money. How could this happen? It launched a plan based on the "truths" of 1979-80. When these conditions shifted, the GM plan was not readjusted. Also, GM overspent the budget by 50 percent; and during 1988, GM produced a million more cars than the marketplace wanted. It assumed that during the time that they were upgrading their own facilities and processes, the Japanese automakers would remain constant. Of course, nothing could be farther from the case; during this time the Japanese automakers were equally busy in a process of improvement, although much less willing to spend the sums of money that GM did. As a result, while GM had reduced the gap between their products and those of the Japanese, substantial gaps still existed, and these gaps have continued to negatively impact GM's market share. The moral of this tale is two-fold: Always check your assumptions and adjust the plan as assumptions change; and always think down-board.

Strategies have also been developed on the expectation that the gaps identified in the gap analysis were going to be bridged. Bridging or closing those gaps typically is not an instantaneous process; it takes time. However, the successful implementation of most strategies depends on actually having the gap bridged or at least having made substantial progress toward closing the gap. This requires the planning team to monitor regularly the organization's internal environment to verify that such progress in gap reduction is actually being made. For example, at BA the gap in customer service was substantial, and it was recognized that even partially implementing the strategy could not be delayed until the customer service gap was closed. This meant, however, that there was a continual need for the planning team and top management to monitor the progress in closing this particular gap and to push for greater and greater progress. Otherwise, the goal would never be accomplished.

Attention must also be paid to *indicator control,* that is, whether the important CSIs are driving behavior in the desired direction and not leading to abuse. For example, consider an organization that developed a series of CSIs about reducing its TCT. A potential abuse of these CSIs could result in a decrease in quality. In other words, employees—in their desire to move work through the system—could become sloppy about the quality of their product, a risk inherent in adopting a TCT approach. Monitoring the impact of CSIs for both their intended and unintended impact on behavior is necessary if the organization is going to be successful in implementing strategy.

Strategic planning, even Applied Strategic Planning, does not necessarily lead to success. The Edsel was a monument to the failure of the strategic planning process, as are the more recent attempts of the oil (or energy) industry to develop oil shale as a major fuel source. In these cases of failure, the reason is simply that there was no way to know (until after the fact) whether or not the necessary ingredients were present. Proper assumptions, continual testing of them, sophisticated environmental surveillance, a high degree of organizational competence, and just a little bit of luck are all necessary.

Managing strategically takes time, effort, and resources. At American Airlines, every Monday CEO Robert Crandall and his senior management team spend all day in strategic-management sessions. Crandall has been quoted as saying this is *not* sufficient time, given the turbulence in the airline industry, but it is all that they can spare from operational concerns. This is certainly a far cry, however, from the typical management pattern of spending virtually no time on strategic issues.

The real measure, however, of the success of Applied Strategic Planning does not take place until the second or third year of the process. Many organizations "do a plan." They commit the time and energy to a planning effort that they hope will set the organization's direction for the next three to five years. They put the plan in place and hope that it works. Our model of Applied Strategic Planning requires continuous strategic management and continuous surveillance of the appropriate environments. The results of this effort are not immediately apparent. It ordinarily takes several years for the impact of even the optimal planning effort to bear fruit, and that fruit is borne only by diligent effort and by regular mid-course corrections that are necessary in the execution of any plan. The Applied Strategic Planning process needs to be repeated on a regular basis. Chapter 15 returns to the process of recycling Applied Strategic Planning.

Figure 14-6 provides a convenient checklist for the planning team to use in verifying that all the necessary steps involved in implementation have been addressed.

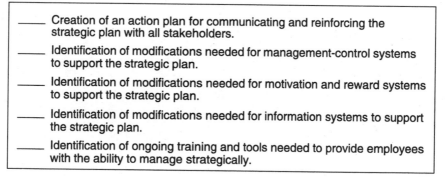

Figure 14-6. Checklist of Specific Outputs Required in Implementation Phase

SUMMARY

The payoff of strategic planning is in the implementation of the strategic plan. The acid test for any strategic planning process is the degree to which it impacts the ongoing behavior of the organization. Implementation is not only the final phase of the Applied Strategic Planning Model, it is also an ongoing process throughout all the other phases. In order to succeed, the organization's strategy must fit the organization's structure. Four typical growth strategies are (1) expansion of volume, (2) geographic dispersion, (3) vertical integration, and (4) product or service diversification. Each of these strategies should be considered in light of what organizational design issues emerge from each. The implementation issues will vary dramatically from one strategy to another. The strategic plan needs to become a road map by which the organization travels and the template on which organizational decisions are based. The final announcement and presentation of the plan needs to be accomplished with the pomp and ceremony that signal an important event in the life of the organization.

REFERENCES

Chandler, A.B. (1962). *Strategy and structure.* Cambridge, MA: M.I.T. Press.

Galbraith, J.R. (1971). Matrix organization design. *Business Horizons, 14,* 29-40.

Galbraith, J.R. (1973). *Designing complex organizations.* Reading, MA: Addison-Wesley.

Galbraith, J.R., & Nathanson, D.A. (1978). *Strategy implementation: The role of structure and process.* St. Paul, MN: West.

Kotler, P. (1980, May-June). Strategic planning and the marketing process. *Business,* pp. 2-9. Reprinted in J. W. Pfeiffer (Ed.). (1991). *Strategic planning: Selected readings* (rev. ed.). San Diego, CA: Pfeiffer & Company.

Lawler, E.E., III. (1990). *Strategic pay: Aligning organizational strategies and pay systems.* San Francisco: Jossey-Bass.

Peters, T.J. (1984). Strategy follows structure: Developing distinctive skills. *California Management Review, 26*(3), 111-125. Reprinted in J. W. Pfeiffer (Ed.). (1991). *Strategic planning: Selected readings* (rev. ed.). San Diego, CA: Pfeiffer & Company.

Reid, D.M. (1989). Operationalizing strategic planning. *Strategic Management Journal, 10,* 553-567.

Sellers, P. (1991, April 22). Does the CEO really matter? *Fortune,* pp. 80-94.

Thomas, P.R. (1990). *Total cycle time: An overview for CEOs.* New York: McGraw-Hill.

TIME: The new strategic frontier. *Planning Review, 18,* 1-48.

Chapter Fifteen

Conclusions and Recycling Considerations

Make no small plans...for they have not the power to stir men's blood.

Niccolo Machiavelli
The Prince, 1514

This concluding chapter has three major sections. It starts with an analysis of some of the pitfalls that exist in strategic planning and ways they can be avoided. This analysis is followed by a checklist that summarizes the outputs of each phase of Applied Strategic Planning that are necessary for its success. Some important issues involved in the regular recycling of the Applied Strategic Planning process are then discussed.

AVOIDING PITFALLS

Every process, especially strategic planning, involves some potential pitfalls. An awareness of these pitfalls and where they are encountered can help both the planning team and its consultant(s) to avoid them. Stringer and Uchenick (1986) identify fifteen such pitfalls or traps that are endemic to strategic planning. These authors argue that the majority of these traps occur in implementing the plan, not in formulating it. Nevertheless, they point out that the typical major obstacle to good implementation is the concentration in the planning process on the *content* of the plan with a consequent neglect of the *process* of strategic planning—a flaw that the Applied Strategic Planning model directly addresses. As a further check on the quality of the Applied Strategic Planning model, the fifteen specific traps named by Stringer and Uchenick are listed below, and the extent to which Applied Strategic Planning addresses them will be examined.

1. Bigger is better.
2. Spreading yourself too thin.
3. Stuck in the middle.
4. Not being customer-driven.
5. Cheaper is better.
6. Underestimating our competition.
7. If it ain't broke, don't fix it.
8. What they don't know won't hurt them.
9. Sloppy communication.
10. Eloquence in everything.
11. Failing to raise the bar.
12. Making the numbers.
13. A good athlete can run any business.
14. Analysis paralysis.
15. Ignoring the corporate culture.

We contend that the first seven traps can occur in the formulation phases, and the first three frequently stem from the organization's naive attempts to grow the business. The first, "Bigger is better," comes from the belief that there are always significant economies of scale. While sometimes true, this belief becomes a trap when factors other than volume impact profits, especially management time and attention. Analyzing how each component of the cost base responds to scale as part of planning can help avoid this trap. Another potential trap involved in rapid growth is "spreading yourself too thin." This trap is sprung when the organization's efforts exceed its capacity, for example, when it fails to recognize the differences in its markets, does not identify the target market(s), and cannot develop an efficient distribution system. In an effort to serve a too-broad market, the business ends up not serving any market well. Avoiding this trap involves trade-offs, which require strong discipline in the planning process. The third such growth-derived pitfall is the classic strategy trap described in detail by Porter (1980), where there is not a clear choice of a marketing strategy. Since one cannot simultaneously be both a low-cost leader and a differentiator, one gets "stuck in the middle" if there is not a clear choice about marketing strategy before resources are allocated to any choice. In reviewing these three potential strategic traps, we realize that we have raised all of these issues earlier in this volume, at least to some degree. Nevertheless, it is useful to resurface them here in this final chapter.

The next four traps emerge in the formulation of strategy but stem from issues in increasing profitability rather than growth. The trap of

This Is a Common Trap

"not being customer driven" is sprung when marketing is not a high-priority driving force in the organization. In that case, products, technology, or something else drives the decisions in strategic planning (e.g., GM's overproduction of one million autos in 1988). Misidentifying the needs of the marketplace can only be avoided by paying careful attention to what the customers have to say. The "cheaper is better" approach simply pays no attention to the even more important "value-added" concept. The temptation is to price products on the basis of cost rather than of potential benefit to the consumer. Avoiding this pitfall involves making pricing decisions in the broadest possible social context, one that pays close attention to the marketplace and how this product or service meets the needs of that market. It is far too easy for organizations to end up "underestimating their competition," assuming that their competitors will continue to respond to the marketplace in the same way and not be similarly forced by circumstances to change and adapt. Cool, analytic, down-board thinking will help avoid this pitfall. The final formulation trap is "If it ain't broke, don't fix it." Planners caught in this trap assume that what worked for the organization yesterday and today—products, market segmentation, quality, and so on—will work equally well tomorrow. Since those strategies still *are* working, it can be difficult to shake that kind of complacency. The envisioning process of developing the best possible future for the organization on a regular basis is the best and only way out of this potential pitfall.

The eight traps that occur in the implementation of the strategy divide conveniently into three subsets:

1. Failures to adequately communicate the organization's strategy;
2. Failures to change the performance-management system; and
3. Neglect of the intangible aspects of the organization.

Failing to Communicate

The first subset involves the trap of assuming, "What they don't know won't hurt them." The idea that *only* senior managers of the organization need to know and understand the strategic plan has been around for a long time, with enormously negative consequences. As this book has continually noted throughout, widespread understanding of the organization's strategy is the best mechanism for avoiding this trap and securing enthusiastic commitment to the strategy. Failure to communicate a clear sense of direction is involved in the "sloppy-communication" trap. Stringer and Uchenick correctly recommend a highly participative approach to strategy formulation as the way to avoid springing this trap. "Eloquence in everything" is the trap that is sprung when the strategy is formulated by a small top team that believes whatever the limitations in process, it can be sold to the rest of the organization through eloquence. However, as this book has repeatedly pointed out, broad participation in the planning process is the *sine qua non* of success.

Failing to Change
Performance-Management System

New strategies require new performance standards; under this subset, Stringer and Uchenick include two potential traps. The first is "failing to raise the bar," which refers to the common failure of top management to require more from the organization to meet the requirements of implementing the new strategy. Higher standards must be communicated and vigorously enforced to avoid this pitfall. "Making the numbers" is a related trap if management is concerned with meeting short-term financial goals rather than implementing the longer-term strategic plan. Banks and Wheelwright (1979) also provide a number of worthwhile suggestions about how to deal with the continuing pressure on managers to attend to short-term objectives rather than long-term strategic goals. As suggested earlier, tying the performance-management system to the CSIs of the strategic plan has a positive impact on implementation, indicating that this book has indeed addressed the avoidance of these two traps.

Neglecting Intangible Aspects

Stringer and Uchenick's final three pitfalls are included in the subset of managing the organization's intangibles and the first of these is "A good athlete can run any business." This trap gets sprung when there is a poor match between the talents, attitudes, and style of a manager and the strategy of the organization for which that manager is responsible. A strategy for becoming a low-cost leader requires a disciplined, structured, and patient manager, a rather different person from the creative, intuitive, and market-sensitive person necessary for a market-driven strategy. A further analysis of the need for matching managers to strategies is found in Herbert and Deresky (1987). This potential trap can readily be avoided by ensuring this job-person match. The "analysis-paralysis" trap is sprung when the organization cannot stop formulating a strategic plan and start to implement it. Developing a clear-cut timetable for formulation and implementation and sticking to it avoids this trap. Although this book has continually addressed the need to avoid analysis paralysis, we want to stress at this point the need to match the manager to the strategy. Raising the issue here should alert readers about the risks involved in not attending to this potential trap. The final potential trap results from "ignoring the corporate culture," the most critical of the three traps in the intangible area. However, in view of all this book has said on corporate culture, there is simply nothing that needs to be added at this point.

The conscientious application of the Applied Strategic Planning model would go a long way in helping any organization avoid the strategic traps described by Stringer and Uchenick. While no planning process is without its own problems, we appear to have successfully by-passed this particular set.

OUTPUTS OF THE APPLIED STRATEGIC PLANNING PROCESS

The Applied Strategic Planning model must be rigorously applied if it is to be effective and if the traps and pitfalls discussed above are to be avoided. The several phases of the process must be completed in approximately the order presented in this book, as each phase is highly dependent on the preceding phase. Since each phase of the process has a number of discrete, specific outputs associated with it, Figure 15-1 provides a checklist that enumerates them. It also provides a comprehensive list to supplement the checklists given in the relevant other chapters.

Planning to Plan:

_____ Identification of planning-team members and their roles.

_____ Clearance of contract, individual commitment, planning schedule, locations.

_____ Stakeholder's considerations clearly identified and involvement defined.

_____ Awareness of competitive environment and preferred planning horizon.

_____ Awareness of the Applied Strategic Planning model and process.

_____ Consideration of factors that support successful strategic planning.

_____ Determination of organizational interventions to enhance the planning effort.

Values Scan:

_____ Comparison of individual values.

_____ Agreement on shared organizational values.

_____ Statement of organizational values.

_____ Understanding of the organization's culture.

Mission Formulation:

_____ Identification of organization's primary product, service, function.

_____ Identification of organization's target market or client base.

_____ Identification of organization's primary technique for providing product, service, or function to the target market or client base.

_____ Identification of the organization's reasons for existence.

_____ Agreed-on statement of organization's mission.

_____ Agreed-on distinctive competency or competencies.

Strategic Business Modeling:

_____ Identification of organization's strategic profile, including innovation, risk orientation, proactive futuring, and competitive stance.

_____ Agreement on the organization's major lines of business or program areas.

_____ Identification of the critical indicators of success for the organization.

_____ Determination of the necessary strategic thrusts.

_____ Specification of the culture necessary for the organization to achieve its mission.

Performance Audit:

_____ Determination of how the performance audit will be conducted in terms of data types, responsibilities, and schedules.

_____ Identification of organizational strengths and weaknesses relative to direct competitors, to be considered in validating the strategic business model.

_____ Identification of opportunities and threats within the environment, to be considered in validating the strategic business model.

_____ Measurement of the current performance of the organization relative to its performance targets, establishing a performance gap.

Gap Analysis:

_____ Identification of gaps between the current performance of the organization and the desired performance defined in its strategic business model.

_____ Development of strategies to bridge each gap.

Integrating Action Plans:

_____ Consideration of an appropriate organizational structure to support the strategic direction.

_____ Identification of functions that must submit supporting plans.

_____ Collection, review, and integration of action plans by functional and line managers.

_____ Collection, modification, and acceptance of budgets consistent with action plans.

Contingency Planning:

_____ Identification of the most important and probable internal and external vulnerabilities of and opportunities for the organization.

_____ Identification of trigger points at which to initiate action on each contingency.

_____ Agreement on actions to be taken for each trigger point identified.

Implementation:

_____ Creation of an action plan for communicating and reinforcing the strategic plan with all stakeholders.

_____ Identification of modifications needed for management-control systems to support the strategic plan.

_____ Identification of modifications needed for motivation and reward systems to support the strategic plan.

_____ Identification of modifications needed for information systems to support the strategic plan.

_____ Identification of ongoing training and tools needed to provide employees with the ability to manage strategically.

Figure 15-1. A Summary Checklist of the Required Specific Outputs of each Phase of Applied Strategic Planning

This checklist should be used as the planning team moves through the Applied Strategic Planning process. Not only does it provide a check that all the necessary steps in each of the phases has been satisfactorily completed, but checking off the items as they are completed also has a strong, positive motivational effect on the planning team as it moves through the planning process, developing a tangible record of its accomplishments. The basic question to answer for each of these items is whether or not there has been a clear, consensual decision on each of these items. One effective way of using this checklist is to begin each session with a review of the accomplishments of the last session and inquire whether there is anyone who would like to revisit any of the outputs from that session. As mentioned earlier, this kind of "second-chance" meeting helps preserve the view of Applied Strategic Planning as an open, ongoing process.

Applied Strategic Planning begins with an envisioning process that is *future based,* providing a conceptual, values-based strategy to reach a desired future. This process of envisioning is followed by a planning process that is *issues based,* producing a structural, detailed set of tactical plans for reaching that desired future state. The planning process itself is followed by an implementation phase that is *action based,* providing a set of operational steps and procedures and ensuring that the desired future state produces its desired outcomes. Finally, there is an anchoring phase when Applied Strategic Planning becomes institutionalized as a future-based process of ongoing management, which involves the recycling of the entire process. It is to this process of recycling that we now turn our attention.

RECYCLING APPLIED STRATEGIC PLANNING

As mentioned several times in this volume, Applied Strategic Planning is meant to be an ongoing process. In most organizations, this ongoing process involves an annual planning cycle in which the organization's key decision makers assemble for several days to re-examine both the ideal state and the current state of the organization. In other words, when a planning team has completed one cycle of Applied Strategic Planning, it moves into the next cycle. This annual process is expected to make certain that the Applied Strategic Planning process continues to be the source of the direction of the organization. It further enables the organization to keep an emphasis on a future-oriented direction and to think and manage strategically.

As the organization completes its initial cycle of Applied Strategic Planning and moves on into its second and third year of the process, the planning becomes both more exciting and more complex. The excitement stems from the fact that the planning team has moved from an initial learning phase to a more sophisticated mode of operation that is more empowering. Regardless of how well supported the first year of Applied Strategic Planning was, there is no way to avoid the fact that a great deal of energy was spent in learning how to work together and how to use the model. The following years tend to be far less encumbered with learning the process and thus much more likely to produce

Applied Strategic Planning Is an Ongoing Process

higher potential results. Topics and issues that were either not seen or put aside in the rush to complete the first cycle of the planning process can now be considered in some depth, and issues that were ignored can be fully examined.

The second and subsequent years of Applied Strategic Planning also differ from the first in several other ways. It is common for the time spent on the various phases of Applied Strategic Planning to differ in subsequent years from the initial year and from each other. For example, in a subsequent year the planning team may decide to invest considerable time and energy in redoing the values scan but to review only briefly the mission statement, or vice versa. These choices are determined by the level of comfort that the planning team has with the results of its previous work in each facet of the planning process and what has occurred in the organization during the intervening year.

Even if the planning-team members have spent twelve to sixteen days in meetings in the initial planning process, it is typical for them to feel dissatisfied with some element of the work and wish to return to spend some quality time in that phase. The necessity to move on to the next phase in the planning process, thus keeping the process on schedule, simply precludes developing completely satisfactory answers to some of the questions that were raised, important areas of discussion that could be explored and rich alternatives that could be further developed. All these potentials should have been captured in a contemporaneous "notes for next year" file maintained by a member of the planning team. The planning to plan phase of each subsequent year should begin with a comprehensive analysis and priority setting of the items in this file. One way to focus the program of activities for the subsequent year is to consider which phases of the planning process have the largest number of important, unresolved issues that should be addressed and budget the planning process accordingly. While each of the phases of the model should be revisited, even if briefly, the planning group should be empowered to decide in which phases they choose to spend the bulk of their time and on what issues in that phase. Also, of course, much will have transpired in the life of the organization during the year since the planning team developed and published its strategic plan. While the strategic-management process should be tracking the progress of the implementation of the strategic plan on a day-to-day basis, the annual recycling provides an opportunity for a broader review, one that is both more comprehensive and in greater depth than is otherwise possible.

The complexity of strategic management is increased as the planning team moves into the second year. This complexity is a function of the requirement for a number of tasks and their CSIs to remain from the first year of the planning cycle and a number of new tasks with CSIs to emerge from the second cycle. During the integration phase of the second cycle, the planning team needs to be particularly attentive to this issue and make certain that there is clarity about priorities and timetables for both sets of marching orders and that they are truly integrated. This issue of overlap and even conflicting marching orders will emerge with each recycling of the planning process. Commitments should be made in light of the multiple demands being made on each team member.

Unit Level

Another set of issues may emerge at the unit level of the organization. Given that many organizations have divisions, offices, plants, and other subunits embedded in their structures and that each of them might have developed their own plans that were derivative of the overall strategic plan, the managers of those units may be involved in planning on three different levels:

1. They are continuing to implement and track the CSIs of their own unit;

2. They are at the planning table working on the next cycle of Applied Strategic Planning for the organization as a whole; and

3. In their own functional area of responsibility, they are working intensively on the development of a detailed functional plan for marketing, finance, manufacturing, or whatever.

While the shifting focus can be more than a bit disconcerting to the manager from time to time, all these processes must be done and, often, by many of the same people. However, none should outweigh the others in emphasis or support. Another consideration is where these otherwise busy people can find the time for this work. The strategic-management process involves doing all these things in an effective and coordinated fashion. Strategic management consists of equal parts of a constant planning process and an effective, day-to-day implementation of that plan. This clearly involves marrying together the strategic and tactical views of the future—the vision and the practicalities for achieving that future.

Changing Group Membership

As the planning group moves into the next year's work, typically, the membership of the group will change somewhat. In most organizations, it is not wise to keep the membership of the planning team identical year after year, and there are multiple reasons for changing the planning-team membership. One message that the organization should not send is that the planning process will be in the hands of the same people forever. Such a message would reduce the likelihood of broad organizational ownership of the planning process. Participation leads to commitment—in planning as in all other forms of organizational life. While a small core of the planning team—the chief executive officer, the chief financial officer, and a few other key guiding members of the organization—should remain constant for the Applied Strategic Planning process to continue to be vital to the future of the organization, others can and should be replaced by newcomers. If these key guiding members of the organization, however, drop out of the process or begin to miss many of the meetings, the planning process soon becomes an exercise that will have little long-range importance for the organization.

Other members of the strategic planning team, who were selected initially because of their expertise or their role or status in the informal power structure of the organization or their ability to think strategically, should be regularly rotated. Furthermore, when such members are invited to participate, they should be told that their participation will be temporary and that they may be replaced after the first cycle in order to give others the same opportunity. It is important to choose people as replacements for their personal and professional skills as well as for their formal role in the organization. In the recycling process, it is important to choose replacement members on a sensible basis, one that the other members of the organization will recognize and respect. After all, no one wants to entrust their future to someone that they do not respect. The actual decisions regarding group membership should be made and announced by the CEO as either a command or a consultative decision. Under no circumstances should the decision be left to the planning team itself so that the group could be accused of simply perpetuating itself with no regard to the real needs of the organization.

Notwithstanding what has just been said, the rotation of members off and on the membership of the planning team must be handled in a thoughtful and considerate fashion. Those who leave must be made to feel that their leaving is not a reflection of the quality of their contributions but rather represents the needs of the team for new perspectives and a fresh approach. Participation in the planning process is an emotional high for most people, even in small organizations. They have a high degree of influence on the future of the organization, they have access to information that many others do not have, and they consort with the formal power structure of the organization. Even when one knows that one's tenure on the team is limited, it is difficult to give up the status that membership on the planning team brings. Some appropriate ceremony with some tangible award for his or her service is a helpful way of easing the process of leaving. There are also highly useful and creative ways to use former team members in subsequent rounds of planning, such as serving on the various tasks forces that need to do project work.

The timing of this change in the planning-team membership is also an important issue. To be maximally effective, a member has to experience the entire cycle—from the beginning of the process through its implementation phase. Because of this consideration, a number of organizations opt to make membership on the planning team a term of two years, rather than one. The first year involves a great deal of learning for all those involved in the planning process. During the second year, there is a greater opportunity to apply that learning and make a real contribution to the process. In essence, during the second year, each team member makes a return on the investment made in him or her during the first year of membership on the planning team.

The Consultant's Role

As the planning group moves from the first year to the next cycle, the role of the consultant will subtly yet clearly shift. The overall role of the consultant is to maximize the quality of the work of the Applied Strategic Planning group. By necessity, therefore, in the first year of the cycle, the consultant carries a heavy educational, training, and guiding responsibility. In the first year the group typically is highly dependent on the consultant to guide it through this somewhat foreign process. As the group becomes more knowledgeable and sophisticated about the process, there is less and less need for the consultant to help the group understand the Applied Strategic Planning process, leaving the facilitative and perhaps the strategist roles as the primary ones for the consultant to fulfill.

This is not to say that the educational and training roles will disappear. The group will still be learning more about the planning process as a group and can still often benefit from the shared insights of the consultant, but these will become less and less frequent in the second and succeeding years of the ongoing planning cycle. The consultant will also have a major role in working with any new members joining the planning group after the first year. These new members will need to learn the Applied Strategic Planning model at the same time they are participating in that process with others who have been through that process at least once before. An ideal way to approach this need is for the internal and external consultants to team up and run an intensive tutorial for the new members. The group usually does not want to slow down its work to help the new members learn the model, thus making the entry process for the new members somewhat difficult. The continuing members of the planning team are simply eager to get on with their work and have a sense of urgency about tackling the issues that they have identified as important, and integrating the new members is just not one of them. The consultant can play a key role in facilitating the integration of new members into the group while, at the same time, teaching the new members the details of the planning model and sharing parts of the group's history with the newcomers. This can involve one-on-one and small-group meetings between the new members and the consultant(s), internal and/or external. The Applied Strategic Planning process is also well supported with reading materials designed to accelerate and support this process of learning about the approach.

The consultant may also have a more significant involvement with some of the subunits of the organization as the various functional and other units attempt to do their own planning by using the same model.

They typically need the same kinds of help that the original planning team needed the first time it went through the process. They need to learn and apply the model. They need to examine and test their team work, which requires facilitation. They need to scan their values, develop a mission statement, do business modeling, and so on, for which training, facilitation, and strategizing by the consultant are required. In very large and complex organizations, this process can be even more detailed and time-consuming than the first cycle at the corporate level. In fact, some of these divisions are larger than many good-sized companies and require more time and energy in their planning process than do smaller companies in their corporate planning. In other organizations, however, the subunits essentially need only tactical planning set within the context of the overall strategic plan. The consultant needs to spend a good deal of time understanding the overall corporate structure and culture in order to understand what kind of strategic planning is required on the subunit level in each of the organizations in which he or she is involved.

Time Involved

Time-conscious and task-oriented organizational leaders often dream and hope that strategic planning can be done in less time than it really takes. As the planning team moves from the first year into the first repeat cycle, this is more often than not the case. If the organization has already spent twelve to sixteen days in the initial strategic planning cycle, they reason, it certainly should take much less time this cycle. However, this is not often the case. In fact, a number of our client organizations have spent more time during the second year than the first, as they could see the payoff from the time spent in this work. Although, as indicated above, the content of how these days will be spent will change from year to year, there is little reduction in the time required for adequate recycling until the organization is quite far along in the recycling process—and that happens only if the organization's growth is static and its environment is fairly stable (not a likely description these days). If senior management is doing its job competently, a significant portion of all managers' time will be committed to a longer-range strategic view of the organization and its work. If this is the case, then the time required for Applied Strategic Planning should not be seen as an intrusion in the manager's job; it will be seen *as* the manager's job (recall the example in Chapter 14 of the view of American Airlines' top management on the this issue).

The consultant should keep in mind that the multiple agendas that appear during the later years in the cycle may require the organization to commit additional time to the strategic planning and strategic-management processes. Such time is necessary to recover and integrate the data required to track the plan's progress from the previous year and/or support or guide the tactical planning process that should be driving the implementation of the overall strategic plan.

Continually Extending the Plan

The process of Applied Strategic Planning as it recycles itself is a process of constantly "rolling the plan out" one more year into the future—the future that is never reachable. If a team is planning a five-year span, it is really working with a rolling five-year plan. If the horizon is longer or shorter, it may have a rolling three-year or a rolling ten-year time frame for the planning process. Generally the minimum time frame should be three years and the maximum ten years. So much of the work of an organization requires at least three years to change plans already set in motion that a time frame less than that is not advisable.

As the planning team seeks to roll the plan out for another year, it is important to remember that the key difference between strategic and long-range planning is that strategic planning involves envisioning the organization's future and then examining the gap between that future and the organization's present reality in order to determine what must be done to achieve that future. Long-range planning simply involves extrapolating the organization's present reality into the future. It is imperative that the organization not lose this distinction in subsequent recycling.

This means that the planning team cannot simply add new elements to its first-year plan. Rather, in each subsequent year a new ideal future needs to be created and tested against the new current reality—thus the need for rejuvenating the planning team by including new members if the envisioning is not to become a stale exercise. Through this continual search for the organization's ideal tomorrow, the organization maintains its vitality; and the Applied Strategic Planning process provides for this maintenance. This process is very different from simply fine-tuning the Applied Strategic Plan created in year one.

The excitement that the Applied Strategic Planning process generates in an organization over time should be obvious from the above discussion. It enables the organization to work to cast off its current limitations and transform itself into the best possible organization. It is a particularly empowering process for members of the organization, because it has as its core assumption that the organization can—and must—influence its own future and that it not necessarily be held hostage by its past and present. The key to the success of any planning process is not the elegance of the process nor of the final plan; it is the implementation of that plan. The Applied Strategic Planning model has as its focus a broad organizational involvement in the process. Over seventy-five years of research in both laboratory and field settings have strongly supported the conclusion that participation in any planning process leads to greater commitment to the execution of the plan coming out of that process. Recent research by Woolridge and Floyd (1990) extended that body of research to the strategic planning process and how participation affects organizational performance. Their study of twenty organizations (eleven banks and nine manufacturing companies), indicated that having middle managers involved in the planning process led to an improvement in organizational performance as measured by overall financial performance and a number of other, more subjective factors. Surely one would not expect better support for our continually highlighting the importance of making strategic planning a process with broad organizational involvement.

Applied Strategic Planning is also a process that—through its design—lessens the risks present in occasional or episodic planning. The constant scanning of the environment and the annual process of planning reduces the need for any one person in the organization to be omnipotent. Since it is clear that no one can ever have a perfect fix on the future, the constancy and regularity involved in this planning process lessens the need for any one person to be perfect in projecting future conditions. Applied Strategic Planning also results in a continually increasing sophistication in understanding marketplace conditions, competitor analysis, organizational innovation and creativity, and, most importantly, organizational effectiveness. It is critical to the long-term health of an organization to increase its ability to understand and adapt to changing market conditions while maintaining its search for its ideal future. Well done, the Applied Strategic Planning model gives an organization the tools to identify and achieve its ideal future.

SUMMARY

Strategic planning involves some potential pitfalls or traps, and Applied Strategic Planning addresses the fifteen posed by Stringer and

Uchenick. The first seven can occur during the formulation stage of strategic planning; the other eight, during implementation. To be effective and to avoid these traps, the Applied Strategic Planning model must be rigorously applied. The phases of the model should be completed in approximately the order shown in the model. When the first-year cycle of Applied Strategic Planning has been completed, this ongoing process must start all over again. In the second and subsequent years, the time frame for each phase may vary from the preceding year, but seldom should the total time decrease. Except for the top decision makers, the membership of the planning team should vary from year to year. An optimal tenure for most of the members is two years. Consultants can play an important role in bringing new members up to speed with the others.

SOME CONCLUDING COMMENTS

After some ten years of our involvement in developing and applying our model of Applied Strategic Planning, we firmly believe that this process, in which the key guiding members of the organization envision its future and develop the necessary procedures and operations to achieve that future, is valid for achieving organizational vitality and growth, especially in today's turbulent world environment.

Our approach to strategic planning can give organizational leaders the ability to shape the future of their organization. Applied Strategic Planning can provide managers and other employees with the sense of control that is all but absent in many organizations. This sense of control comes from the clearly apparent excellent execution of a fundamentally sound strategy that has the total concentration of the organization's limited resources on its key strategic goals (Yee, 1990).

Applied Strategic Planning provides a model for transforming organizations and contains the seven ingredients that are necessary for such transformations. That is, Applied Strategic Planning:

1. Is future focused.
2. Is leadership driven, not leader driven.
3. Provides for a high level of organizational involvement.
4. Produces a plan that is widely understood and accepted.
5. Produces a plan that is both comprehensive and detailed.
6. Is a model that can be rigorously applied.
7. Provides the energizing force to drive the transformation.

If applied with intelligence, commitment, and conviction, Applied Strategic Planning will enable an organization to create and achieve its ideal future.

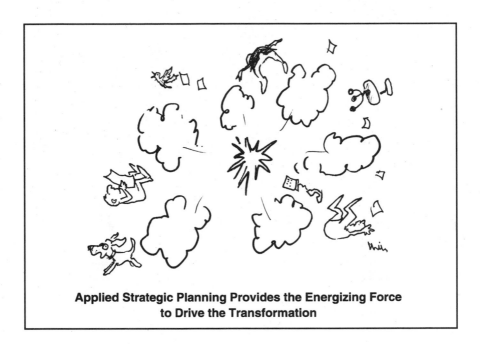

**Applied Strategic Planning Provides the Energizing Force
to Drive the Transformation**

REFERENCES

Banks, R.L., & Wheelwright, S.C. (1979, May/June). Operations vs. strategy: Trading tomorrow for today. *Harvard Business Review*, pp. 112-120. Reprinted in J.W. Pfeiffer (Ed.). (1991). *Strategic planning: Selected readings* (rev. ed.). San Diego, CA: Pfeiffer & Company.

Herbert, T.T., & Deresky, H. (1987). Should general managers match their business strategies? *Organizational Dynamics, 15*(3), 40-51.

Porter, M.E. (1980). *Competitive strategy*. New York: Free Press.

Stringer, R.A., Jr., & Uchenick, J. (1986). *Strategy traps and how to avoid them*. Lexington, MA: Lexington Books.

Woolridge, B., & Floyd, S.W. (1990). The strategy process, middle management involvement, and organizational performance. *Strategic Management Journal, 11*, 231-241.

Yee, D.K. (1990, May/June). Pass or fail? How to grade strategic progress. *Journal of Business Strategy*, pp. 10-14.

INDEX